REFERENCE BOOKS
IN INTERNATIONAL EDUCATION
VOL. 27

LEARNING
TO TEACH IN
TWO CULTURES

GARLAND REFERENCE LIBRARY
OF SOCIAL SCIENCE
VOL. 870

LEARNING TO TEACH IN TWO CULTURES

Japan and the United States

Nobuo K. Shimahara
Akira Sakai

GARLAND PUBLISHING, INC.
New York & London / 1995

Library of Congress Cataloging-in-Publication Data

Shimahara, Nobuo.
    Learning to teach in two cultures : Japan and the
United States / Nobuo K. Shimahara, Akira Sakai.
        p.   cm. — (Reference books in international
education ; vol. 27. Garland reference library of social
science ; vol. 870)
    Includes bibliographical references.
    ISBN 0-8153-1081-1 (hardcover)—
    ISBN 0-8153-1924-X (pbk.)
    1. First year teachers—Japan—Case studies.
2. First year teachers—United States—Case studies.
3. Teaching—Cross-cultural studies.   I. Sakai, Akira,
1961–   . II. Title.   III. Series: Garland reference
library of social science ; vol. 870.   IV. Series: Garland
reference library of social science.   Reference books in
international education ; vol. 27.
    LB2844.1.N4S545   1995
    371.1'02—dc20   94-36321
                                                          CIP

Paperback cover design by Patti Hefner

Printed on acid-free, 250-year-life paper
Manufactured in the United States of America

Contents

For
Mark
&
Motoko

Series Editor's Foreword

This series of scholarly works in comparative and international education has grown well beyond the initial conception of a collection of reference books. Although retaining its original purpose of providing a resource to scholars, students, and a variety of other professionals who need to understand the role played by education in various societies or regions of the world, it also strives to provide up-to-date information on a wide variety of selected educational issues, problems, and experiments within an international context.

Contributors to this series are well-known scholars who have devoted their professional lives to the study of their specialization. Without exception these men and women possess an intimate understanding of the subject of their research and writing. Without exception they have not only studied their subject in dusty archives, but they have also lived and travelled widely in their quest for knowledge. In short, they are "experts" in the best sense of that often overused word.

In our increasingly interdependent world, it is now widely understood that it is a matter of survival that we not only understand better what makes other societies tick, but that we also make a serious effort to understand how others, be they Japanese, German or Chilean, attempt to solve the same kinds of educational problems that we face in North America. As the late George Z.F. Bereday wrote: "[E]ducation is a mirror held against the face of a people. Nations may put on blustering shows of strength to conceal public weakness, erect grand facades to conceal shabby backyards, and profess peace while secretly arming for conquest, but how they take care of their children tells unerringly who they are" (*Comparative Method in Education*, New York: Holt, Rinehart & Winston, 1964, p. 5).

Perhaps equally important, however, is the valuable perspective that studying another education system (or its problems) provides us in understanding our own system (or its problems). To step outside of our own limited experience and our commonly held assumptions about schools and learning in order to look back at our system in contrast to another places it in a very different light. To learn, for example, how the Soviet Union or Belgium handles the education of a multilingual society; how the French provide for the funding of a public education; or how the Japanese control admissions into their universities enables us to understand that there are alternatives to our own familiar way of doing things. Not that we can often "borrow" directly from other societies; indeed, educational arrangements are inevitably a reflection of deeply rooted political, economic and cultural factors that are unique to a society. But a conscious recognition that there are other ways of doing things can serve to open our minds and provoke our imaginations in ways that can result in new approaches that we would not have otherwise considered.

Since this series is intended to be a useful research tool, the editor and contributors welcome suggestions for future volumes as well as ways in which this series can be improved.

Edward R. Beauchamp
University of Hawaii

Acknowledgments

The research project that led to the publication of this volume began in January 1989. That year, Nobuo K. Shimahara was invited to the Faculty of Education, University of Tokyo, as a senior research fellow of the Japan Society for the Promotion of Science (JSPS) and as a visiting professor to conduct research. Dr. Ikuo Amano, Professor of sociology of education at the University of Tokyo, was his host and provided him with generous assistance. Professor Shimahara wishes to express his deep appreciation for Professor Amano's support during his research in Tokyo and for the funding provided by the JSPS. The JSPS also granted Akira Sakai a fellowship, which enabled him to participate in the project in Tokyo and in the United States during 1989–1991. Additionally, Nanzan University (in Japan) generously offered him a Father Pache Research fellowship (1-A) to support his research.

We are especially indebted to Mr. Katsuji Tampo, former superintendent of schools of Ota Ward in Tokyo, for his extremely generous assistance in locating study schools and gaining cooperation from administrators and teachers. He offered us a variety of guidance and support during the entire project in Tokyo. It suffices to say that our research would have been impossible without the unselfish cooperation of beginning teachers, experienced teachers, and administrators at the three Tokyo schools and the two schools in the United States we studied. Unfortunately their names must remain anonymous to maintain their confidentiality. We cherished both Japanese and American beginning teachers' interest in participating in our research, and we are truly grateful to them for the generous time they provided us.

Finally, gratitude is expressed to Professor Sarah Pickert of Catholic University of America who kindly read our manuscript and offered valuable comments.

Small portions of the text have appeared previously in the works listed below. This material is reprinted by permission of the publishers concerned.

- Nobuo K. Shimahara (1992). Overview of Japanese education: policy, structure, and current issues. In Robert Leestma and Herbert J. Walberg (Eds.), *Japanese Educational Productivity*. Ann Arbor: Center for Japanese Studies, University of Michigan, p. 19.

- Nobuo K. Shimahara and Akira Sakai (1992). Teacher internship and the culture of teaching in Japan. *British Journal of Sociology of Education*, 13 (2): 157.

Nobuo K. Shimahara
Rutgers University

Akira Sakai
Nanzan University

Learning
to Teach in
Two Cultures

CHAPTER 1

Introduction

Since the end of World War II Japanese educators and officials have studied American education, including teacher education extensively. But their interest in American education originated even earlier, prior to 1872, when Japan laid out its first modern educational system and followed Western educational models. It was in that year that the first normal school was founded in Tokyo by the Department of Education, the precursor of the Ministry of Education. Marion M. Scott, an American teacher who was initially invited to Japan to teach English, was appointed for a three-year term as the first instructor of the school. Using instructional methods and materials then current in the United States, Scott was responsible for teaching 24 students chosen from various prefectures (equivalent to states in the United States). This inception of teacher education in early Meiji Japan (beginning in 1868) typifies the initial educational development—drawing on Western experience while searching for advanced models of schooling.

American interest in Japanese education started to flourish a century later. Beginning in the late 1970s, books and articles on Japanese education flowed from the pens of American authors and journalists, who watched with fascination the effects of education on Japan's industrial development and competitiveness in international trade. Without exception, these writers extolled the virtues of Japanese education to an American audience relatively unacquainted with the subject but keen to learn. The reason for their keenness was twofold. First, both business leaders and scholars sought to understand in detail the precise part education played in the ascendancy of Japanese industry. Second, educational internationalists, baffled by the apparent deterioration of American schools, found the Japanese system attractive as a high-quality comparative reference. Such recent publications as *The Japanese School: Lessons for Industrial America* by Benjamin Duke (1986), *Japanese Education Today* by the U.S. Department of Education (1987), *The Japanese Educational Challenge: A Commitment to Children* by Merry White (1987), and *The Learning Gap: Why Our Schools Are Failing and What We Can Learn from Japanese and Chinese Education* by H. W. Stevenson and J. W. Sigler (1992) unswervingly continued to reflect that trend in the 1980s and the early 1990s.

Only a few publications on the subject available in either English or Japanese, however, are based on detailed ethnographic accounts. Cummings (1980) and Rohlen (1983) pioneered ethnographic research on elementary and secondary schools, respectively, in Japan, and recently Tobin et al. (1989) and Peak (1991) published excellent ethnographic accounts of Japanese kindergarten and preschool education. But to date, no ethnographic findings have been published contrasting teaching in the United States and Japan.

Our assumption is that learning to teach is a culturally patterned process, and we will explore how teachers learn to construct the process of teaching in two cultures, the United States and Japan. Our aim is to offer a cross-cultural perspective on teaching. To accomplish this exploration, we will focus on beginning elementary schoolteachers in both cultures so that we may appreciate from their perspectives the process of learning to teach.

There are common characteristics in the ways in which American and Japanese teachers learn to teach. They both construct the concept of teaching through the intersubjective process that is often identified as apprenticeship. Despite cultural differences, apprenticeship is the most commonly practiced, most pervasive process by which the social reality of teaching is interpreted, constructed, and reinforced. Nevertheless, what American and Japanese teachers learn through interacting with each other is that the content of their apprenticeships is more often than not different. The cultural knowledge of teaching that they acquire through the intersubjective process in their workplace is unique to their culture.

That knowledge plays an important role in defining various aspects of schooling, including the purpose of teaching, the role of teachers, the curriculum, teaching methods, and classroom management. Teachers in the two countries articulate and emphasize different types of cultural support for schooling (Hess & Azuma 1991).

Few researchers have attempted to inquire into the socialization of beginning teachers from a cultural perspective. This book will fill this gap.

Teaching as a Reform Issue

Our study of beginning teachers took place against the background of the education reform movements in the United States and Japan in the 1980s.

Improving teaching has been a pivotal part of the education reform agenda in the United States during the 1980s. Individual states and institutions of teacher education launched initiatives to upgrade standards for entry into the teaching profession, to improve preservice education, to offer higher salaries, and to attract better-qualified applicants to the profession. These initiatives were bolstered by professional task forces organized in the mid-1980s to offer an intellectual framework for enhancing the quality of teaching. The Holmes Group (1986) and the Carnegie Forum on Education and the Economy (1986) were two outstanding examples of such task forces. These initiatives in the 1980s responded to what was perceived to be the mediocrity of both teacher preparation and the teaching profession, a characterization of teaching that appeared in a provocative national reform report, *A Nation at Risk* (National Commission on Excellence in Education 1983).

During the 1980s over 1,000 pieces of new teacher-related legislation were proposed in the states, and at least 27 states required tougher admissions standards for teacher-preparation programs (Bennett 1988). Furthermore, many states were demanding more course work in the liberal arts in these programs (Darling-Hammond & Berry 1988). Member institutions of the Holmes Group were not only strengthening liberal arts training but also extending teacher preparation with intensive graduate-level course work leading to a master's degree (Holmes Group 1989).

Obviously one of the most salient assumptions of the national drive to improve teaching was that teaching could be improved if initial teacher preparation was grounded in solid intellectual training (Holmes Group 1986; Carnegie Forum 1986). This assumption led to a greater emphasis on the liberal arts component of teacher preparation. There was also a renewed stress on internship in the school as part of teacher preparation (Carnegie Forum 1986) and on partnership with schools (Holmes Group 1986). Hurling-Austin (1990) reported that at least 31 states offered and were planning internships or apprenticeships for beginning teachers by 1990.

Japan's latest education reform was a culmination of the series of national drives to improve education that began in the late 1960s (Central Council of Education 1971). One of the major recommendations made by the National Council on Educational Reform (1988), a task force appointed by the prime minister in 1984, was to improve the quality of public schoolteachers. This recommendation represented a host of proposals for a mandated one-year internship for beginning teachers at all levels, the modification of certification standards to upgrade teacher preparation and to recruit competent applicants from outside the field of teaching, and the remodeling of in-service education for teachers, of which the proposed internship was a part.

For three decades the Ministry of Education had sustained interest in teacher internship. Ministry-sponsored proposals to re-educate teachers had been made since the late 1950s. In its reform report of 1971, considered to be a major proposal to reorganize schools in the postwar period, the Central Council of Education, which is an advisory body to the minister of education, urged the introduction of internship, stressing the critical importance of practical training for beginning teachers. Subsequent proposals for internship were submitted in 1972, 1978, and 1983 to the Ministry of Education by its advisory council, the Council for Educational Personnel Training (Yokohama National University Institute for Modern Education 1983). But these proposals failed because of a lack of political and fiscal support. But upon the recommendation of the National Council on Educational Reform, the national legislature approved mandated internship for all beginning public schoolteachers and authorized the funding for its implementation in 1988.

Learning to Teach—A Paradigmatic Issue

Learning to teach is part and parcel of the socialization of beginning teachers. To clarify what we mean by teacher socialization, we will briefly review recent studies on this subject. Until recently, the literature on the socialization of beginners by and large focused on the outcomes of socialization and on the factors that influence the outcomes (Wells 1984). These factors are conceptualized in terms of the effects of preservice education, the impact of the school bureaucracy, and the influence of role models identified in neophytes' biographies. As carefully documented by Veenman (1984), until the early 1980s most studies employed a questionnaire method that required respondents to rate their experiences on a scale. These quantitative methodological approaches, however, failed to capture the process of socialization and context-specific interactions and adaptations (Veenman 1984; Tabachnick & Zeichner 1985).

Moreover, partly because of the methodological and conceptual limitations of past research, research findings are often conflicting and suggest that there is little consensus on the effects of preservice education, student teaching, and beginning teacher socialization (Zeichner 1984). Such findings are also influenced by the fact that teacher socialization is context-specific and that situational variables affect individual students differently.

For example, on the one hand, the literature that supports a continuity model in developing perspectives highlights biographic factors and the role of anticipatory socialization, including preservice education and student teaching (e.g., Lortie 1975; Mardle & Walker 1980; Denscombe 1982; Petty & Hogben 1980; Tabachnick & Zeichner 1985). Lortie's contention that the socialization of teachers is profoundly affected by the internalization of teaching models through close contact with teachers in the early years predating teacher education is supported by the studies just cited.

On the other hand, a number of studies suggest significant shifts in the first year of teaching, which are often viewed as "washing-out effects" (Veenman 1984). These studies tended to concentrate on the themes of authority, discipline, and bureaucratic control (Feiman-Nemser & Floden 1986). They support the evidence of changes from liberalism to authoritarianism, humanism to pupil control, and progressivism to traditional orientation (e.g., Liguana 1970; Hoy 1986; Edgar & Warren 1969; Lacey 1977).

Encouraging research initiatives on teacher socialization in recent years have attempted to surpass methodological and paradigmatic limitations. Unlike the quantitative approach, which concentrates on collecting data only from pretests and posttests, these studies examine the process and context of socialization. They conceptualize socialization as a process in which the socialized plays an active role, and qualitative methods are employed to collect data. The following paragraphs will selectively review the literature built on these studies, paying particular attention to the paradigms used for the studies and their shortcomings.

The research paradigm that Becker, Geer, Hughes, and Strauss developed for their study of medical students in the late 1950s has had a significant impact on studies of teacher socialization through the 1980s. Their work, *Boys in White: Student Culture in Medical School* (1961), a sociological classic that resulted from that study, is one of the last landmark achievements in sociological ethnography to date. Its influence is still felt because researchers of teacher socialization (Crow 1986; Etheridge 1989; Janesick 1978; Lacey 1977; LeCompte & Ginsburg 1987; Sharp & Green 1975; Smyth 1989; Tabachnick & Zeichner 1985) have a renewed interest in the theory of symbolic interactionism (Cooley 1956; Dewey 1930; Mead 1934), which is the conceptual underpinning of the Becker study. Becker et al. focused on the development of medical students' perspectives, the concept that underlies recent studies in teacher socialization. They define *perspective* as "a co-ordinated set of ideas and actions a person uses in dealing with some problematic situation. . . ."

(1961, p. 34). This definition gives prominence to situational learning: individuals' adaptive abilities to deal with problematic situations.

Colin Lacey, a British educational sociologist, has singularly contributed to the popularization of the construct of perspective among educational researchers. In his ethnographic study of student teachers in a graduate teacher training year at Sussex University in Britain (1977), he employed the term *perspective* as his central conceptual instrument, with some modification. He stressed Herbert Blumer's (1966) view that "[the individual] acts towards his world interpreting what confronts him and organising his action on the basis of the interpretation" (p. 536).

Lacey's redefinition of perspective focuses on "social strategy," which includes "internalized adjustment," "strategic compliance," and "strategic redefinition" (1977, pp. 72–73). These types of perspective represent variations of social strategy constructed by individual teachers in response to the situations they face. He states: "Social strategies are, therefore, selected or created and guided by a wide range of factors including . . . the individual's interpretation of the situation . . . [and] the ability of the performer" (1977, p. 73). But Lacey's concentration on individual social strategies offered only a lopsided account of teacher socialization that ignored reproductive forces in that socialization process (Atkinson & Delamont 1985).

In the United States, Tabachnick and Zeichner's longitudinal study (1984, 1985) best represents recent research on teacher socialization based on the paradigm developed by Lacey. It is a quasi-ethnographic study, the prominent feature of which is to gather and interpret interview data and descriptive accounts of events. Its purpose was to examine the development of the perspectives of teacher trainees in two stages: student teaching and first-year teaching. Tabachnick and Zeichner (1985) insist that they paid special attention to "the interrelationships between social context and individual abilities and dispositions in the process of learning to teach" and the influence of both individual and contextual factors on the development of perspectives. In their view the development of perspectives is mediated by "individual intent" and "institutional constraints" (Tabachnick & Zeichner 1985). Nevertheless, their analysis of findings suggests that they were primarily concerned with the "action-idea systems" developed by the beginning teachers, whereas the influence of contextual factors, elements critical in cultural transmission in the reproduction of teaching, was not adequately captured.

In a similar vein, using Lacey's construct of social strategy, Ross (1987a) explored how 21 student teachers interacted with the agents of socialization. Like Tabachnick and Zeichner's research, his study emphasizes the role that student teachers played in developing their teaching orientations.

Another related study was conducted by LeCompte and Ginsburg (1987). Its primary relevance here is in the use of the perspective paradigm discussed previously. It is guided by the theory of symbolic interactionism. The purpose of the study was "whether or not individuals involved in occupational training programs were active or passive participants in their indoctrination" (LeCompte & Ginsburg 1978, p. 6). LeCompte and Ginsburg contrasted teacher perspectives using a continuum of responses ascribable to symbolic interactionist and structural functionalist positions.

A recent study of beginning teachers by Etheridge (1989) also reflects the influence of Lacey's paradigm. It is a "three-year" study with a focus on the first year of teaching. It concentrates on how beginning teachers developed "strategic adjustment strategies" in response to what she calls "constraints," such as time realities, work conditions, teaching assignment, and student behaviors. Etheridge asserts, "Adjustment strategies were consciously selected based on perceived situational need" (p. 310). The thrust of the study was obviously to determine the nature of situational learning, or what Atkinson and Delamont (1985) call the "hidden curriculum" of beginning teachers. Etheridge characterizes that situational learning as "active participation in their socialization" (p. 299). It is apparent that neophytes' socialization into the occupational culture of teaching received little attention in both the LeCompte and Etheridge studies.

Our ethnographic research (1992) highlighted the development of perspectives of elementary teachers in Tokyo. Our findings suggest, however, that the construct of perspective does not encompass some critical aspects of the process of teacher socialization in Japanese schooling. The beginning teachers we studied not only engaged in situational learning in their process of induction into teaching, but also made active use of a large repertoire of cultural knowledge of teaching shared by experienced teachers to cope with various situational demands. Our findings (1992) indicated that the ecology of teacher interaction, in which the reproduction of this repertoire occurred, is governed by collective values and norms. In short, the construct of perspective does not fully capture these aspects of teacher socialization.

Likewise, Atkinson and Delamont (1985) are critical of the symbolic interactionist approach, because it views socialization as situational learning and as a recurrent process of adjustment to cope with daily activities. They point out that "detailed ethnographies of everyday life in training and work settings which document the process of socialization, the hidden curriculum of training, the development of occupational cultures, trainees' survival strategies" are most strikingly lacking (p. 308). Such ethnographies are needed, especially in view of the fact that most "ethnographic" studies conducted to date are of short duration and fall far short of the ethnographic requirements of intensive and prolonged observation.

The prominence of the interactionist approach to teacher socialization in the past decade may be viewed in part as a reaction to the functionalist approach (Lacey 1977; Atkinson & Delamont 1985; LeCompte & Ginsburg 1987; Etheridge 1989). The latter approach emphasizes common functional requirements, relevant competencies and values to be acquired by novices, the continuity of professional socialization, and the correspondence between training and practice. In contrast, as already pointed out, the symbolic interactionist approach accentuates the role of the individual in socialization, individual intent and needs, conflicts of personal and institutional interest, and situational learning. These two approaches represent contrasting paradigms. As suggested by Atkinson and Delamont

(1985) and Pollard (1982), we need a paradigm that links these two strands of research, to generate data that will offer a better understanding of teacher socialization.

Our study, on which this book is based, attempted to fill the gap by giving attention to both the recurrent patterns of situational learning developed to cope with problems and the transmission of occupational knowledge, including the cultural knowledge of teaching that beginners acquire. Cultural knowledge of teaching refers to work-related beliefs and knowledge. Some of it results from what Martyn Hammersley calls the "typifications of situations and lines of action" (1980, p. 58). It reveals the shared character of teachers' ideology and perspectives. Teachers draw upon their cultural knowledge to interpret and generate classroom events. The cultural knowledge of teaching is not acquaintance with scientific theories of instruction and management, but teachers' practical knowledge for creating solutions to the problems they encounter in everyday life. This knowledge constitutes a significant part of the occupational knowledge of teaching that teachers learn. They learn it through casual conversations and observations. In significant measure, cultural knowledge of teaching accounts for the contrasts between Japanese and American beginning teachers.

Methodology

Study Schools

The data to be presented in this volume come from our research projects in Tokyo and the East Coast of the United States. In Tokyo our fieldwork began in April 1989 (the beginning of the Japanese 1989 academic year, which ended the following March), and continued through December 1989. In the United States our research began in September 1990 and was completed in June 1991. Gaining access to a research site and securing cooperation for the implementation of research is always a critical and difficult first step in ethnographic research. Likewise, selecting our research sites was a truly trying process for several reasons.

First, we had to choose schools where beginning teachers were appointed. That considerably narrowed the range of our choices. Second, because our research required prolonged, intensive observations of beginning teachers and the events that involved them, school administrators, who were concerned with protecting beginning teachers from the adverse effects of research, were often reluctant to grant us permission to undertake research. Third, beginning teachers usually felt uncomfortable with our request to observe them for an extended period at a time when they felt vulnerable and uneasy because their induction into teaching had just began.

These factors, among others, contributed to our difficulty in securing cooperation from schools. In Tokyo, with the generous assistance of a former superintendent of schools who was well acquainted with schools in several wards, we launched our search for suitable schools in February 1989 and identified possible research sites. But we were not informed that beginning teachers would be assigned to these schools until the middle of March, when personnel decisions were announced by the Tokyo Metropolitan Board of Education. We started to visit schools on March 15 to seek cooperation from principals, superintendents of schools, and research participants. Two schools in one ward agreed to participate in our study by March 31, but we could not gain permission from a third school in another ward until the middle of April, shortly after the academic year had begun.

In the United States we began selecting schools in March 1990, one in an urban district and another in a suburban district. We met superintendents of schools to present our request and sent our research proposal to them for approval by the board of education. Nearly two months passed before we received their responses. We were denied the opportunity to study the schools we originally selected. Therefore, in May we began seeking cooperation elsewhere. Two school districts in suburban communities granted us permission to conduct research in July. In late August we met with principals and beginning teachers in two schools each of which had been chosen by the assistant superintendent of schools in its district to request their participation in the study. Through this process we secured two suburban schools for research.

Research Participants

We studied a total of seven beginning teachers in Tokyo and four beginning teachers in the United States during 1989–1991. Our study of Japanese teachers took place in 1989, when the teacher internship program referred to earlier had just started. Seven beginning teachers were assigned to the three elementary schools of our study: Komori, Ikeshita, and Taika. Three beginning teachers, two male and one female, were appointed at Komori, which is situated in the commercial, middle-class area of a ward; and two beginning teachers, one male and one female, were appointed at Ikeshita, which enrolls pupils from middle-class residential neighborhoods of the same ward. The third school, Taika, which is in another ward, is located in the heart of one of the busiest commercial centers in Tokyo. Two beginning teachers, one male and one female, were assigned to this school. The first two schools are medium-sized, public elementary schools with an enrollment of approximately 700 pupils, but the third school, which is also public, enrolls fewer than 300 pupils because residences in its school district are being gradually replaced by business establishments.

In 1989 there were 23 classroom teachers, a principal, and an assistant principal at Komori Elementary School. Ikeshita had a total teaching staff of 22 classroom teachers, a principal, and an assistant principal. Taika had only 14 classroom teachers but had two administrators like the other two schools. At each school one veteran teacher was appointed by the principal to serve as a full-time supervisor of interns. Beginning teachers were responsible for full-time teaching duties and for participating in the internship program.

Unlike the schools we studied in the United States, Japanese schools do not closely link kindergarten and elementary programs. The Japanese schools we studied are six-year primary schools. Pupils attend elementary school for six years and middle school for three years. The nine years of schooling at the elementary and lower-secondary level constitute compulsory education, which is followed by noncompulsory, upper-secondary education for another three years. This represents the pattern of schooling in postwar Japan.

In the United States, we studied one beginning teacher, at Westville Upper Elementary School and one at Southtown Elementary School for a period of one year (1990–1991). Located in an upper-middle-class suburban community, Westville is a new, unusually large 4–6 school that had just opened in 1990, when our research began, and enrolled over 1,200 pupils. The rapid growth of population in Westville necessitated the construction of this new school. It had a large staff of 67 classroom teachers, of whom 7 teachers were new to the district, and 2 of these 7 teachers were the female beginning teachers whom our research focused on. The remaining 60 teachers previously taught at other elementary schools in the district. Westville had a principal, two assistant principals, and a large supporting staff, as well as 16 specialized teachers.

In contrast, Southtown is a much smaller K–6 school with an enrollment of 490 pupils, and it is located in a suburban middle-class community 10 miles north of Westville. It had 23 classroom teachers, a principal, and an assistant principal. Of these 23 teachers 14 were nontenured teachers and 8 were beginning teachers. There has been a frequent turnover of teachers at the school. Our study focused on a kindergarten teacher and a first-grade teacher, both of whom were female. Southtown integrated its early childhood programs, including kindergarten, first-grade, and second-grade pupils.

Data Collection

We employed an ethnographic method as the major methodological approach for data collection. It is designed to focus on ongoing events in a natural setting, the linkages between these events, and their social and cultural context (Erickson 1986). We were interested in capturing social actions taking place in the classroom and the school setting as they occurred, and we were interested in the meanings of these actions to the actors. We inductively sought patterns of actions and learned cultural principles that govern everyday life in the classroom and school setting, as well as relationships between events in the classroom setting and events at other system levels. The ethnographic approach was best suited to gathering data pertaining to these aspects of life in schools.

Our approach involved prolonged observation and interviewing of participants to ensure the validity of the data collected. In Tokyo, as well as in Westville and Southtown, the study generally developed in four progressive phases: the initial descriptive observation phase and the three succeeding phases of intensive observation and interviewing that focused on the beginning teachers.

In the initial phase our primary research participants were observed for two to three weeks so that descriptive data on their overall activities in their school settings could be gathered. Unstructured interviews were also conducted to obtain the participants' "personal documents" (Bogdan & Taylor 1975): descriptive, first-person accounts of their reflections on their education and significant events that had a bearing on their selection of teaching as a career. A domain analysis (Spradley 1980) was conducted to identify orienting categories for the study. Our approach was to discover those categories grounded in the data. The categories identified in Tokyo, Westville, and Southtown were compared with the categories developed in other studies, especially by Tabachnick and Zeichner (1985). The orienting categories were used as the basis for deciding the categories for focused observation and interviewing.

In the second phase, using the inductively constructed categories, each of the primary research participants was observed for two to three weeks. After the observations, structured interviews were conducted with all participants to gain their interpretation of the actions that occurred in these categories. Following the second phase, we analyzed descriptive and interview data to construct patterns from the actions observed and to develop hypotheses.

The third intensive phase, a focused observation-of-participants facet lasting two to three weeks, was launched and primarily followed the same procedures as in the second phase. The hypotheses generated in the second phase guided observation and interviewing at this stage of research. At the conclusion of this phase, we analyzed the data to determine the extent to which the patterns and hypotheses generated in the second phase were supported by data and to compare similarities and differences between the patterns of socialization at the schools studied. At this stage weak hypotheses were eliminated and new hypotheses were added. The frequency of interviews was increased in this phase.

The final, two-week phase of research was launched toward the end of our study. The emphasis of this phase was to contrast and compare the socialization of the beginning teachers studied.

The research participants were observed in not only their classrooms but also the broader settings of their schools throughout the entire duration of the research, where they interacted with significant others who served as agents of cultural transmission in the reproduction of teaching. We interviewed significant others to gain data pertaining to their participation in the socialization of neophytes. When intensive observations and interviewing were not conducted, we made at least two visits to each study school every week for unstructured observation and interviewing. In addition to observational and interview data, other relevant information, such as school documents, was collected.

Synopsis of the Book

This volume consists of eight chapters. Chapters 2–4 will focus on American beginning teachers, and chapters 5–7 concentrate on Japanese beginning teachers. Chapters 2 and 5 will provide detailed accounts of how beginning teachers in two cultures learn to teach. The purpose of these chapters is to offer an analysis of events: what beginning teachers did, what problems they encountered, and what strategies they employed to solve them. Chapters 3 and 6 will focus on the strategies that beginning teachers developed to deal with child motivation and control, which are critical concepts in teaching. Special attention will be given to classroom routines, management, interaction, and the development of child attitudes toward learning. Chapter 4 and chapter 7 will examine the perspectives that beginning teachers developed in the process of socialization. Chapter 8 will offer a comparative cultural perspective. It will highlight common and contrasting characteristics in teaching that teachers learned in the induction year in both cultures.

Special attention will be given to the role that the culture of teaching plays in shaping the process of learning to teach. Comparative comments will be made throughout the volume so that contrasts in teaching between the two countries may enhance the reader's appreciation of teaching.

CHAPTER 2

How American Teachers Learn to Teach

Introduction

This chapter parallels chapter 5 in its conceptual organization. This parallel structure will enable the reader to identify similarities and contrasts between beginning Japanese and American teachers in the process of learning to teach. Here we will explore three thematic questions: How do beginning American teachers organize routines in the classroom? How do they learn to teach? and What do they teach? Our overall purpose is to understand, based on ethnographic data, how beginning teachers learned teaching, especially in the first five to six months, the most crucial period in the socialization of neophytes. We will first provide biographical information on neophytes relevant to the theme of this chapter. We will draw upon observational data to construct the neophytes' routines. This will offer a context for the sections that follow and for chapters 3 and 4. Learning to teach occurs in special settings and involves interactions with particular individuals. We will explore these settings and interactions. Finally, we will look at how neophytes construct their curriculum and at the difficulties involved in this process.

We will focus on Nancy Smith at Westville Upper Elementary School and Ellen Steinbeck at Southtown Elementary School. Our aim is to describe and interpret the events in which both teachers were immersed. We will refer to Janet Montana at Westville and Gail Fisher at Southtown whenever their comments shed light upon the socialization of beginning teachers. These four young, female teachers were our major research participants.

Beginning Teachers

Unlike the Japanese teachers depicted in later chapters, the American beginning teachers we studied all had graduate education. Three of the four teachers already had a master's degree prior to assuming teaching, and the fourth teacher had completed two-thirds of the graduate course work required for her master's degree. Moreover, they had far more extensive student teaching experience than the Japanese beginning teachers.

Nancy graduated from a state university in 1988 with a major in English literature and took a job as an editor in a publishing house in a large city for a year. Subsequently she decided to get teacher certification at a state college that had just started a new, "experimental" certification program. She enrolled in the program as a full-time student and received both teaching certification and a master's degree in 1990. Nancy did not like the top-down structure of the publishing company, where she had little autonomy and only followed orders from above. In contrast, she felt teaching would permit her total involvement ("every part of me")—including cognitive, emotional, and physical qualities—and liked that challenge. She looked for a stimulating job that would satisfy her intellectual and creative needs. That motivation led her to seek admission into a graduate teacher education program.

Nancy's program was intensive, and she devoted 14 months to complete it. It included student teaching for one entire year, which was divided into internship, course work, and a thesis. In the first semester she was placed in a second-grade class for six weeks for observation and some teaching practice, followed by six weeks in an eighth-grade class for intensive student teaching. In the second semester she taught a fifth grade class from January through May. Nancy explained that clinical teachers—cooperating teachers—were most influential in shaping her orientation toward teaching and teaching skills. They permitted her to organize lessons according to what she thought was appropriate and insisted that she had to try everything and organize it herself. She was told she should not be "enclosed in the curriculum." "You really are the curriculum," suggested a clinical teacher. She reminded Nancy from time to time, "Do not fall back on the textbook. Do not lock yourself into what is safe for you to teach. Pressure yourself beyond what is there."

In contrast, Nancy's college supervisors had little influence on her at all. In fact she was afraid to comment on them to us because it might hurt the reputation of the college. Likewise, her course work hardly had any impact on her.

Nancy applied for a teaching job in the Westville district because of its reputation as a progressive, exciting place, not just a traditional school district. She had heard that the district encouraged an individualized approach to stimulating an interest in reading and writing and emphasized a "new language-teaching approach" that required students to take the initiative in reading. She was first interviewed by the assistant superintendent at the Westville board of education and subsequently by the principal and two assistant principals at Westville Upper Elementary School. They reviewed her academic transcripts, evaluations of student teaching, letters of recommendation, and personal statement on her beliefs on teaching. The principal told us that interviews were critical for discovering applicants' strengths and weaknesses and that Nancy's interview had lasted for nearly three hours. She was hired because of her excellent English literature background and intellectual strength, and she was assigned to a fifth-grade class.

Ellen Steinbeck began preservice teacher education at the undergraduate level and completed her program in elementary and special education at a state university. Subsequently she enrolled in a large private school to receive a master's degree in special education. She chose the state university for her B.A. program because of its depth in fieldwork and student teaching. She began observing classes and student teaching for two days a week as early as the sophomore year and student taught for three days a week in the junior year. In her senior year she intensively student taught a third-grade class every day for 18 weeks. During her master's course work at the private university, she spent most of her time during the first semester observing a special education class and, in the second semester, student taught four days a week in a resource classroom. She took evening courses and completed her master's program within one year. Like Nancy, Ellen felt that student teaching gave her the most valuable preparation for teaching. Her cooperating teachers also left a strong impact on her. Although student teaching was an unusually extensive part of her programs, she felt that going into a classroom and teaching as a student was not enough preparation for teaching. But what her student teaching enabled her to understand was "what is real in the classroom"—the complex reality that is not represented in textbooks.

Ellen liked children and wanted to be a teacher in early childhood. She attributed her fascination with teaching to a kindergarten teacher who remained a reliable source of guidance for many years. She learned the lasting meaning of teaching from that teacher. Having completed her master's degree, she began to work as a substitute teacher at Southtown in April 1990 and was impressed with the "innovative things" the school did. Consequently, when she learned of an opening at the kindergarten level, she immediately applied for it. Ellen was particularly interested in the K–2 level, because she liked little children and also because she did not want to teach math at a higher level. She liked the Southtown school district especially for its emphasis on an innovative approach to reading and writing and for the freedom it granted teachers to explore their own original ideas. She pointed out the whole-language approach adopted by Southtown Elementary School as an example of a new approach whereby children learn language through their personal experience. In her view learning is "holistic and influenced by the total environment."

We will briefly introduce the remaining two beginning teachers. Janet Montana was appointed at Westville and assigned to a fourth-grade class. After she had received a B.A. degree in human resources at a state university, she worked for a private company for a year. Subsequently she enrolled in a 48-credit M.A.T. program as a full-time student at a state college for one year and earned 36 credits and teaching certification. Gail Fisher, our second research participant at Southtown, got a job as a first grade teacher. She worked for a state association of principals and supervisors for two years immediately after she received a B.A. degree in journalism at a state university. In her second year at the association, she began her master's course work in elementary education as a part-time student and subsequently devoted another full year to full-time study for her master's program. She received a master's degree in 1990. She did student teaching in the Southtown district, which helped her to get employment in the district.

The shared motif that evolved from our initial interviews with Janet and Gail was that their student teaching for 16 weeks was the most profitable and significant part of their master's programs. They referred to the intimate, attentive guidance they received from the cooperating teachers on a daily basis and to the emphasis that the cooperating teachers put on their initiatives. Their cooperating teachers' "hands on" approach to daily problems had an impact on both Janet and Gail. However, they found their college supervisors to be detached from the classroom and ineffective in providing the needed guidance. That these are common themes shared by the four beginning teachers is noteworthy.

Learning to Create Routines

In his remarkable study, *Life in Classrooms*, Philip Jackson (1990) presents an ethnographic sketch of American elementary classrooms characterized by the elements of repetition, redundancy, and ritualistic action, which provide a fairly "constant social context." The classroom offers the space in which activities are organized, roles are performed, and expectations and rules provide regularity for these activities. The teacher's task is to develop a structure and sequence of events that occur in the classroom. Given these characterizations of classroom management, the beginning teachers' shared commitment is to create a classroom social context that is controlled by regularity. The primary goal of our American beginning teachers was to establish routines for their classrooms. This was an important part of learning to teach. These routines reveal how beginning teachers orient themselves toward teaching, classroom control, teaching strategies, school in general, and the chief problems they have to cope with.

In Westville and Southtown, "buddies" were designated by the principals to guide beginning teachers. Buddies saw their task as informing beginners of "classroom" procedures, a term commonly used by teachers that refers to a variety of habitual activities. The procedures include making an inventory of student interests, a weekly schedule, homework assignments, and a supply list; writing a request for parent volunteers; developing a classroom management strategy, developing rules, and determining the consequences if rules are broken; writing lesson plans; and school operations. Buddies viewed the induction of beginners into teaching largely in terms of acquainting them with the operational procedures of the classroom. Procedures are what build uniformity and continuity in the social context of the classroom. Indeed, for Nancy Smith building classroom procedures were so consequential that she declined our visit during the first week of the year, because she was so busy developing procedures.

What follows is a sketch of one day in late September 1990, when Nancy was still trying to put routines in place. We arrived at Westville Upper Elementary School at 7:45 A.M. on September 17 and, upon entering the building, met Nancy in the hall. She was approaching her classroom to get ready for the day. Shortly after 8:00 school buses began to arrive in the front parking area of the school, and by 8:10 more than a dozen buses lined up. No one in the buses was standing or moving, and the buses looked as if they were empty. Four administrative staff members, including two assistant principals, were standing and watching the buses in the parking area to supervise the unloading process. Everyone knew the procedures to be followed when the buses arrived. The unloading of children from the bus started at 8:12, and the children quickly filled the spacious entrance area. They proceeded to the main hall and then to divided corridors leading to 57 separate classrooms equally distributed in the east and west wings of the building. As the unloaded buses each left the parking area, more loaded buses arrived in turn. Transporting 1,200 children from their homes every morning is a process that requires coordination and efficiency. The students' arrival was smooth and orderly. School bus arrival is unfamiliar to the Japanese, because in Japan all public school children walk to school.

By 8:17 children began to enter Nancy's fifth-grade classroom, located at the end of the west wing, where she waited for them. They were orderly and quiet, but unlike Japanese schools no formal greetings were exchanged between the teacher and students. The children started to move their chairs from desktops to the floor and to unpack their knapsacks to get ready for the first period. By 8:20 all 24 children (3 Asians, 2 blacks, 1 Hispanic, and 18 whites) were present in the classroom. Nancy promptly reminded them of the homework to be handed in, and she asked one boy to return to the students the homework she had previously checked. Every day, the students took turns discharging classroom responsibilities. Nancy reminded her students that they must obtain their parents' signatures on the returned homework and bring it back to her. This was part of the homework policy that she developed and distributed to parents early in September. There was also a schoolwide homework policy that was included in the student/parent handbook and that outlined the rationale for homework. Nancy attached special importance to homework.

Nancy's classroom was rectangular and conventionally arranged: two long rows of desks parallel to the front chalkboard and two short rows of desks at right angles to both ends of those long rows. She created a large space between the chalkboard and the students' desks; she called this a family room, and it was where students gathered when she read to them. Part of the chalkboard was used to post daily assignments. Children's tests were posted on the front wall. Next to the tests was a big poster on which a banner proclaimed in block capitals: GIVE CREATIVITY A BOOST. The rear wall was decorated with students' inventories (called "Look What's Ahead!") and colorful clippings from science magazines. Next to them was a large piece of paper with a list of classroom rules in large letters:

1. Listen and follow directions.
2. Raise your hands and wait for a turn.
3. Listen to others.

These three rules were chosen from a longer list of rules, an important aspect of classroom management that Nancy and her students worked out in the first week of the year. A piece of paper listing these rules was also pasted to the desk of each student. Above the entrance door was displayed a small American flag. Students' hangers were located between the entrance and the front wall. Nancy's desk, which was adjacent to the windows, was situated opposite the entrance and to the side of students' desks.

On the large front chalkboard was the schedule of the day that Nancy had written:

First period: gym
Second period: math
Third period: reading/spelling
Fourth period: writing workshop
Fifth period: lunch
Sixth period: social studies
Seventh period: science
Eighth period: reading aloud

Each period is 40 minutes long, and there is a break of five minutes between periods. Forty minutes are allowed for lunch. Nancy had math, reading, writing, social studies, and science every day. This was her own lesson schedule, and there was no grade-level uniformity with respect to the amount of time allocated to each subject. Unlike Japanese schools, no time was allocated to such common activities as a morning meeting of teachers, short morning and afternoon meetings of the class, cleaning, a long break for play, and student activities. Another notable contrast is the larger number of class periods than is found in Japanese schools.

At 8:25 Nancy announced to the class that it was time to pledge allegiance to the flag and requested the pledge leader of the day to move to the entrance where the flag was displayed. All the children stood up and routinely pledged allegiance in unison, a practice not seen in the Japanese classroom. Subsequently Nancy directed her class to line up in the hall to go to the gym for the first period and told the students that they should be quiet and orderly when they walked in the hall. Then she led the class to the gym, where a male gym teacher was waiting. She immediately returned to her homeroom to work on "Progress Update," a report to parents about each student's progress in the class. Physical education is the responsibility of special gym teachers at Westville, which has five such teachers on staff. By comparison, Japanese classroom teachers are invariably expected to teach physical education. Students at Westville did not change their clothes for a gym uniform, and the only requirement for gym is that they wear sneakers. After a five-minute exercise, the gym teacher took the class out to the spacious lawn for a kickball game.

At 9:05 Nancy came to the gym to escort the students back to the classroom; students were not expected to return to their homeroom without the supervision of their teacher. At 9:12 she distributed to each student the progress update, which included the student's test results and evaluations of assignments for the past week. This was to be inspected and signed by the parents. She urged the class to sit quietly to begin a math lesson on rounding numbers and exhorted them to wake up. Nancy wrote several numbers on the board to demonstrate how to round them to the nearest tenth, hundredth, and thousandth. She then added a dozen numbers for exercise and instructed the class to round one number at a time and flash their answer on a piece of paper. The students raised their hands to offer answers. However, they were not permitted to talk unless permission was granted, and as a rule students must raise their hands first and wait for the teacher's recognition. This exercise continued for 15 minutes.

Nancy gave the class additional problems from the math textbook, a standard textbook used throughout the school. When a few students began to chat, Nancy immediately reminded them of the classroom rule. As the class started to work on the new problems, she walked past their desks to monitor their work. Toward the end of the period Nancy stood in front of the chalkboard and asked students to volunteer answers. She assigned additional questions from the textbook for homework and directed the class to write the assignment in the weekly assignment sheet and to obtain their parents' signatures on the sheet.

At 10:05 without a break, Nancy switched to reading and instructed students to put away their math homework and place on their desks their journal and the novel they had been reading, Jean George's *My Side of the Mountain*. (Incidentally, Westville replaced basal readers with a literature-based reading program.) Nancy told students to come to the family room, the open space that she created, and to sit down on the carpeted floor. A couple of boys lay down on small cushions belonging to the class, while several other students sat in their own chairs facing her. Nancy wanted them to relax during this period. She started recitation with the class reviewing what they had read thus far. She initiated dialogue with the students, asking questions, to which they quickly answered by following the classroom rules. However, a couple of students started to whisper to each other. Nancy immediately stopped them by suggesting that it would be very impolite for them to talk when someone else was talking. She demanded that the students concentrate on their work at hand and told them that even a minor infraction of her expectations would be improper. She asked the class to volunteer to read the book aloud, and students took turns, each reading a short passage. This was followed by another series of prompt questions and answers. She hastily suggested that the reason the group worked together was to offer a model of reading and that students would be expected to read the book themselves soon.

At 10:30 the students returned to their regular seats. Nancy instructed them to write in their journal the following question: What do you expect the book to be about based on what you have read so far? She also wrote down five new words that she told students to define with the use of a dictionary. Students were also told to identify whether each word was a noun, an adjective, a verb, or an adverb and to use each word in a sentence. Her announcement of the assignment was followed by questions and answers for several minutes.

At 10:45 Nancy announced snack time and told the class that students had to be quiet lest they disturb their neighbors. They got snacks from their knapsacks. While they were enjoying both the snacks and a brief opportunity to speak with each other, Nancy asked three volunteers to borrow copies of *Language: Skills and Use*, a grammar book, from her buddy. Because the entire school was adapting the whole-language approach, according to which grammar was expected to be taught holistically as part of reading and writing when necessary, the school stopped purchasing grammar books. But Nancy and her buddy believed that it was necessary to teach grammar methodically. On their own initiative, they used *Language: Skills and Use,* a fact they did not want to publicize because they knew such usage was not school policy.

At 10:55 the class was told to remove snacks from the desk and get ready for the writing workshop period. Nancy paired students together and instructed the class to open the grammar book. She made a brief presentation on subject and predicate as the topic for her lesson and engaged in recitation with the class for a while. Subsequently she gave worksheets to students to take home. They wrote down a new assignment on their assignment sheet. Three students were asked to collect the grammar books and return them to her buddy.

When Nancy was reiterating the assignment and the fact that a test was to be given, several students started to talk. Immediately they were told that talking displayed disrespect for the class. Nancy shouted, "Freeze! What's wrong with this?" when some students started to sharpen pencils. She told them to be more orderly and quiet.

At 11:40 Nancy announced the lunch period and told the class to line up in the hall. She accompanied them to the large cafeteria where 400 other children were having lunch under the supervision of teacher aides. Nancy left the cafeteria to join her colleagues at lunch in the staff room. Lunch time is regarded as a private time for teachers in American schools, though it is shared time for students and teachers in Japanese schools. In Japan student lunch monitors serve school lunch under the supervision of the classroom teacher, and the teacher has lunch with her students in the classroom. When lunch was finished, the students at Westville were permitted to go outside to play for 20 minutes.

At 12:20 Nancy went outside to bring her students back to her homeroom. The sixth period was social studies. Nancy and her fifth-grade colleague agreed to switch classes for social studies and science to reduce the burden for preparing for two periods. Nancy taught science for her colleague's class in the sixth period and her class in the seventh period, and in turn her colleague taught social studies for the same two periods. At 12:35 Nancy had her students line up in the hall and escorted them to her colleague's classroom for social studies. In turn, her colleague brought her class to Nancy's classroom.

Nancy started a lesson on plants and photosynthesis. She instructed the class to open the science textbook. Her science lesson closely followed the textbook, as her math lesson had. Through recitation her students identified the materials needed for photosynthesis and the functions of various parts of plants. No observation and experiment was involved in her discussion. She directed the class to write "job descriptions" for these parts of the plants. For homework she handed out worksheets that required identifying the functions of the plant parts. The class was dismissed at 1:15, and Nancy's students returned to their homeroom. Without a break Nancy repeated the same lesson for her own students in the seventh period.

At 2:10, as Nancy's science class was ending, the students began to show signs of fatigue and to talk. Nancy called out, "Please freeze!" Students appeared to be a little frightened. At 2:15 she announced that it was time for reading aloud and directed students to pack up their belongings before they came to the family room for reading. She repeated the request. Meanwhile some students were copying assignments from the board, and one girl started to clean the board with a wet sponge. A group of eight students sat in the family room to listen to Nancy read a book for them. Two were working with a computer. Nancy started to cough, and a girl was asked to take over the reading. Students were permitted to sit or lie on the floor as long as they did not make noise as the girl continued to read. Nancy took another turn at reading and stopped at 2:45. In contrast to Japanese schools, there was no class meeting to reflect upon events of the day.

At 2:50 the loudspeaker started to announce the arrival of the buses, identifying them by numbers. All the students were anxiously standing, listening to the announcement. Children were kept in the classroom until their bus was announced. They started to leave the classroom in an orderly manner as their bus number was called. By 3:10 all the students had gone.

This brief sketch of a single day's activities identifies the patterns of routines that Nancy was establishing. Universal to schooling in the United States and Japan, the daily lesson schedule provides a structure and flow for classroom activities. When students came to the classroom in the morning, Nancy expected them to attend to a few routines, including submitting homework, getting ready for the first period, and reading if there was time. The pledge of allegiance to the flag, a taken-for-granted routine, preceded the first period. Thereafter there was a succession of lessons without a break between them except for the lunch period, which both Nancy and the students considered their private time. This was the only time slot over which the students had any control, a period during which they were not directly supervised by teachers.

The classroom rules that Nancy developed with her students regulated the students' interaction with her, as was clearly pronounced in the first rule, "Listen and follow directions." She attached great importance to these rules and classroom order. She expected the class to be quiet and orderly and often reminded students of their infractions of her expectations and rules. Her expectations were that students' engagement in some form of interaction with each other was inappropriate unless it was permitted by her. Suffice it to suggest that Nancy placed significant stress on order and control. Unlike Japanese teachers, Nancy was not concerned with how and where her students sat, her primary concern being their concentration on the task at hand. Japanese teachers demand that students sit upright to concentrate on their task.

Nancy's teaching methods were characterized by a predominance of recitation and working at one's desk. Reflecting her beliefs and school policy, she organized a heterogenous group and rejected ability grouping in any subject including reading and math, the subjects for which students are often ability-grouped at the elementary level. Nancy used textbooks for math and science lessons, whereas she constructed her own materials for reading and writing lessons, as other teachers at Westville did. Likewise, the colleague who taught social studies used a textbook for those lessons. Homework was an important part of Nancy's teaching strategy. She diligently implemented her homework policy to encourage independent study and insisted that the policy be complied with.

Nancy's students had two gym periods and one music, one art, and one computer period a week. Her teaching responsibility, however, excluded gym, music, art, and computer because those subjects were regarded as areas taught by specialized instructors. That enabled her to concentrate on teaching math, science, reading, and writing. Her overall charge was to provide not only the constant social context of the classroom but also to supervise students outside the classroom. This required her, for example, to escort her students to and from the gym, the cafeteria, the music room, the art room, the library, etc. As a rule, except for those occasions, her students were confined to the classroom all day. Yet because there was no break between periods, students had few opportunities to engage in interactions initiated by themselves.

Let us now turn to Southtown Elementary School to explore how Ellen Steinbeck was creating routines for her class. Ellen taught a kindergarten class that included 4 four- and 15 five-year-olds, 18 of them white and one black. Kindergarten was considered part of the integrated early childhood education program, which included first and second grades. Shared activities for kindergarten and first-grade children were thought to be important, especially for the former to be assimilated into schooling. Although obvious differences existed between Nancy's fifth-grade class and Ellen's class with respect to the children's social and intellectual development, there was a parallel in the teacher's attempts to establish routines related to control and order. We will take a look at activities in Ellen's class in early October.

Southtown Elementary School had both conventional closed classrooms and open-space classrooms. The former were in an old building and the latter in a new building. The four kindergarten classes were evenly divided into conventional and open-space areas. Ellen and her buddy, Susan Taylor, were assigned to open classrooms, as were two first-grade teachers. These two kindergarten classrooms were partially separated by a wall and a kitchen situated in the middle. One side of Ellen's classroom was used as the children's work area, where there were four large tables and chairs. Ellen had her desk adjacent to these tables. On this wall were hangers for knapsacks and coats and cubbies for lunch boxes and snacks. The other side was carpeted for children to lie down during the "quiet hour" and to play. This area contained several activity centers for blocks, housekeeping, reading, puzzles, drawing, and listening to tapes, as well as a chalkboard. The walls were colorfully decorated with the children's latest drawings and clippings from magazines. However, unlike Japanese kindergartens, where a piano or organ is thought to be essential, there was no piano in the classroom, because at Southtown singing and activities that involve music were not a customary part of the curriculum.

School at Southtown began at 9:15 A.M. and ended at 3:15 P.M. Children were transported by school bus and arrived by 9:00, at which time they were permitted to enter the building. As kindergarten children started to come in, Ellen greeted them saying good morning to each, but no children returned the greetings. They placed their knapsacks on the table in order to take out a communication folder and lunch money. She told them to hang the knapsacks and coats immediately and put their magnetic name plates on the chalkboard to indicate their presence. As the children arrived, she directed them to start to work at their tables, where she placed crayons and drawing papers. These routines were practiced throughout the month of September. Ellen complained that Michael was talking and told him to start coloring the paper at the table. She nervously added that the children were talking too loudly to do work, although they were making relatively little noise, and demanded that they be quiet. Her expectation was clearly that children should minimize talking and maintain quiet in the classroom even before the first period begins. Obviously Ellen's expectations were quite similar to Nancy's view that students should sit at their desks and read books as soon as they arrive in the classroom. Children in both classrooms were not expected to socialize among themselves before the first period. Ellen's concern was to build what she hoped to be "right habits." To promote these habits, she spent a couple of days, as Nancy did with her fifth-grade class, discussing classroom rules with her children.

By 9:15 all the children were present. At the kindergarten level there is no pledge of allegiance to the national flag; that begins in the first grade. Ellen's first business was to check attendance, find out who wanted to buy lunch, and collect money from the children. As she was attending to housekeeping business, she told the children to put their work in the basket and go to the reading center in a corner of the room that Ellen used for early morning lessons. At 9:30 all the children convivially sat on the carpeted floor in the reading center, and Ellen sat on a stool facing the class. She began a lesson using a calendar. The purpose of the lesson was to teach numbers, days of the week, and months, holidays, birthdays, weather, and special events. She was also interested in establishing good order when the children were interacting with her during the lesson, and she even reminded them of how they should sit. Such a reminder is quite common in Japanese first-grade classrooms, but not at the kindergarten level. This early morning lesson using the calendar was repeated almost every day through the spring.

Around 9:50, as the calendar lesson was over, children were permitted to have snacks, a favorite event of the day. However, they were quickly reminded that they must maintain order. They were told that they should get snacks in the alphabetical order of their names and sit at the table quietly when they were eating. Ellen raised her voice as she warned the class not to call to each other across the table after she heard Corey call to a boy in this way. Children were relaxed during the snack time but could use only their "indoor voices" when they talked to each other. At the end of snack time Ellen praised the class for being quiet.

At 10:15 Ellen directed her children to go to Susan's classroom for another lesson and apprised them that they should not touch each other, another rule that she insisted on. Ellen and Susan, her buddy, regularly combined their groups for reading. All the children sat in front of Susan, who was seated on a stool by the stand holding a "Big Book," a large picture book with a story printed in large letters. The Big Book, which was adopted by all kindergartens in the district, was used to teach reading. Susan took charge of the combined class and read the story of a T-shirt boy aloud, and the children repeated it after her. Subsequently she played a tape of the T-shirt boy song and placed her finger on the words. Ellen sat in a chair to watch Susan as she taught and occasionally told children to sit straight and be quiet. The class was attentive and enjoyed the story and song.

In contrast to typical Japanese kindergartens, where the primary emphasis is on the development of emotional maturity and social skills in a group setting with comparatively little attention to the academic area (Lewis 1989; Tobin et al. 1989), the Westville kindergarten program stressed the instruction of reading, math, writing, art, and gym as mandated aspects of the curriculum to provide the academic foundation for first grade. After the reading lesson was over, Ellen directed the children to line up for gym and asked the line leader of the day to stand in front of the group. She told the children they should not hold hands when they went out and escorted her class to the playground, where a young gym teacher was waiting for them. As noted earlier, unlike Japanese schools, even at the kindergarten level gym was considered a specialized area where particular skills were imparted and taught by one of the two full-time gym teachers at the school. Instead of watching her class do physical exercise, Ellen returned to her homeroom and worked on children's evaluation packets.

At 11:20 Ellen came to the door leading to the playground to escort her children back to their homeroom. In the room she distributed lunch tickets to the children who had ordered them and instructed all the children to line up to go to the cafeteria, and then she led them to the cafeteria. During lunch and the subsequent playtime the children were supervised by two paraprofessionals. One paraprofessional was assigned to Ellen and Susan each, to assist them every day. Meanwhile Ellen and her colleagues had lunch in the teachers' room. Lunch break constituted a private time for teachers, who were released from their duty of overseeing their children.

At 12:40, the children for the two classes were waiting outside the hall, with two supervising paraprofessionals, so Ellen gave them permission to enter the building. The children walked into the hall and to their classrooms. The first afternoon period was a joint class for reading which included two kindergarten and two first-grade classes. When everyone was sitting on the floor in Ellen's classroom and order was restored, a first grade teacher took charge of the entire class and started to read a story book. At 12:55 this short reading class was over and children left for their homerooms. Immediately Ellen directed her children to get folded sponge mats and spread them on the floor to lie down for a rest. Although this period was designated as a quiet time, the children were permitted to do other things as long as they did not disturb the class. A dozen children were lying down on the mats, several children were drawing pictures at the table, and the remaining children were looking at books on the floor. Meanwhile Ellen was watching her class from her desk. She heard children on the floor chat and warned them that they would be denied center activity if they made further noises. She named individual children who were talking and told Brian to "sit out" at an isolated table. Ellen frequently used this method of isolating children whom she regarded as not following classroom rules. She started to do work at her desk, but it was often interrupted by policing activity. She separated children when they spoke to each other and told several children to lie down several times. This was a difficult time for the children. No one was sleeping.

Ellen told the class that children could sign books out when she called out their names, and urged them to hurry and check books out quickly. When these activities were going on, the children were permitted to whisper to each other. At 1:40 Ellen announced that it was time to clean up. Children rolled up their sponge mats.

Ellen announced center activities, which included Legos, watercoloring, puzzles, blocks, and spelling. Children chose centers of interest, and six children sat at the table to practice writing their names. The paraprofessional distributed pencils and paper, with each child receiving a sheet with his or her name printed on it. With the help of the paraprofessional, the children traced the printed names while Ellen worked with children who were painting with watercolors. All the children were engaged in activities of their choices. Ellen emphasized the importance of center activities because they reflected the children's choices. In the group-oriented Japanese kindergarten, children's activities are largely uniform and tend to exclude personal choice.

At 2:15 children were told to clean up and went back to their seats. Ellen distributed papers and told the class to draw their portraits with crayons and reminded children that they must do the work quietly. These portraits were to be included in the children's evaluation packets, which she had been working on for a few days. After completing their portraits, the children were permitted to go to play centers. One group of active boys was playing with wood blocks, three girls were listening to a taped story, seven boys and girls were reading books, and several girls were playing with housekeeping kits. Suddenly, Ellen sternly demanded that the boys at the block center stop playing because they were getting excited and making noise. She asked them how they should play in the center. A boy replied, "Be good." Ellen said, "What else do you want to be?" "A star of the day," replied another boy. Following this exchange, she told the boys at the center to clean up the blocks and sit out.

At 2:55 Ellen told the class to clean up promptly and sit at the table. She checked the books the children had borrowed from the library and told them to take all their papers, lunch boxes, books, and pencils home. Kindergarten children were encouraged to borrow books from both the bookshelves in the classroom and the school library. It was Ellen's routine to keep a record of these books. She then watched the children pack their knapsacks and sit on the floor in a circle. Ellen gave the children their folders, which contained a communication form and a notice for a show at the school. Finally Paul was named the star of the day for his exemplary behavior.

Reviewing this sketch of Ellen's activities, we see two types of routine that contributed to creating the regularized social context of the classroom. One is the development of "correct" habits, including patterns of orderly and quiet behavior. She did not condone the children's failure to meet her expectations and often issued directions to restore order. While establishing the order and quiet of the classroom was her pedagogical aim, a concern with classroom management, she attributed its importance to her personality. She admitted that she could not stand noise and was a "stickler" with respect to rules. Meanwhile, Ellen was not interested in promoting peer-initiated interaction as part of classroom routines, although it did occur when she did not impose control on all the children. As in Nancy's classroom, kindergarten children were expected to sit at their tables to do work, such as coloring on paper and reading under the supervision of the teacher, when they arrived in the classroom. Moreover, they were not supposed to talk to each other across the table because that would create noise. When talking was necessary, they were expected to use their "indoor voices." Common to Nancy's and Ellen's classrooms is also the fact that the children had little space and time in which they could control themselves. Instructional activities were initiated and controlled by the teachers, and no break for peer interaction was given between periods.

The second type of routine is instructional activities. Ellen had a planning conference with her buddy, Susan, every day, to make sure that she followed Susan's plans. So both classes had an identical schedule. It typically began with teaching numbers using the calendar, followed by reading the Big Book, gym or art, and center activities. Center activities were offered to give children a choice of interest. The afternoon program included quiet time, story reading, and another opportunity for center activities, which included the practice of writing one's name. Once or twice a week, first-graders participated in story reading. Although a majority of the children could not yet read, teachers encouraged them to borrow books from the library, to foster their interest in books. Thus borrowing and returning books was an important part of the program. Lessons for each day were constructed with flexibility, and there was a clear emphasis placed on the instruction of reading, writing, and math.

Learning to Teach

How do neophytes learn to teach? Although there are individual differences in terms of what and how they learn to teach, there are some common paths through which neophytes learn to teach, regardless of the level of teaching. These common paths are distinctive of teaching as an occupation. Teaching involves anticipatory occupational socialization, commonly identified as preservice education, which includes professional studies and clinical experience. It is followed by in-service education, part of the occupational socialization of neophytes. The extent to which anticipatory socialization has a distinct influence on teaching is an empirical issue. But recent research studies (Bullough 1989; Crow 1987; Ross 1987; Tabachnick & Zeichner 1985) suggest that it has only a limited effect on the development of an orientation toward teaching and tends to negate the functionalist assumption of anticipatory socialization.

Yet student teaching is often cited by neophytes as the best experience for providing a critical footing for the first year of teaching (Haring & Nelson 1980; Nosow 1975). As noted earlier, both Nancy and Ellen supported this observation and further suggested that the most influential individuals throughout their preservice education were cooperating teachers in the classroom. Cooperating teachers situate student teachers in the classroom setting for the first time, where they give a first lesson and must learn to cope with problems of control and authority—a ubiquitous issue of classroom management. Teacher trainees begin to understand the complex reality of the classroom for the first time through student teaching. As already mentioned, both Nancy and Ellen had extensive student teaching experience. In the United States there is a much greater stress placed on clinical experience than in Japan. Nancy student taught for one entire year as part of her master's program in teaching, and Ellen began student teaching in her sophomore year and continued through her master's program.

The Japanese teachers we studied student taught for a maximum of only eight weeks, however, and had no graduate course work at all. Yet, as will be discussed later, to compensate for the lack of student teaching, in 1989 the Japanese government started a mandated one-year internship program for all beginning public schoolteachers at all levels throughout the nation with each beginning teacher under the supervision of a full-time mentor (Shimahara & Sakai 1992). Our Japanese research participants took part in the internship program.

Both Westville and Southtown offered a variety of in-service educational opportunities to help beginning teachers learn to teach. There were differences between the two schools in their approach to in-service education for beginning and new teachers. Westville offered them opportunities to participate in in-service education, but their participation was voluntary and not monitored by administrators. In fact, administrators were hardly involved in in-service education. In comparison, the principal at Southtown took a hands-on approach to in-service education. He was known to be paternalistic and sometimes domineering among experienced teachers. The difference between the two schools in their approach to in-service education may have resulted in part from the variation in the sizes of the schools. The fact that Westville had nearly three times as many students and teachers as Southtown may have contributed to the Westville administrators' inability to give personal attention to new teachers. However, Westville had only 7 new teachers and 3 beginning teachers whereas 11 teachers out of a total of 23 teachers at Southtown were new teachers, 7 of them beginners.

In late August, the Westville school district held a two-day human relations workshop for all beginning and new teachers. This provided them with their first opportunity for in-service education in the district. The workshop was a districtwide orientation session designed to promote an understanding of cultural diversity, communicative competence in a culturally diverse context, and the student's self-concept. During the summer, the Westville Upper Elementary School planning committee prepared for beginning teachers a packet titled, *Helpful Hints for New Teachers*, a 120-page collection consisting of hints and excerpts from magazines and books. This packet offered information on procedures for classroom management, beginning activities for children, suggestions for student activities, weekly plans, assignments, rules and consequences, and the like. Beginning teachers also received curriculum guides and a teacher handbook that covered classroom-related procedures. As noted earlier, the emphasis on procedural information is ubiquitous and suggests that the process of induction of beginning teachers is to acquaint them with procedures.

Beginning in September, Westville also offered "Inservice Monthly," a one and one-half hour session once a month, which was coordinated by a guidance teacher and in which experienced teacher volunteers met with beginning teachers to discuss a topic of interest. "Inservice Monthly" covered such topics as back-to-school night, classroom management, lesson plans, report cards, and parent conferences. Further, the reading-writing committee of the Westville district sponsored a credit-bearing biweekly seminar on fostering literacy development, which was offered in the library of Westville Upper Elementary School. The seminar was taught by a professor at a local college, and the three neophytes at Westville were among the expected participants.

Nancy, however, relied more on informal interaction with her buddy and a few colleagues located near her classroom than on formally organized programs to steer her through her induction into teaching. Conversation with her colleagues served as an especially rich, useful vehicle for learning to teach. The functional significance of conversation is articulated well in the field of sociology of knowledge. As Berger and Luckmann (1966) point out, "The most important vehicle of reality-maintenance is conversation. One may view the individual's everyday life in terms of the working away of a conversational apparatus that ongoingly maintains, modifies and reconstructs his subjective reality" (p. 152). The social construction of everyday life occurs through the conversational apparatus that individuals manipulate.

Likewise, everyday conversation in the school setting plays a pivotal role in the social construction of teaching. Nancy's induction into teaching was grounded in her active commitment to conversation with her colleagues and took on a form of apprenticeship—seeking advice from peers and observing what they do. In contrast to the packaged procedural information that is prepared in anticipation of the potential demand for it, conversation has three unique features. It is preceded by the rise of a problem calling for attention. Second, it immediately responds to the need for particular information defined by the problem that a neophyte is undergoing. Third, conversation is concrete and contextual rather than abstract and generates information that is most meaningful to the context of ongoing classroom events.

One may recall that Nancy had a buddy designated by the principal to assist her. They were the same age and teaching the same grade, but the buddy's advantage was that she had two more years of teaching experience. At both Westville and Southtown, buddies were peers with two or three years of teaching experience who were not significantly different from the beginning teachers in their career development. This presents a sharp contrast to Japanese practice. Japanese beginners were paired with well-experienced teachers on the assumption that long experience and the knowledge grounded in that experience are a legitimate basis for mentoring. Their classrooms were located in the same area, and they were seated next to each other in the staff room to promote interaction between them.

Nancy relied heavily on her buddy, Pat Busch, for the first two months at least. They regularly chatted with each other several times each day. Pat saw her role as familiarizing Nancy with the "school procedures" that were called for by the special situation in which Nancy was involved. As suggested earlier, in this sense Nancy's apprenticeship was a process of learning appropriate classroom and school procedures from her peers. Information on such matters was included in the packets mentioned earlier but became contexualized in the conversation between the neophyte and the buddy. The procedures Pat shared with the neophyte included establishing a smooth classroom operation but not how to teach. Because nobody advised Nancy on how to teach, she relied on the strategies of teaching that she learned when she was a student teacher.

Like student teachers, Nancy was ambitious and tried to compress three lessons into one. Pat gave practical advice to Nancy on how to develop lesson plans. The rules of thumb that Pat used in advising Nancy on procedures were "workability" and "comfort" in adopting them. Pat insisted that the neophyte should develop "reasonable" and "realistic" lessons, rather than the award-winning lesson that Nancy hoped to give every time. In her view, what worked well for Nancy was the most important, and a sense of "appropriateness" comes from experience. Given this advice, Nancy stopped comparing her lesson with other teachers' lessons. Pat summed up her advice:

> We worked a lot at the beginning of the year, especially when we had more time. We worked together setting up our own rooms. . . . We worked on room arrangements that work best to facilitate activities. I helped her with lesson plans. . . . And one thing I've got to tell her is that she's got to teach, she's got to grade. All procedures you use are something you have to feel comfortable with. Everyone can give you advice, but it has to be something that works for you. Something must work well for someone. But you have to feel comfortable with it. Otherwise it may not come off well for you. I think she got it all.

The advice Nancy frequently sought before and after school was exceedingly useful to her, especially because she found it difficult to relate what she learned from college to the practical situations of the classroom.

Janet followed the same path and told us:

> When Betty [another beginning teacher at the school] and I first got here we had to come up with a reading program. We looked at each other and said, "Where shall we start?" But we talked to Kate a lot. She told us her program which she had been teaching for a while. She gave us all kinds of ideas without which we would not have known what to do. By just talking to other people we learned a lot.

The back-to-school night, held late in September, was a trying experience for Nancy and illustrates how heavily she depended on her buddy and peers. In preparation for it she went to Pat and another fifth-grade colleague asking for suggestions, agenda items, and materials to be given to parents. She also talked to the two other beginning teachers at the school who already had the back-to-school night a couple of days earlier. Using their suggestions, she was able to construct her own agenda for the night and cover what she thought was important. During her presentation Nancy had a stomach upset and felt flushed, but felt the night was successful.

During September and October Nancy often approached her buddy and other colleagues and simply asked "Can you help me on this? How do you do this?" She felt they were always on target every time she asked for their assistance. By November, however, she had become better acquainted with procedures and had gained confidence and independence in handling daily events. And when she met her peers, it became more of an occasion to chat about their mutual concerns.

Conversation with buddies and other peers served as a major vehicle through which occupational knowledge was transmitted to neophytes. The three neophytes at Westville actively sought such conversation. But they did not gain as much knowledge from formally planned meetings. For example, Nancy felt she learned relatively little from the monthly in-service meeting. It focused on the procedures to which she was already exposed. Nancy evaluated the monthly in-service program and revealed her skepticism:

> It is very informal. It provides opportunities to meet other teachers. I appreciate it in that sense. But I caution about the value of in-service itself. However, you do get good materials, articles, things like that. But after a while, you are simply collecting papers and you will never look at them again. You are just a big paper collector, paper chase, you know. It gets absurd to a point. . . . But there are somewhat profitable, worthwhile ones once in a while.

Likewise, Nancy felt that the biweekly seminar on literacy development was not useful because it was very formal, general, and repetitious and presented no new knowledge. To her this seminar looked like a pep rally to promote a whole-language program. She eventually quit attending the seminar, although she feared her absence would reflect badly when she was evaluated. Janet Montana and the other beginning teacher continued to participate in the seminar.

Obviously what Nancy was looking for was not just information but also sharing and applying it to teaching in the classroom. But one veteran teacher suggested that although Westville had an excellent staff it provided few opportunities to discuss "the formal component of the teaching craft." In this large school every teacher is "an island to herself," in his phrase, with a lot of individual freedom but little opportunity to interact in groups. He suggested small interactive groups of teachers, especially for beginning teachers. Small groups of teachers at the same grade level for sharing problems of teaching, he pointed out, were not built into "the system" at Westville. Meanwhile, formal meetings, such as staff and grade-level meetings, were designed to provide only decontextualized procedural information. These structural problems made Nancy's casual conversation with her buddy and other peers a much more important vehicle for learning to teach.

Turning to Southtown, the induction process was more personalized, as pointed out earlier. Ellen, along with 10 other beginning and new teachers, participated in at least three in-service workshops organized with the express purpose of promoting the induction process. The first one was what the director of instruction for the Southtown district called an early childhood summer laboratory. It was a two-week session offered in early July in which beginning teachers and children in the district were invited to participate. Ellen, paired with Susan as her mentor, developed a project on police stations as a theme to enrich the experience of the small group of kindergartners that participated. This was Ellen's first exposure to students and gave her an opportunity to learn how to work with them under Susan's guidance. Ellen and Susan volunteered to run a second session for another two weeks.

The summer lab was followed by a four-day, intensive classroom management workshop sponsored by the district and run by a team of experts invited from a southern university. Ellen and seven other beginning teachers at Southtown were among the participants. It involved the presentation of theories and procedures (described in a 200-page packet distributed to participants) and simulations. The packet included six topics: organizing the classroom, planning and teaching rules and procedures, managing student work, maintaining good student behavior, planning instruction, and constructing instruction.

In late August, the principal of Southtown Elementary School offered what he called "an integrated workshop" for beginners and new teachers for four days. The assistant principal and experienced teachers also participated in the workshop as "trainers." The principal summarized its purpose:

> We give beginning teachers a chance to do the first day in
> school more than once. If you think teachers have only one
> first day in their careers, they may get a bad start. I try to
> make sure that they will have a good start. This workshop
> is to be as practical as possible. When you go into the class
> what are you going to teach? What impression are you
> going to make on your kids? How are you going to set the
> time for that? What are you going to concentrate on first
> among various subjects? How are you going to connect all
> other pieces to it? These are some of the questions we ask.
> In other words, we try to give beginners enough practice
> before they actually do it in their classroom.

The principal started this workshop as a whole-staff
meeting in which every teacher was involved. He used discussion, small interaction groups, and simulation games to conduct
the workshop. He characterized this in-service program as
integrated because it was designed to integrate the relevant
knowledge and skills that the neophytes learned during the
summer. It was the principal's undertaking to leave his personal
mark on the beginning teachers. Hereafter, he would continue to
play an important role as a mentor for the beginners throughout
the year.

For Ellen the first summer offered her rich learning
opportunities that contributed to her confidence about teaching
in the fall. In her assessment, the workshops provided "a set of
ideals and direction," rather than a framework of concrete
activities in the classroom. She learned how to teach kindergarten children and how to cope with potential problems in the
classroom setting. But she feared that she knew very little about
what to teach. This necessitated her frequent consultation with
Susan, who had taught the kindergarten level for two years.
Ellen's conversation with Susan assumed a critical role in her
process of learning to teach.

From the first day of school Ellen actively sought Susan's
guidance. They sat down regularly to make weekly and monthly
activity plans. To discuss daily lessons, they met for thirty
minutes before the children arrived at school. As Ellen put it,
Susan served as her curriculum. She saw her new situation as
follows:

What is important for me now is not so much a matter of
having freedom as working with Susan to learn about
what to teach. Susan's teacher passed the curriculum to
her, and in turn she is passing it down to me, just as a
folktale is passed down. It is passed along that way. Here
is a class that works with Susan, not a class that goes for
every teacher. I have to learn what Susan knows. She is
my curriculum. She knows where to go up until December. So I have to check with Susan before we do anything.

Susan elaborated on Ellen's remarks:

We do team teaching. So she learns experience from me.
We do the daily schedule together. Basically I review with
her what I previously did. We might look through books
for ideas, and I might look through my past lesson plans,
things I did previously. That's the way to help children
together.

Ellen also chatted with the principal and assistant
principal at least twice a week to get their suggestions. Talking
was frequent among teachers in her area and was an important
source of relevant information. Ellen's extensive reliance on her
buddy stemmed from the fact that she did not receive any
detailed curriculum guide. She was not able to determine by
herself the curriculum content to be covered for a given week
and month. There was a districtwide curriculum, but it did not
specify the content. But by December Ellen began to feel that
she could identify "semi-instinctively" some of the materials that
she used, although her consultation with Susan continued
throughout the spring.

Ellen's other area of concern from the outset was classroom management, a problem she was very conscious of
throughout the year. She feared that she might lose control of
some of the children in her class. Our description of her
routinized activities presented earlier reveals that she was rather
stern in enforcing classroom norms. She frequently issued
directives and warnings to the class to restore quiet and
attention. Ellen often perceived loud talking, excitement, and
playful behavior as disruptive, disorderly, and inconducive to
learning. She sent one boy to the school's student assessment

team for what she considered to be his unmanageable behavior problem. But the team evaluated the problem as being less seriously disruptive than Ellen had made it out. One boy was transferred to Susan's class at the request of his parents—a shocking event that affected her for a long time. From early in the year, she began to be known among the administrators and her colleagues as a "crier." Ellen's concern with classroom management encompassed other matters as well. She wanted children to be independent and take responsibility for themselves. When her children failed to meet her expectations, she issued warnings and punished them by isolating them.

Ellen was not able to get much help from Susan and her other peers with respect to classroom management. It was something that she had to work out herself and became a source of lonely struggle. Nevertheless, by January her primary concern became three boys whom she regarded as having behavior control problems.

As early as October Ellen started what she called a positive reinforcement schedule, a technique she learned when she was a special education student. Every day she named a star of the day and gave a certificate. She gave an award to the three boys for displaying good behavior. By December she began to realize that she must improve herself and bought a book on alternatives to punitive discipline to learn a better way of handling behavior problems. Ellen learned that she should be more patient and sit back. She confessed, "I discovered that children at this age need a lot of freedom. They need you to sit back." Meanwhile the majority of her children learned what she expected of them, although the three boys continued to be a problem throughout the spring.

What Beginning Teachers Teach

At both schools, the difficulties that beginning teachers encountered in teaching were in significant part related to the whole-language approach that these schools adopted. At Southtown this approach replaced the conventional basal program and led to the development of an integrated curriculum. In principle, the integrated curriculum of early childhood education was guided by a series of themes around which instruction of skills and knowledge in language, math, science, and social studies evolved. Each of these areas was taught as part of the project under a particular theme. Teachers chose the theme, on which they spent two to three weeks.

The integrated curriculum makes a standard approach less effective and relevant. Moreover, as the assistant principal at Southtown stated, because children's readiness for academic work at the K–2 level varied considerably, that variability made standard materials less appropriate. Accordingly, the district replaced conventional tests with the "portfolio" of the individual child, an evaluation packet used continually from kindergarten to second grade. Instead of giving the tests, teachers must collect materials for the portfolio, including a self-portrait, interviews with the child and parents, word/writing awareness, a reading sample, a writing sample, and the class record. The portfolio individualized the evaluation of each child. Southtown's rationale for banning the standard curriculum for K–2 was related to the above-mentioned changes that took place in the past four years. Southtown's approach posed a challenge for Ellen as well as for Gail Fisher. They were expected to construct a curriculum that would meet the different needs of kindergarteners and first-graders. This caused Ellen anxiety from the outset. She resolved the problem by accepting the notion that the curriculum is a folktale handed down to her by her buddy. Ellen's metaphor that "Susan is my curriculum" was a form of adaptive response that she invented in her struggle to learn to teach. But Gail, who as a beginner was also placed in the same situation as Ellen, noted, "You have so many choices and so many creative things here. Sometimes it is overwhelming. But you have to design your program."

At the same time, Ellen was not reluctant to accept whole language as the basis of her instruction. She explained how whole language was used in her teaching:

> What we do revolves around whole language. Right now we are doing monsters [the monster theme]. Whether we work on monsters or math, every activity is guided by whole language. We are studying a lot of literature about

> monsters, wild things, a monster party, doing reading on
> monsters, doing extended activities. All these revolve
> around monster stories. . . . Whole language is a means to
> integrate all topics and subjects we deal with.

Ellen was quite comfortable with the monster theme because
Susan guided her in developing it.

Ellen defined the chief academic objectives for kindergarten as language development, story writing, talking, and the
development of math skills and social skills. Theme-based
projects, the calendar, reading, writing practice, the sharing
circle, and activity centers made up Ellen's curriculum, designed
to meet these objectives. Notice that art and gym were not
included in her program, because they were taught separately by
specialists. For Ellen, the development of what she called
"correct habits" was important but secondary to the improvement of cognitive skills. It is also relevant to note that the
portfolio, the evaluation packet, was primarily a profile of
literacy development and excluded evaluation of the child's
moral and social development. In other words, moral and social
development did not have as much weight as cognitive
development in Southtown's official curriculum even though
learning and obeying school rules was an important component
of each school day.

Turning to Westville, the introduction of whole language
to the school was also the source of sustained concern for all
beginning teachers. The Westville district began to adopt whole
language as early as 1987. By the time Westville Upper
Elementary School opened in 1990, the transition from the traditional basal approach to literacy development based on literature
was nearly complete and whole language was gaining credibility
as the central concept of the new approach. Accordingly, in 1990
the district's reading committee was rewriting the curriculum
guide for reading and writing at the elementary level. But this
was not available yet to the beginning teachers; instead, they
received the guide used in the past. Westville had a reading
specialist, whose primary assignment was to promote a literacy
development campaign based on whole language and a half-
dozen veteran teachers who developed expertise in literature-
based reading. These teachers, along with the principal, who was

also an ardent adovocate for whole language, orchestrated the initiative in promoting the new approach at the new school. It was against this background that beginning teachers started to teach reading and writing in 1990.

Beginning teachers spoke of two categories of curriculum. The first category included math, science, and social studies, which were said to be "clear cut" in terms of objectives and content. They and their buddies adopted textbooks for these subjects. There was a correspondence between the curriculum guides for these subjects and the textbooks. As we saw, Nancy followed the textbooks literally when she taught math and science. Because the textbooks provided materials and the framework for objectives, Nancy had little sense of ambiguity or ambivalence about the instruction of math and science. Likewise, Janet Montana felt "comfortable" in teaching these subjects.

The second category of curriculum was reading, writing, and English. It made the beginning teachers "panic." Nancy's buddy discussed the problem for beginners and some other teachers:

> Since we are moving into a wholistic reading and writing program, a literature-based program, there is a lot of confusion among many teachers as to how to teach reading and writing. In this district that is the hardest thing you come into. When I moved into this district [in 1988], people were still using a part basal and part literature program. And I am still doing that. I feel comfortable doing it. I think many new teachers, besides Nancy, feel a kind of panic. You are kind of thrown into a literature program out of college. You don't understand how to teach or what it is about. That's the kind of curriculum that is a gray area.

Nancy concurred with her buddy's characterization of the difficulty that beginning teachers encountered. Although she, unlike Janet and another beginner who specialized in science and math at college, was an English major at college and was confident in teaching literature to students, she felt that the whole language approach was too elusive and lacked requisite operational strategies. She was committed to promoting the literature-based program but needed structure in teaching language. Consequently, she and her buddy used the grammar book to teach grammar and used a spelling book to teach spelling. As we saw earlier, she admitted that she was in what she called a "lecture mode" when she taught reading and writing, but insisted that that was necessary to give the students basic knowledge. With the help of her buddy, she targeted district guidelines to select materials and literature in reading and writing.

Although Nancy was in the first year of teaching, it is evident that she held a firm view about teaching language and insisted that there must be a coherent and guiding structure in teaching language. By comparison, the whole-language approach, she felt, was devoid of that structure and placed priority on the process of learning language, in which children's needs took precedence. When she came to the district, she was first enthusiastic about whole language and hoped to learn it. In the course of the first three months, however, she became disillusioned with it.

With respect to Nancy's overall instructional schedule, as pointed out earlier, Nancy constructed her own weekly lesson plan, with emphasis on reading and writing. She devoted two periods each day to reading and writing and four additional periods a week to some aspects of language instruction: 35 percent of the total weekly lessons were allocated to language instruction. She allocated one period each day to math, science, and social studies: 12.5 percent of the total lessons to each. In addition, each week had two gym periods; one period each for music, art, and computer; one period for current events, and one period for "family" meetings to discuss students' interests. The latter two periods, however, were usually used for either reading aloud or silent reading.

By comparision, the allocation of time to subjects in the Japanese school is uniform throughout the nation. The allocation of time at the fifth-grade level is currently: 19 percent for Japanese; 16 percent for math; 10 percent each for science, social studies, and gym; 6.5 percent for art, music, and home economics. In addition, there is one period for moral education, and two periods each for special student activities and student projects. It is noted here that time is much more evenly distributed for various subjects than it was in Nancy's class. Further the Japanese school assigns a significant amount of time to music, art, home economics, moral education, and student activity each week.

Nancy taught three subjects—language, science, and math—and was primarily concerned with activities that enhanced the cognitive growth of the student within the classroom. There is a remarkable consistency in the emphasis on the cognitive aspect of schooling between the kindergarten and fifth-grade levels.

Summary

Both Nancy and Ellen received master's degrees and had extensive clinical experiences by national standards. But their induction into teaching was hardly guided by what they had learned at college. For them, learning to teach for the first year scarcely involved an application of theoretical knowledge but, instead, was directed toward a constant search for the practical knowledge needed for teaching. Knowledge of teaching is generally viewed as encompassing two types: theoretical-technical and practical (Carter 1990). The neophytes we studied saw learning to teach as enlarging practical knowledge and integrating it into a personal frame of reference. In brief, it was an experiential, craft-oriented process. Our preceding analysis reveals that it was not theoretical knowledge but practical knowledge that dominated the neophytes' concern. As Ellen put it, "It was not until I became a teacher that I began to feel I was learning what teaching was all about."

Learning to teach in the first year, especially for the first several months, occurred in a highly intense and unsettled social context hitherto unfamiliar to them. Their encounters with the children and incessant and interminable classroom events called for their immediate response. The routinization of classroom activities we saw provided stability and constancy to these activities. It was in these situations where practical knowledge was most applicable and useful. Following the advice of their buddies, for example, the neophytes dealt with problems of classroom management with the rules that they created jointly with students—a universal practice of which classroom teachers invariably avail themselves. These rules, part of the practical knowledge, were an instrument to attain control of activities, space, and time in the classroom. Nancy's buddy suggested, "Consistency is of number-one importance in making these rules effective."

Both the neophytes and their buddies interpreted learning to teach as attaining familiarity with rules of practice (Elbaz 1983). While the neophytes were exposed to an array of procedures that included school policy and procedures to deal with classroom and school events and parents, they sought context-specific rules of practice by working closely with buddies. Practical knowledge for teaching is rooted in the shared character of teachers' experiences and in the perspectives that evolve from them, that is, the culture of teaching (Hargreaves 1980). In this sense, learning to teach is a form of learning the culture of teaching, that is, apprenticeship through conversation and observation.

The mode of learning teaching as an apprenticeship does not readily accommodate learning innovations that are not embedded in the culture of teaching. Although she was interested in promoting literature-based reading and writing, Nancy's rejection of whole language finds its basis to some degree in this mode of learning to teach. Nancy was initially attracted to Westville for its innovative approach and wanted to learn whole language. She projected to herself this image of the school, and she took it as a challenge. But after a couple of months teaching at Westville, she found herself in conflict with the whole-language approach. She needed structure instead of the elusiveness of the whole-language approach. For the identical reason, Ellen decided to take a job at Southtown. In her case, she liked the concept of whole language but did not know how to implement it. She was expected to develop curriculum materials appropriate for the instruction of whole language, but, instead, complained about the absence of a detailed curriculum guide that would have informed her about how to teach. She fell back on the metaphor that "Susan is my curriculum," and Susan as a buddy accepted that metaphor and passed down her experiences with teaching to Ellen as a folktale is transmitted to a younger generation.

Emphasis on practical knowledge in learning to teach is common to both American and Japanese beginning teachers. But there is a sharp contrast in their definitions of the content of practical knowledge. American teachers see it exclusively in terms of enhancing the cognitive process in the classroom, whereas Japanese teachers view it much more inclusively and broadly.

Where did all the rules for student behavior fit in at the American schools we studied? A hidden curriculum predominantly dealt with "appropriate school behavior." We will deal with this issue in the next chapter.

CHAPTER 3

Expectations and Classroom Control
The Case of American Teachers

Our ethnographic account presented in chapter 2 focused on the process of learning to teach in the school setting. Here our aim is to explore the expectations that beginning American teachers had of their students and the pattern of control they adopted to create a learning environment conducive to realizing those expectations. More specifically, we will first discuss the student motivational orientation that beginning teachers sought to promote and then discuss classroom management and related activities designed to enhance control of students. To appreciate the distinctiveness of American school practices, we will contrast them to Japanese practices when appropriate.

The Purpose of Teaching: Cultural Embeddedness

Teachers' expectations of students are closely related to their perceptions of the purposes of schooling that society defines by virtue of the fact that teachers are considered agents of cultural transmission (Spindler et al. 1990). It follows that there are appreciable differences as well as similarities in what American and Japanese teachers view as the goals of education. As we have seen earlier, American classroom teachers framed them primarily in terms of cognitive achievement and academic performance. Indeed, from the time students arrived at school until they left, beginning elementary teachers devoted little time to activities other than the academic. The domains of physical and aesthetic education were delegated to specialists and viewed as aspects of teaching outside their primary responsibilities. Such an emphasis on the cognitive process was noticeable to an appreciable extent, even at the kindergarten level. In contrast, Japanese classroom teachers saw the basic goals of education much more broadly, encompassing competencies essential to the cognitive, moral, physical, social, and aesthetic development of the students. These findings are supported by previous research (Cummings 1980; White 1987; Sato & McLaughlin 1992).

These differences in educational goals are highlighted in school handbooks in the United States and Japan. Southtown's handbook, for example, states its "philosophy" as follows:

> We recognize the importance of our children as individuals with specific needs, and we strive to provide a strong educational program that meets those needs at each step of development. . . . In order to implement this philosophy, we focus on the following goals:
>
> 1. To provide a strong foundation in math, reading, and language arts.
>
> 2. To help children to explore and investigate the world through science and social studies.
>
> 3. To help each child communicate in the most effective ways possible through oral and written language.

This statement epitomizes the fact that the dominating concern at school is academics and related individual needs. Compare it with the following excerpt from the handbook of a Japanese elementary school:

> Our school philosophy is to strive to accomplish the aims of elementary education stated below:
>
> 1. To foster children who have healthy minds and bodies.
>
> 2. To foster children who cooperate with others, make efforts, and take the initiative.
>
> 3. To foster children who have the ability to think profoundly and have generous hearts.

The elementary course of study issued by the Ministry of Education further stresses: "It should be a basic principle that moral education in school should be provided throughout all the educational activities of the school." Here an emphasis is given to the development of the mind and body, cooperation, individual initiative, effort, fostering warm and generous hearts, and moral education. Although only one weekly period is provided for moral education, it is expected to be implemented broadly in all aspects of schooling.

Differences in educational goals between U.S. and Japanese schools can be further elucidated by comparing the weekly schedules of classes. As decribed in the previous chapter, Nancy Smith's class schedule consisted of lessons in reading, writing, spelling, math, and science (social studies was taught by her colleague). Additionally, two periods of gym and one period each of art, music, and computer were offered by specialists. Students were confined to the classroom all day and were allowed little time to engage in social interaction among themselves, except during the 40-minute lunch period. Clearly Nancy's chief interest was to concentrate on the cognitive process in the classroom, and hardly included other domains of interaction with students. Moreover there was a significant degree of isomorphism between her orientation and that of other teachers at Westville.

By comparison, the weekly schedule of classes for a Japanese beginning fifth-grade teacher whom we observed included a variety of areas: Japanese language, math, social studies, science, arts/crafts, and gym plus one period each of moral education, classroom assembly, club activity, and classroom guidance. In addition, two periods of music and home economics each were offered by specialized teachers. As this example makes clear, Japanese elementary classroom teachers are expected to design teaching broadly on the assumption that it is multifaceted. This expectation is embedded in what the Japanese call *zenjin kyoiku*, "whole-person education" (Sato & McLaughlin 1992).

Moreover, Japanese schools organize events outside the classroom (such as sports, cultural and music festivals, and interschool contests in which classroom teachers are involved) much more frequently than do U.S. schools. Sports and cultural festivals especially are big schoolwide events that require the coordination and preparation at all grade levels for a couple of weeks—events where parents also take part as spectators. In short, the scope of teaching assumed by Japanese elementary classroom teachers is much broader than that of their counterparts in the United States.

As explored in another chapter, Japanese students have more opportunities than do American students for social interaction designed to improve skills in human relations, and Japanese teachers' routine responsibilities include mental, moral, aesthetic, physical, and social development. Moreover, it is assumed that student guidance, personal habits, motivation, and interpersonal relations are important parts of the activities that classroom teachers are expected to address (Kataoka 1992; U.S. Department of Education 1987).

In contrast, in the U.S. schools we studied, the division of work is such that much of the responsibility for these noncognitive areas of education (such as guidance, music education, and physical education) is assumed by specialists. Even at the kindergarten level, there is a clear division of work. As discussed earlier, Ellen's primary responsibility in her kindergarten classroom was to focus on the cognitive domain, with concomitant emphasis on social skills and personal habits and excluding physical, music, and art education. No Japanese elementary schools, by comparison, have specialized counselors and gym teachers, although they have music specialists. Music, however, is usually taught by classroom teachers at lower elementary levels. In short, American elementary classroom teachers generally see their role as specialized in the academic area, while Japanese counterparts view their role more broadly. These different notions of teaching are culturally embedded and reflect what society expects the school to perform.

Teacher Expectations and Instrumental Activities

We will turn to American beginning teachers' expectations of students and to the relevant activities through which they tried to achieve these expectations. There was a remarkable consistency between Ellen Steinbeck, a kindergarten teacher at Southtown, and Nancy Smith, a fifth-grade teacher at Westville, in terms of their expectations of students. This by and large applies to the two other beginning teachers we studied. What this consistency suggests is that pervasive cultural expectations existed that influenced their orientations toward teaching. The extent to which these expectations were internalized and operationalized varied with individual teachers. To elucidate cultural influence on teaching, we refer to Hess and Azuma's fascinating article "Cultural Support for Schooling: Contrasts Between Japan and the United States" (1991).

The authors suggest that culture provides models for learning and teaching that are adopted when children are socialized at home and that are carried over to the school, where teachers make use of them. On the one hand, Japanese parents and teachers avail themselves of a cultural practice that enhances what Hess and Azuma call "adaptive dispositions" for effective learning and teaching. Adaptive dispositions are characterized by diligence, compliance, and accommodation. On the other, American parents and teachers emphasize quite a different model, which focuses on dispositions characterized by self-reliance and self-assertiveness, which we may call "independent dispositions." In socializing children during the preschool years, this model underscores the precedence of one's own goals and desires and regards socializing agents to be others in a position of authority. In contrast, the Japanese practice relies on modeling, with special attention to close identification with others, in which the difference between the child and the socializing agent is minimized.

These dispositions are brought to bear in teaching and learning at the elementary level, when children enter school. Hess and Azuma suggest that American teachers typically capitalize upon children's independent dispositions to facilitate learning by stimulating intrinsic motivation. Teachers' strategies are to provide a stimulating environment to induce children's engagement in learning, instead of exploiting their adaptive dispositions. Therefore, submit the authors, "the primary method of motivating students in the United States has become the managing of the social context of learning to provide stimulation" (p. 7) with acknowledgment of the individuality and independence of the student. Meanwhile, Japanese teachers typically rely on students' adaptive dispositions—diligence and receptivity to the demands of school to stimulate effective learning. Thus, "In Japan teachability is an internalized receptive diligence. . . . Overt control by the teacher is minimal. . . . Students perceive the situation, realize what is expected of them" (p. 7).

Hess and Azuma's thesis, which we described here briefly, is reflected remarkably in our beginning teachers' practices. As will be seen shortly, both Ellen and Nancy sought to strengthen students' independent dispositions. We will explore their pedagogical beliefs and practices.

Our field notes reveal that in Nancy's frequent evaluative comments to her students and us, one frequently used word invariably stands out: "independent." She believed that her students did not have disciplined independent dispositions and were passive in their attitudes toward learning. In her view they were pampered "upper-class" children who often expected entertainment and fun in their lesson; they expected "a pony show, to be entertained." She insisted that her "job is to set you up so that you are self-directed." A self-directed student was the ideal that she strived to actualize through teaching, and she saw her goal of teaching as making her students "independent of her" in doing their work. Other terms and phrases Nancy often used in her talks to the class to convey the importance of independence were responsibility, initiative, maturity, accountability, and taking charge of one's own activities—terms that represent a self-directed student. She often used expressions that combined sarcasm with admonition when she was disappointed with her students and felt they were not taking responsibility for their work. She often told them: "You are immature." "Are you still in fourth grade?" "I will be glad to send you back to Brighton" (a K–3 school). "Don't you understand this is a two-way street? When I give you everything I have, I expect you to give me back 100 percent of you." "Don't rely on me for your work." "You are the ones who are looking at yourself 10 years from now, not me." In the words of a veteran teacher at the same grade, "They need to know that they are in charge of themselves."

The concept of self-direction was already part of Nancy's pedagogical ideology when she started to teach at Westville. She

related it to her biography and suggested that she began to realize the importance of independence when she was in second
grade and saw her brother as a model to follow because he was
"mature" and independent. Her following comment articulates
her belief:

> It has been a part of my personal philosophy. I was a
> good, successful student throughout my life and some-
> what an academic type starting from a very young age.
> I was kind of self-motivated and took my own initiative. I
> was just like a goal setter. I did not know why I was very
> hard on myself for perfectionism. But I have always
> thought that throughout my life experiences, it basically
> comes down to what I have thought I have to accomplish.
> It is a kind of existential stance that you create yourself.
> That was roots. I have a philosophy that as a person you
> are ultimately responsible for yourself. I think that it is the
> real object of education. It is a way of life, so that it
> continues beyond the classroom. You have to have that
> initiative to learn as well, and seize an opportunity to
> learn whenever you can. In any event that's how I want
> my kids to be.

Nancy was much more emphatic about self-direction than two
other beginning teachers and several experienced teachers we
interviewed at Westville. Although she felt it might be too arro-
gant for her to assume that her "way of life" is right for every
child, she was consistent in insisting that her students be more
self-directed.

To accomplish her expectations, Nancy chose several
instrumental activities that, incidentally, were also practiced by
other teachers at Westville. One type of instrumental activity was
reading. As pointed out earlier, it was the policy of the school
that basal readers not be adopted. Drawing upon her rich background in English literature (unlike the two other beginners at
her school who had different training), Nancy readily selected
books from children's literature as materials in reading. She
believed that reading is an area where she could encourage students to engage in self-directed work most effectively, and her
goal was to enable them "to be on their own books." She
earnestly exhorted them to choose their books from the list of
literature she selected, to study them, and frequently to write

what she called "journal letters," personal impressions about the books they read. Because Nancy did not fail to suggest that students read whenever there were opportunities for reading, reading became a dominating concern for the entire class.

Incidentally, there is a clear contrast between Nancy's approach to reading to foster students' independent dispositions and Japanese beginning teachers' approach to instruction in the Japanese language. In Japanese schools, reading, writing, and spelling are typically combined, and teachers use an officially approved textbook that contains selections from literature. It is equivalent to the conventional basal reader used in the United States, but much more condensed. Teachers usually concentrate on the textbook and emphasize the comprehension of materials presented in the textbook. Our observations in Tokyo suggest that students were not encouraged to explore literature as part of the language curriculum, the emphasis being on cultivating students' diligence in comprehending the textbook. As noted earlier, there is a clear distinction between the two approaches.

Viewing homework as self-directed work, Nancy underscored it as essential to building independent learning attitudes in her students. Because homework requires students to take the initiative themselves, organize their time, and have the discipline to complete it, she saw its merit in terms of developing these habits. Indeed, she frequently gave homework and spent a considerable amount of time explaining it. On the front chalkboard she regularly posted a list of homework and reminded her class of it. That Nancy attached importance to homework was supported by her persistent adherence to the homework policy that she developed and distributed to the class and parents, who were requested to sign it to acknowledge its legitimacy.

The policy stated:

1. If a child comes to class without completed homework or a written excuse from home, then a notice will go home that evening to be signed by a parent.

2. The child will have the opportunity to complete the work that evening without any effect upon his or her grade.

3. If the child does not make up the incomplete work that evening, then a zero will be given for the assignment.

4. After a total of three late assignments, I will call your home to arrange for a plan to get homework completed on time.

5. Homework assignments will be excused for illness and/or emergencies, provided I receive a written note from a parent. Work missed due to absence will be made up over a period of days when the student returns to school.

Nancy also included this policy as part of the handout that she prepared for a back-to-the-school night and reiterated its importance to the parents. Likewise, the schoolwide homework policy was elaborately stated in four full pages and defined the responsibilities to be borne by teachers, students, and parents. Its "philosophy" underscored the notion of independent work: "Homework may be defined as an assignment given by a teacher to increase proficiency in particular skills, reinforce concepts presented in the classroom, develop lifelong study habits, and foster independence and self-discipline."

Nancy also developed "Progress Update" and a point system to monitor students' progress. "Progress Update," designed to inform parents of her evaluation of students' work including homework, was periodically sent home to the parents. Within the classroom she used a point system to measure students' performance in homework and other areas. These were some of the devices that Nancy used to reinforce her homework policy.

Nancy attempted to foster an independent disposition toward learning by other methods as well. For example, she required a "research" paper to be completed in the spring. She wrote an impressive nine-page research handbook for students to use in conducting research and writing a paper, an elaborate research guide that could be used even by high school students. She carefully outlined how to choose a topic, develop questions, categorize them, establish the order of categories, and find and use sources of information. Students were granted three weeks to complete the papers, which were lengthy and rich in content, and they were displayed in the hall with Nancy's comments. She attributed the success of this project to students' disciplined independent work.

Nancy saw her role as that of a "director" promoting students' self-directed activities. Her role was to provide a stimulating environment for nurturing independent dispositions and self-directed work. Nevertheless, in other areas her ethos of self-direction was not consistent with her actual conduct of teaching. This was a source of her persistent dilemma as a beginning teacher, which she could not resolve in the first year. For example, Nancy assumed that to do independent work students first had to master requisite knowledge and skills, and she conducted teacher-directed lessons in writing-spelling and grammar. She by and large used recitation and seatwork as "a social context for learning" (Weinstein 1991) in which student activities were controlled by her. As noted in the previous chapter, she felt uncomfortable with the unstructured approach advocated by her colleagues in the school, in which, in her view, basic skills were not systematically taught. As a result, she admitted that she was in "a lecture mode" for the first several months, but in the spring her lessons gradually involved more student-directed activities, focusing on the materials that students read independently. Likewise, her math and science lessons were entirely textbook-centered and employed recitation and seatwork throughout the year. During our observations, student-directed experiments and observations of nature never occurred in the science class.

We now turn to Ellen Steinbeck, who taught kindergarten. We have already pointed out the significant degree of continuity between Ellen and Nancy, in terms of their expectations of children. Speaking of order in Japanese society, Thomas P. Rohlen, an anthropologist, suggests: "Recent intensive observations in early education give reason to conclude that even in the earliest learning environments practices and understandings are found that echo distinctive features of Japanese law, government, and management" (1989, p. 5).

Rohlen is pointing out the isomorphism and continuity that exist between the two practices—between socialization in early childhood and institutional practices in society. This suggests that these practices consistently reflect the pattern of

Japanese culture. This is an insightful observation that, we believe, can be applied to American education. Given this perspective, we need not be baffled by the continuity of expectations for students between the kindergarten and the upper elementary levels.

Ellen wanted to accomplish two chief expectations. One was the development of independent attitudes and behavior in children, and the other was classroom control. We will discuss the latter concern later in this chapter. Ellen ambitiously stated her first goal as follows:

> I want to get to the point where they can run this class-room without my being here. They come in the morning and totally get to work without my saying "You have to do this." I want them to do it themselves. My goal is to turn the classroom over to children and give them more air time, so that it's their class not my class. And that's the main goal whether or not that will happen.

For Ellen independence meant that without her directives four- and five-year-olds would independently follow the routines that we described in chapter 2. What often annoyed her was that she had to issue directives from time to time throughout the day to focus children on their task. She viewed independence as the assumption of responsibility and repeated its importance throughout the year:

> Developing children's responsibility is very important. Children must develop a sense of responsibility in ful-filling what is expected of them. For example, bringing money to school, buying lunch, etc. Children are respon-sible for taking homework home and returning it to the teacher. It is not mom's or dad's responsibility. Children will learn that they have to put it in their folder. I am very emphatic about this matter. They can be trained to develop a sense of responsibility at this age.

Ellen linked the development of ability to manage routines to the growth of independent dispositions. She expected children to manage their folders that contained money for lunch, parents' communications, and the like. They were expected to place these folders on their desks every morning and make sure that every-thing was in them. Ellen considered this type of routine as providing an opportunity to develop a habit of responsibility without her assistance.

As Nancy did, Ellen regarded homework as consequential at the kindergarten level to develop a sense of responsibility. She used punitive strategies if children did not perform their expected responsibility. For example, she commented:

> I give homework in order to develop their sense of responsibility. If they forget it, it is not their parents' problem but theirs. They have to sit out in the classroom. They will have no centers. If they forget it, they have to suffer the consequence by not having a recess period.

To develop children's independent dispositions, Ellen believed that she must be emotionally detached from her children and stressed the acceptance of her authority by children. To put it differently, she saw her relationship with children as one based on what she called respect, but not on emotional ties such as friendship. She insisted that mutual respect must exist between her and them to develop good relationships. She viewed herself as the "other" in the position of authority and suggested "formal relationships" with them, an emotional distance conducive to a good classroom environment where children could develop self-reliance. She could be friendly to children only on the condition that they accepted her as the authority.

In contrast to the emotional distance that both Ellen and Nancy maintained with their children, Japanese teachers emphasize emotional closeness and attachment as a fulcrum to achieve their pedagogical goals (Lewis 1989; White 1987; Shimahara & Sakai 1992). As will be noted in chapter 6, they saw the motivation for learning and achievement as being stimulated by the emotional ties, often called *kizuna*, created between the teacher and children. *Kizuna* are interpersonal relationships that foster empathy and what is characterized as the "touching of the hearts." To cultivate it, teachers promote intrinsic, unpretentious, interpersonal experience that engages children. That interpersonal experience results in enriched companionship and thorough familiarity with children.

The adaptive dispositions that Japanese children bring to school are supported and further developed by interdependence and trust based on ligature, or bonding. These dispositions are fostered through what Hess and Azuma (1991) call osmosis. They refer to two closely related but distinctive modes of cultural transmission of values: osmosis and "teaching." Osmosis involves nurturance, interdependence, and emotional and physical closeness, which provide exposure to adult values. It encourages identification with significant others. "Teaching" involves direct instruction, injunctions, frequent dialogue, and explanations and does not require emotional closeness between children and adults; this was the form of cultural transmission that the beginning American teachers employed.

We turn next to other instrumental activities Ellen used to develop independent dispositions. The reader is already acquainted with the curriculum that Ellen adopted—one that her buddy, Susan Taylor, introduced her to. Although Ellen articulated her pedagogical goals independently of her buddy, she diligently followed Susan's lead in devising and implementing the curriculum. Within this shared framework Ellen placed importance on the notion of choice, the freedom to choose one's own activity, which required independent initiative by a child.

She allocated half the space available in her classroom to a half-dozen centers of activity. Once or twice a day, children chose their own activities and enjoyed them. The centers where they organized their activities and the time spent on them were designed to provide fun for the children and an opportunity for cooperation, but the activites were not academic. But Ellen occasionally used the concept of centers to devise academic activities. For example, with the assistance of a paraprofessional she organized three academic activity centers (the alphabet, painting, and number recognition), which children chose and which rotated. She explained the meaning of choice:

> Our curriculum is based on choice. It is rare that children have to do only one thing as a group. When they have options, they are expected to control their actions, and they control what they learn. Of course, they have to do some things without having a choice. For example, they have to practice counting. When I give them choices, I preset them in my mind, to enable them to make right choices.

Again, the contrast between what we saw here and Japanese practice is interesting. Japanese kindergartens offer group-oriented activities where children do not choose individualized activities (Yuki 1992; Tobin et al. 1989). Children are typically put into small groups, to develop an identity with the group, social skills, cooperation, and shared responsibility for activities. Instead of engaging in diverse activities, small groups engage in the same activities as are designed for the entire class. Here the emphasis is not on independence and choice but on interdependence, cooperation, group activity, and a sense of belonging (Yuki 1992).

The evaluation of student performance adopted by the district in which Southtown Elementary is located was also conducive to the development of student independence and choice. Two years prior to our study, the district replaced standard tests with what was called a "portfolio," an individualized assessment package—the "Red Folder," as most teachers referred to it, because the portfolio was contained in a red folder. The Red Folder was used from kindergarten through second grade. Its chief characteristic was to recognize the uniqueness of each child and the diversity of student performance as natural.

Patterns of Control

What concerns many American and Japanese teachers—especially beginning teachers—is what they commonly identify as control. In this section we will explore patterns of student control. Controls are universal practices that induce members of a society to conform to the expected patterns of their culture. Likewise, control is ubiquitously exercised to achieve students' conformity to the expectations of schools and teachers, regardless of the cultures to which the schools are oriented. However, there is a marked difference in the degree to which American and Japanese elementary teachers exercise control over their students. We will explore American beginning teachers' control of students in terms of time, space, and activity (with attention to classroom routines and student-teacher interactions as control mechanisms) and highlight some differences between American and Japanese teachers' styles of control. Then we will discuss two approaches to control, identified as cognitive and affective (or interpersonal), which respectively represent the American and Japanese styles. In this section we will focus on classroom management.

Control is the exercise of power, and power is relational. A power relationship exists where interests conflict, for instance, between a teacher and her students, especially when the students must comply with the demands of the teacher, who can threaten to invoke sanctions against the students when compliance is not achieved. In this case, power refers to the teacher's ability to control the behavior of students to produce a desired outcome. Power is vested in and generated by the authority of the teacher, who is in the cognitively and normatively superior status. In this sense, the authority represents institutionalized power. By the same token, it is a relational concept which addresses the process of communication in which the teacher generates power. Jackson (1990) eloquently addresses the power relationships that confront children:

> The school child, like the incarcerated adult, is, in a sense, a prisoner. He too must come to grips with the inevitability of his experience. He too must develop strategies for dealing with the conflict that frequently arises between his natural desires and interests on the one hand and institutional experiences on the other. (p. 8)

As White (1989) describes in her ethnographic study, most teachers are exposed for the first time in their professional careers to power relationships and authority status when they engage in student teaching. Many student teachers initially hold an idealistic view about their relationships to students, a view that is characterized by equality of status and power. For example, when they are introduced to students as Mr. Smith and Ms. Jones, their immediate reactions are expressed by a variable degree of discomfort such as giggles and blushes. "Why can't I be Sandy to the kids?" is a typical reaction. It is not atypical that student teachers value developing a warm, nurturing climate of relationships with students, but the first thing that the cooperating teacher suggests to them is, "Don't make the mistake of trying to be friends with kids" (White 1989, p. 183). White comments:

> Becoming a teacher means being inducted into a structured, differentiated, and hierarchical system in which there is status inequality between the teacher and student. A corollary is that teachers must establish and maintain a relationship with a group of children that differs from the relationship an individual adult can establish with an individual child. The position of teacher carries with it the right and obligation to establish and maintain control over a group of pupils. (p. 182)

Eventually student teachers learn that proper control of students is indispensable and critical to effective teaching. Indeed, both Ellen and Nancy recollected that controlling students was the most challenging task they ever confronted during student teaching. Ellen further revealed that as her concern with control heightened during her student teaching, she became more uncompromising in her interaction with children. Although teachers do not want to discuss publicly their relationships to students in terms of control, suffice it to suggest that control is their universally shared, deeply rooted concern.

Time as a control variable refers to the extent to which a teacher and his or her students regulate their time. Let us first reflect on how Nancy and her students controlled time. As we saw in the previous chapter, on a given day her students proceeded to their classroom as soon as they got off the bus in the morning, and she was physically present to supervise their movements before class formally began. No sooner did they enter the classroom than they lost control of time. Nancy urged them to unpack their knapsacks, submit their homework to her, and sit at their desks to read. Shortly before class started, she reminded the class of the pledge of allegiance. Immediately after this event, students were told to line up in the hall to go to the gym, and they were told of the code of behavior they had to observe in the hallway while Nancy escorted them. At the gym she relinquished her supervision of the class to the gym teacher.

When gym was about to be over, she stood at the entrance to the gym to bring her class back to the classroom.

Immediately after the students returned to the classroom, Nancy told them to get ready for a math class. A break would have offered students brief control of their time. The math lesson was followed by a reading lesson in the third period and the writing workshop in the fourth period, in which she taught grammar. All morning long, she never lost control of time because there was no student-controlled break. However, she did provide a snack time toward the end of the third period, during which students were told to remain quiet. They were permitted to talk quietly while they were seated at their desks. In the fifth period, designated as lunch, Nancy lined her students up in the hall and escorted them to the cafeteria. In the cafeteria they were not under the supervision of their teacher, although they were supervised by teacher aides. But they were not under strict time control there. Students gained complete control of time for 20 minutes after lunch, when they played outdoors.

Toward the end of this period, Nancy went outside to escort her students back to the classroom. The lunch period was followed by two lessons offered in succession without a break. The last period, designated as silent reading, was replaced by "Read Aloud," during which Nancy read a novel to the class. The eighth period was a more relaxed time for students, some of whom were permitted to work with a computer and to copy assignments. But her students were hardly permitted to engage in peer-initiated talking and interaction. Obviously, time was controlled by the teacher. When the eighth period came to an end, Nancy urged her students to pack their belongings and wait for the announcement of their bus. During this time students were in the classroom under the teacher's supervision and were nervously waiting for the announcement.

It follows from our brief summary of events on a given day at the school that Nancy exercised a high degree of control over time, to regulate the occurrence of events. Her students were able to control only the postlunch play time. Our ethnographic data suggest that Janet Montana, a beginning fourth-grade teacher, and another beginning fourth-grade teacher at Westville echoed the same pattern of time control. This suggests a high degree of consistency in time control among the three teachers. The pattern of control displayed by these teachers resulted in part from the schoolwide policy of Westville Upper Elementary School, which provided little time and space for student-initiated activities outside the classroom, other than the postlunch activity time. It was also in part a consequence of classroom teachers' preference not to offer students time and space under their own control within the classroom. Although Nancy's official time schedule allowed for a five-minute break after each lesson, she chose not to use it for student-initiated interaction. We were struck by the fact that students had little opportunity for social interaction with peers outside the domain of teacher control, although they did steal some time to engage in brief talks among themselves whenever possible. But such covert peer interactions represented a student-generated hidden strategy that was not approved by the teacher. In short, in the words of Ann and Harold Berlak (1981), the beginning teachers we studied displayed "a mode of high control of time."

We will make only a brief comment with respect to space and activity as control variables, because these dimensions of control were implicit in the foregoing discussion of time control. The classroom was the space where Nancy constructed her teaching events, and she regulated its use, including the walls, the floor, space for interaction between herself and her students and among the students, and desk arrangements. Use of the hallway was also regulated by the teacher; Nancy's students, like other students at the school, were not permitted to go out to the hallway without permission. Given Nancy's persistent control of time and space, her students could hardly initiate their own activities within the classroom. Suffice it to suggest that we scarcely saw student-initiated activities, except for the reading that her students regularly did before the first class started. As mentioned earlier, all the other activities in the classroom were directed by the teacher. Her students, as well as other students at the school, initiated their activities during the postlunch time when they went outdoors to play: There, they could choose their activities and the space where the activities occurred.

A high degree of control over time, activity, and space suggests that students' behavior is closely monitored and regulated. In other words, it means pervasive control of students. Not only Nancy's but also the other two beginning teachers' classrooms at Westville were characterized by such an extent of control. In contrast, Japanese teachers exerted relatively lower degrees of control over students. To put it differently, Japanese students had more time, space, and activities that they controlled themselves than the American students did. Japanese students controlled time and activity in many of the time segments that we will describe later. Japanese students used these segments of time to organize self-initiated activities ranging from informal interaction among themselves to structured meetings and club activities. It goes without saying that Japanese students add more time and space for activities that they can initiate and implement than do American students. As a result, Japanese schools and classrooms are much noisier, more robust, and livelier than their American counterparts. Such characteristics of schools and classrooms are not just tolerated but expected in Japan. While Nancy and her colleagues promoted interactions between themselves and their students (teacher-student dyadic interaction) and deemphasized student peer interactions, Japanese teachers generally underscored peer interactions so that students could learn to function as a member of a group.

In summary we note that there is a tendency to restrict peer interaction in the classrooms and the school settings that we studied in the United States, whereas there is a reversed tendency in Japan to increase such interaction in these situations. These differing patterns reflect the different purposes of schooling discussed earlier. It seems that because American elementary schools are preoccupied with the cognitive process in the classroom, students' social, emotional, and physical needs are attended to much less than they are in Japanese schools. As noted earlier, Japanese elementary schools display an equal concern with cognitive development, health, physical development, the development of social skills, moral sensitivity, and cooperative attitudes. The various abovementioned time segments at Japanese schools are intended to promote them. Students are expected to share time and activities with teachers during these segments; a student task group takes charge of school lunch; small groups are in charge of the assigned areas for cleaning; teachers, especially beginning teachers, are expected to join children when they play on the playground during the 20-minute break; a student monitor organizes a morning and an afternoon assembly to announce the goals for the day and reflect on major events of the day. Moreover, even schoolwide events, such as annual sports and cultural festivals, are jointly planned and implemented by students and teachers. This partly explains why Japanese schools provide students with more opportunities for self-initiated interaction among students, where control of time and activities is shifted from the teacher to students or shared.

Turning to Ellen Steinbeck's kindergarten classroom, we will present a briefer analysis than we did for Nancy, to avoid redundancy. What the reader will find in Ellen's classroom is that time, space, and activity are controlled just as in Nancy's. Let us first select some distinctive features from Ellen's profile of activities we saw earlier. As soon as Ellen's children arrived in their classroom around 9:00 A.M., she urged them to hang up their knapsacks and place their other belongings in the cubbies and their communication folders in a basket. They were told to sit at their desks and to color the papers that she placed on them and told that they must do their work quietly. The several students who were talking were reprimanded. This work was an expected activity before the first class started, and children were not permitted to engage in free play or talking. When the first class started at 9:15, Ellen attended to business including attendance check and lunch money. Subsequently the class gathered at the reading corner where she taught the calendar, numbers, and events. During this time the teacher demanded undivided attention from the children and stopped any talking and touching among them.

This lesson was followed by a brief snack time, during which all children sat quietly at their tables. It was then followed by a joint reading session with Susan Taylor's (her buddy's) class, where Susan read a Big Book and Ellen watched the children. After this lesson Ellen had her class line up at the entrance of her classroom, escorted her children to the gym, transferred supervision of the class to the gym teacher, and returned to the homeroom to do her work. As Nancy did, toward the end of gym Ellen returned to escort her children back to the classroom. As they lined up to go to the cafeteria, they were reminded that they must be quiet during their passage. Suffice it to say that thus far, without giving any break between lessons, Ellen conscientiously controlled time, space, and activities. Children had no free play or space for their own activities. Our ethnographic data reveal a noticeable parallel between Ellen and Gail Fisher, a first-grade beginner we studied, in terms of the control of time, space, and activity.

Kindergarten children were supervised in the playground area by paraprofessionals during the postlunch playtime, and at 12:20 P.M. Ellen opened the door for them to return to the classroom. Children from Susan's and two first-grade groups joined Ellen's children for another reading session. Gail Fisher read a book to the joint group and engaged in recitation while the other three teachers watched them. This was followed by a 30-minute period of center activities during which children chose activities of interest; this was a fun time that children could control. However, Ellen permitted them to continue these activities only as long as they were orderly and quiet. When this period was over, she announced a rest time during which Ellen's major concern was to keep them quiet. During this time, children could read or look at picture books while lying on the sponge mat or could take a nap. After the rest time Ellen directed the children to draw self-portraits to be included in their evaluation packets. Children who completed their portraits were permitted to play in centers again, but active children at the block center were told to stop playing, because they were boisterous. At 2:55 Ellen told all the children to sit at their desks and check the books they borrowed and other housekeeping items so that they would be ready to go home.

It is obvious that in the afternoon children had more time, space, and activities for themselves. They initiated activities during the postlunch playtime and during the center periods, but because they had to comply with Ellen's expectations when they played in centers, considerable control was exercised over children in the centers. As mentioned previously, if some children made excessive noise out of excitement, they were unfailingly isolated from the class—a form of punishment employed by Ellen.

Like Nancy's class, Ellen's children were confined to their classroom all day except for the gym and lunch period. The teacher entirely controlled morning time and activities. In the afternoon, however, Ellen's control of time and activity was relaxed. This pattern of control was not different from Susan Taylor's, although she issued warnings less frequently to maintain classroom order. Our ethnographic account of Ellen's activities suggests that her control of time, space, and activity was relatively pervasive. She always maintained a high profile as a control agent in all activities.

There is an interesting contrast in patterns of control between Ellen's classroom and the Japanese kindergartens that Lewis (1989) observed. She suggests three characteristics of control in the Japanese kindergarten. First, adults keep a very low profile as control agents. Japanese teachers do not constantly maintain surveillance of children's activities, because they believe it is unnecessary and also impossible when there are 30–35 children in one class. Second, Japanese teachers tolerate a wide range of behavior, including boisterous behavior, and place greater emphasis on free play than academic activities. This would reduce the necessity to control time and activity.

And finally, Lewis comments:

> The observations suggest a third way in which teachers mute their role as authority figures. Preschoolteachers appear to emphasize child-initiated compliance, rather than teacher-directed enforcement of rules. For example, one preschoolteacher attempted to discourage two boys from throwing sand by trying a number of different gambits. After several minutes of unsuccessful attempts, she turned her back and walked away from the boys, who continued to throw sand. (p. 143)

Moreover, Japanese teachers encourage what Lewis calls "self-management by children": Children are expected to assume a significant degree of responsibility for classroom management. For example, children choose monitors or task groups, as in the elementary level, who take responsibility for lining up children, assembling the class for events, etc. This would forgo the necessity for the teacher to direct children all the time.

To summarize, the patterns of student control that we have seen at both Westville and Southtown represent collective significance for they can be applied to a group of teachers at different levels. The context in which control is exercised is the routines we presented in the last chapter and the types of interaction between teachers and students that we have just discussed. The distinctive features of the control patterns become apparent when they are contrasted with the Japanese patterns.

Classroom Management: A Cognitive Approach

American and Japanese teachers have different approaches to classroom management, which account for distinctive patterns, although most teachers in both countries combine elements of both approaches. One is the cognitive approach, which by and large characterizes American strategies for classroom management and which underscores the creation and application of rules to regulate student behavior. Successful classroom management is predicated upon students' ability to develop cognitive linkages between the rules created for them and the goals to be achieved. It is relatively uncomplicated to make rules, but it is a challenging task to establish the internalized cognitive linkages to the goals on the part of students. We are struck by the fact that there are so many rules stipulated in the handbooks for students, teachers, and parents. What is enunciated here is the codification of acceptable behavior. The other approach, interpersonal, is predominant in Japan and underscores emotional ties, interpersonal relations, character development, and moral sentiments. Its success does not depend on many rules, but on a sense of trust and interdependency between the classroom teacher and his or her students and among the students. This approach calls for a personal knowledge of each student. We will make a further comment on Japanese classroom management later.

Classroom management is a broad term that includes a variety of concerns. The handbook on elementary classroom management that Ellen used during a three-day workshop

includes such topics as classroom organization, rules and procedures, management of student work, maintenance of good
student behavior, and organizing and conducting instruction
(Evertson & Harris 1990). When teachers speak of classroom
management, they often refer to some of these items, especially
control of student behavior and promotion of desired behavior.
As Doyle (1986) suggests:

> From the perspective of classroom order, the early class
> sessions of a school year are of critical importance. . . .
> During this time, order is defined and the process and
> procedures that sustain order are put into place. Indeed,
> over 75 years ago Bagley (1907, p. 22) exhorted teachers
> that "the only way absolutely to insure a school against
> waste is to make the very first day thoroughly rigorous in
> all its details." (p. 409)

Ellen, along with other beginning teachers in the Southtown school district, participated in a three-day workshop on
classroom management to learn the requisite skills. The workshop was offered by two professors from a southern university
in the summer of 1990. Highlights of this workshop will be
reviewed as they pertain to planning and teaching rules and
procedures. The 230-page handbook on classroom management
(Evertson & Harris 1990) used by workshop participants states:
"Describe what behaviors are acceptable and unacceptable in
your classroom. Then think about what procedures students
must follow in order to participate in class activities, to learn,
and to function effectively in the school environment" (p. 2.1).
The handbook urges teachers to do the following:

> Teach rules and procedures systematically with (1) expla-
> nation, (2) rehearsal, and (3) feedback. . . . Good classroom
> management is based on children's understanding of the
> behaviors that are expected of them. A carefully planned
> systematically taught system of rules and procedures
> makes it easier for you to communicate your behavioral
> expectations to your students. (p. 2.1)

The handbook defines rules as expected norms of general behavior and procedures as ways of getting classroom activities done.
The function of procedures is to routinize tasks for the sake of
continuity and predictability and to save time.

In accordance with these premises of classroom management, participants reviewed examples of rules and procedures and devised their own appropriate to their classrooms. Some of the procedures discussed included minute everyday routines.

Using the knowledge of classroom management she acquired from the workshop, Ellen sat down with her children in the first week of the year to decide on a set of six classroom rules which are common in many elementary schools:

1. Raise hands.
2. Do not interrupt.
3. Do not hit each other.
4. Be polite and courteous. Share.
5. Use indoor voices when talking to each other.
6. Respect other people's property.

Unlike in Nancy's fifth-grade room, these rules were not posted on the wall or on students' desks, because four- and five-year-olds could not read them, but Ellen frequently reminded them of the rules throughout the year. As our ethnographic account suggested earlier, she was trying to enforce all the rules quite strictly: recall that she called herself a "stickler" with the rules.

Ellen felt that these rules worked well for her group. But she was deeply concerned about several children, and she feared that she "would lose them along the way." She identified their difficulty as a behavioral control problem, and it was her most persistent anxiety since she resumed teaching in September. Their problems became doubly burdensome for her because she was especially interested in establishing a quiet, orderly, "self-directed" classroom for four- and five-year-olds. To achieve such a classroom, she often issued warnings and directives, and she isolated children with "control problems." Thus, in her own words her "biggest fear became classroom management and control." As we noted, she could be friendly with her children only on the condition that classroom control was established. They, she insisted, could never be friends first. It meant children's acceptance of her as the authority in the classroom first. Incidentally, echoing Ellen's view, Nancy articulately addressed the relationship between the teacher and students:

> I feel it is important to maintain formal relationships with
> kids. I need to be in power. I do not have to be liked, I do
> not need to be in a popularity contest. The rapport I would
> have with kids must be professional and appropriate. I
> would like to be in a warm and open environment, but do
> not have to be liked. I want to command respect because it
> is important for effective teaching. It is important to
> communicate to kids clearly the teacher's expectations.

Both Ellen and Nancy unambiguously insisted on their
authority as vested in their position and on their right to use
their power appropriately. Whether use of power in the form of
punishment (isolation, for example) might alienate the punished
children was of secondary consideration. For them, rules constitute a code of behavior that students must comply with, and the
teacher has the power to enforce them. Ellen employed not just
punitive methods but also what she was proud to call "positive
reinforcement," which included giving an award to a child who
displayed good behavior, giving praise, and awarding a certificate to a star of the day. She learned positive reinforcement
techniques from the workshop, as well as her graduate program
in special education, and assessed them as effective.

The Westville school did not offer a workshop on classroom management, but Nancy received a voluminous handbook
titled *Helpful Hints for New Teachers,* which included classroom
management, and was prepared by a committee of experienced
teachers. The reader will recall that one of the first things she did
in early September was to decide on the classroom rules, as did
Ellen. She took full advantage of the handbook to develop the
rules. The handbook warns beginning teachers that they have to
show thoughtfulness in introducing rules:

> Sadly enough one of the first things we are concerned
> about when we get a new group is that they know right
> away that we are the boss, that we have rules and that
> they will have to follow them. The way we approach this
> at first can set the tone for the rest of the year. And if we
> seem too mean or at all unfair, we may lose them for a
> long time. . . . but you know that they know how to
> behave and you would like to do some fun things the first
> few days. Then get around to setting the rules with them
> and deciding on what the consequences are going to be.

The handbook suggests how to set consequences and concludes with the following words: "Once the consequences are set, be consistent and unemotional when telling a child that he has broken the rule. Make sure that he knows exactly what the consequences are and what will happen." Nancy's buddy suggested that consistency is the key in classroom management and that she must be consistent in applying rules and discipline. Using a metaphor of a horse controlled by reins, she suggested that discipline to be imposed on students is the reins.

In working with her students Nancy made general classroom rules and other rules related to homework, to which we have already referred. Awards and consequences for breaking the rules were also decided and announced. If students followed the rules and demonstrated their commitment to learning, they would be rewarded in the following ways: a dip into the candy jar, a 5-minute visit with a neighbor during dismissal time, free time (to do silent reading or journal writing), a homework pass, permission to switch one's seat for a day, etc. On the other hand, the consequences for violating rules included the following:

- First violation: warning (evil eye, verbal reminder)
- Second violation: time out (write in journal what happened)
- Third violation: forfeit privileges and bring a note home
- Fourth violation: classroom detention after school, parent-student-teacher conference

Nancy posted the classroom rules on the wall as her colleagues did and photocopied two-page sheets of rules, rewards, and consequences for students and parents. Moreover, the teacher handbook spelled out schoolwide policies with respect to "student procedures," discipline, homework, and other matters. For example, one page is devoted to describing student passes: "Each teacher must maintain a daily lavatory sign-out sheet detailing the name, time out, and time in for any student leaving a classroom. Each student is to sign the log when leaving and returning to the room." Another page spells out student "rights and responsibilities":

1. Report promptly to class or assigned areas.

2. Respectfully follow directions given by any staff member at the time they are given.
3. Walk quietly on the right-hand side of the hallway.
4. Follow individual classroom rules and procedures.
5. Carry passes for the bathroom, office, nurse, media center, and hallways.
6. Respect the rights and personal property of others.
7. Use a conversational tone when speaking. Use appropriate language. Put-downs, teasing, cursing, and gestures are not permitted.

. . . .

We have discussed enough examples to suggest that the cognitive approach to classroom management underscores the rules for maintaining order and the learning environment. It is important for students to internalize the cognitive linkages between these rules and consequences to maintain good status as students and to avoid negative results.

By comparison, as noted earlier, the Japanese approach to classroom management assumes that interpersonal relations in the classroom constitute centrality in the management of the classroom. As a general concept, classroom management in Japanese elementary schools encompasses a much broader range of concerns than does classroom management in U.S. schools. These concerns include the development of group life, instructional plans, life guidance, moral education, management of classroom and schoolwide events, and improvement of the classroom environment. Basic rules are taught as part of teachers' responsibility to build "basic habits" in students. There is an official bulletin published every year by each school that delineates annual events, plans, and school policy, but there are no handbooks for teachers and parents where regulations and rules are stipulated in detail. Japanese elementary teachers' conception of classroom management is that the classroom is an organization of interpersonal relations that need to be managed to create a conducive learning environment.

Thus, as we will see in chapter 6, attention is naturally given to group life, intersubjectivity, and coordination of classroom activities by students. While American teachers tend to focus on dyadic relations between themselves and their students, Japanese teachers are essentially concerned with students' interpersonal relations, of which their dyadic relations with them are a part. While American teachers assert the primacy of their authority as antecedent to creating friendly relations with students, Japanese teachers are interested in building *kakawari* (relationships) and *kizuna* (bonding) with students as the basis for trust between them. None of the beginning and experienced teachers we interviewed in Japan referred to their institutional authority as a critical element in classroom management. Instead, their concern was to gain a sufficient understanding of students through interaction with them at the personal level. It was not formal relationships that they sought to develop but relationships of trust. They strove to build with students relationships characterized by emotional commitment. In their view, the bond between teachers and students is a pivotal fulcrum for promoting students' academic motivation. In other words, children's adaptive dispositions are cultivated by teachers' encouragement (rooted in ligature) and, in turn, by children's close identification with the teachers—their feelings and desires.

Instead of creating many rules, Japanese classroom management offers opportunities for social interaction and ritualized events, such as a Monday morning assembly of all students and classroom assemblies to reflect upon major events of the day. The Japanese pattern of control of time, space, and activity enhances the objectives of classroom management. Teachers seek personal knowledge to understand students. Several experienced teachers whom we interviewed in Japan told us that they promoted communication by reading student diaries every day. Japanese teachers more often than not encourage students to write diaries routinely where personal knowledge is revealed.

Summary

The beginning American teachers displayed several distinctive features. First, they defined teaching largely in cognitive terms and restricted it to the physical setting of a classroom. This definition of teaching was inherent in the professional culture of teaching and the macrolevel policies of the school districts. The beginning teachers' definition of the scope of teaching did not originate with them, but with the realm outside their initiatives. In other words, it was transmitted to them as part of the professional knowledge of teaching. Second, there is a shared character of the teachers' expectations of students. At different levels of schooling there is a common emphasis on developing independent dispositions, a value central to American culture. There was a remarkable consistency between Ellen and Nancy, two beginning teachers at two different levels, in terms of their identification of the development of independent dispositions as their primary pedagogical purpose.

Third, there was an obvious tension between the promotion of self-direction, which was the beginning teachers' chief goal, and the pattern of control that they developed. However, they saw authority vested in their institutionalized status as a given and as a legitimate source of power that was essential for facilitating effective classroom management. Their strategy for control was to establish a codification of acceptable behavior by creating rules with which students were expected to comply. We called this a cognitive approach, whose character is to enunciate the linkages between the rules and teacher expectations, on the one hand, and student performance, on the other. The beginning teachers at Westville and Southtown diligently learned classroom management strategies and successfully established quiet and orderly classrooms. They also exerted control by the manipulation of time, activity, and space, which were major variables. Students had relatively little control of those variables.

It appears that both Ellen and Nancy by and large took the pattern of control they established for granted. After all, they learned it from student teaching, workshops, experienced teachers, and handbooks. Of course, there were individual differences in the degree to which control was exerted. Ellen was a self-proclaimed "stickler," annoyed by even minor noise in the classroom, while Nancy thought that she had little problem with control but often reminded her students of the need for concerted efforts to maintain concentration on their tasks. She often used warnings, sarcasm, and exhortation to restore that concentration. The two other classrooms at Westville and South-town in which beginners were in charge were more relaxed; corrective measures in the form of warnings were used much less frequently. But we should reiterate that all beginning teachers used the same strategies for controlling time, activity, and space and used the cognitive approach to classroom management.

CHAPTER 4

Development of Teaching Strategies and Perspectives

Introduction

In this chapter our aim is to explore the strategies that American beginning teachers developed to learn to teach. And our interest is to understand how these strategies were adopted by individual beginning teachers and what perspectives resulted from these strategies.

As referred to earlier, based on the symbolic interactionist view (Cooley 1956; Dewey 1930; Mead 1934) of how reality is constructed, Becker et al. (1961) define *perspective* as: "a co-ordinated set of ideas and actions a person uses in dealing with some problematic situation, to refer to a person's ordinary way of thinking and feeling about and acting in such situation" (p. 34). They further distinguish immediate and long-range perspectives. While immediate perspectives are situation-specific and employed in response to everyday problems, long-range perspectives are stable over time and less affected by everyday specific events (pp. 35–36). In his study of teacher socialization, Lacey (1977) introduced the term "social strategy" as a concept that addresses differential strategies that individuals employ to cope with specific situations. Moreover, in contrast to Becker et al.'s emphasis on situational adjustment to problematic situations, Lacey enunciates the potential of individuals not only to adjust to immediate situations but to be creative, diverse, and innovative in defining these situations. To support his view he draws on Blumer (1969):

> With the mechanism of self-interaction, the human being ceases to be a responding organism whose behavior is a

89

product of what plays upon him from the outside, the
inside or both. Instead, he acts towards his world interpreting what confronts him and organizing his action on
the basis of the interaction. (p. 63)

Lacey's social strategies are of three types: internalized
adjustment, strategic compliance, and strategic redefinition. The
first type refers to a pattern of situational adjustment that individuals make by willingly complying with the constraints of the
situation confronting them. The second type is strategic acceptance of authority and the constraints imposed on individuals
in the situation defined by the authority. Individuals who use
this strategy are "merely seen to be good" and retain private
reservations about the constraints, whereas those individuals
who use the first strategy are viewed as "really good" by the
authority who defines the situation for them. The third is a
radical strategy by which individuals who do not have power
bring about change.

In this chapter we will refer to Becker et al.'s concept of
long-range perspective not as an action-idea system but as an
idea system that results from the strategies used to deal with a
variety of situations. We will also draw upon Lacey's definitions
of social strategies in our analysis of the process of learning to
teach, to distinguish the strategies employed by our research
participants. Lacey's concept of strategy, in our view, is useful
for identifying strategic patterns but not the context of individual
coping actions. Later in this chapter we will introduce the concept of coping strategy developed by Pollard (1982) to focus on
the context of actions. Individual beginning teachers differ with
respect to their "latent culture," which reflects biographical
factors, self-image, personality characteristics, preparation for
teaching, and the ability to learn to teach. These differences
account in significant part for the diversity in their approaches
to teaching and the strategies that they use in response to
the situations they confront. Moreover, the diversity of strategies used is influenced by the interactive context of the classroom, the teacher culture, school organization, the pedagogical
ideologies of the school, and the school district. Some strategies
are highly situation-specific while other strategies are more

general and sustained, leading to the development of a long-range perspective.

Nevertheless, for two reasons beginning teachers also use common strategies to confront common situations. First, the school, as an agent of cultural transmission and socialization, imposes common constraints upon all teachers and students. These givens include the school setting, the classroom, students, the curriculum, academic and behavioral standards, power relationships, and parents. Second, these teachers are novices in teaching who have relatively little knowledge about what teachers often call "procedures" and little experience of classroom and instructional management.

The strategies used by beginning teachers range from internalized adjustment to strategic redefinition. All beginning teachers at Westville and Southtown experienced varying degrees of shock in the first several weeks and resistance to institutional demands. Beginners at Westville, for example, were upset and confused in the first week when they were told that reading was entirely literature-based and followed a whole-language approach. For Nancy literature-based reading did not pose a threat, as it did to the other two beginners, because her background was English literature, but the notion of whole language shook her as well. Likewise, Ellen at Southtown was thrown into a state of confusion when she found out that she received little formal guidance with respect to the kindergarten curriculum. Initially she expected detailed curriculum guides that she could follow. Her colleague, Gail Fisher, was also upset when she was told to team-teach first-graders in an open-space classroom, for she had never been exposed to such a classroom. As a result of their initial reactions to the shock, they talked among themselves about the threatening situations and sought assistance from experienced colleagues so that they could develop strategies to respond to the situations. Although their strategies varied from internalized adjustment to strategic redefinition, each strategy was a complex process that involved personal interpretations of the problems and the construction of strategies.

Application of Practical Rationality as a Strategy

Here we will consider teachers' strategies to apply "practical rationality" to teaching. Carter (1990) uses the term *practical rationality* to refer to the personal knowledge acquired from teaching—practical knowledge that encompasses self-knowledge, the milieu of teaching, subject matter, curriculum development, and instruction. It is differentiated from the "technical rationality" of teaching, the knowledge derived from research. Carter suggests:

> Professionals make complicated interpretations and decisions under conditions of inherent uncertainty (Doyle 1986), and to do this they engage in practical thinking that leads to an action appropriate to the particular situation. The knowledge required for practice under these circumstances is experiential, that is, it evolves out of "reflection-in-action" (Schon 1983). (p. 300)

Practical knowledge is, in the words of Feiman-Nemser and Floden (1986), teachers' "beliefs, insights, and habits" that are derived from their experiences and that enable them to do their work in schools. As Carter (1990) points out, "conventional research on teaching is based on technical rationality and ignores the practical knowledge and personal intentions of teachers" (p. 300).

Lortie (1975) characterizes teaching as lacking a technical culture, that is, a shared, systematically organized body of knowledge and skills that distinguishes teaching from other professions. In the same vein Jackson (1990) suggests that teaching is void of a scientific base. Both Lortie and Jackson see teachers' knowledge as inherent in idiosyncratic experience and personal synthesis. Though these observations are appropriate, it is important to understand how teachers construct personal knowledge and what strategies they use to do so. Here we will address teachers' images of self and students and their "tacit theories," which are conceptions of personal values, beliefs, and principles that guide their actions.

Self-image is a social construct grounded in a constant dialectic of social processes where actors adapt to the conditions in which they find themselves (Pollard 1982). In learning to teach, one's self-image serves as a focal reference used to select what is learned. Speaking of "informal exchange" as a critical mode of learning "the tricks of the trade," Lortie (1975) suggests:

> Their [teachers'] talk underlines the idea of adapting others' practices to their personal styles and situations. . . . To be adopted a practice must be seen as consistent with the receiver's personality and "way of doing things." They portray the diffusion of classroom practices as passing through the screen of the teacher's self-concept—of the way he visualizes his peculiar style of work. Thus the individualism and gatekeeping we saw earlier are reaffirmed: the teacher mediates between ideas and their use in terms of the kind of teacher he is. (p. 77)

Thus self-image becomes the mesh or a filter that provides selectivity in adapting strategies for learning how to teach.

We now turn to Nancy and Ellen to explore their self-images and how the self-images affected the strategies that they adopted. Events that occurred in Nancy's early childhood—especially the events associated with her parents' divorce and the absence of parental nurturance in her home when she was in second grade—strongly impinged upon her self-image. She was born into a working-class family. Her father was irresponsible and virtually absent from home, and as a result her mother was extremely debilitated. Nancy was often left alone and received little emotional support from them. As she recollected, it was at that time that she realized that instead of seeking the support that was not afforded her she must be independent. In her words, "There was no other choice but to be self-directed and independent." Fortunately she had a brother who served as her model, in the sense that he was independent and bright and worked exceptionally hard. Throughout her educational career her brother remained a lasting archetype on which she drew to motivate herself, develop her identity, and excel in school.

When she was a college student, Nancy was attracted to William Blake and learned "a lot from him as a poet and as an artist and from the way he was trying to challenge people, a perspective to think independently and inventively." She also cited Maxine Green's (1973) *Teacher as a Stranger* as having provided her with a provocative and existential perspective that she needed when she was student teaching. Nancy's disposition toward being independent, challenging, and striving for excellence were legitimated by her exposure to those intellectual models.

The notion of independence apparently became central to the integrity of Nancy's self-image, for she was apprehensive of the situations where her independence was threatened. For example, she mentioned two relevant episodes that evolved when she was student teaching at a suburban middle school in 1989. The first was what she characterized as student behavior problems in the eighth grade. Low-achieving students in her class were incessantly disorderly and displayed little concern for work. They knew that she was young and not able to control them. Their behavior represented a tenacious challenge confronting her every day for eight weeks. The greater her efforts to motivate the students to focus on their tasks and to get them through a lesson, the more awesome her confrontations with them grew to be. These students were aware that Nancy would be teaching for only eight weeks and found little compelling reason why they had to sit and listen to her. Nancy admitted that she not only looked young, lenient, and unable to control the classroom, but was also insecure. She concluded that the students' defiance and disorderliness were a response to her insecurity.

Another episode involved Nancy's encounter with parents as a student teacher. They often challenged her by asking a number of questions forcing her to defend her position with respect to the materials used in the classroom, her teaching method, and classroom discipline. She felt quite nervous and vulnerable and attributed that vulnerability to her lack of confidence in handling parents and her perception that the parents viewed her as an imaginary daughter who was young and immature, not as a teacher. Nancy realized that the problems depicted in these two episodes were inherent threats to her self-image as an independent and competent individual. That realization reinforced her belief that her self-image as a confident teacher must be fortified. She told us that in light of that encounter with the parents, she would devise strategies that would enable her to handle the parents more effectively at Westville.

These biographic factors, molded in the social processes in which her encounters with people occurred, shaped her idiosyncratic way of responding to a variety of problems she faced at Westville. As we saw earlier, she defined her ultimate goal of teaching as the promotion of student self-direction and identified its "roots" in her biography. Accordingly she devised strategies (such as her reading program, homework policy, and projects) to enhance independent dispositions. Undoubtedly her experiences in student teaching measurably sensitized her to the imperative of classroom management. She wanted to protect her independence in her relationship with her students by promoting their respect for her and their "maturity" in the classroom. She developed formal relationships with her students that distanced her from them, and viewed her power and authority as critical to maintaining these relationships and promoting the cognitive linkages the students had to build between the classroom rules and the goals to be met. To accomplish effective classroom management, she exerted a high degree of control over time, activities, and space in the classroom.

The back-to-school night that Nancy held in late September reveals how her self-image impinged upon the event. For neophyte teachers the back-to-school night is usually the first encounter with a large number of parents, and it makes them nervous. While Nancy's peers, two beginning teachers at Westville, were relatively relaxed at the time of the event, Nancy became more anxious and tense than they were, because she was once challenged by parents when she was a student teacher and, more important, because she wanted to impress parents this time. She spent a few days preparing for the event by seeking advice from her buddy, by studying the agenda items that her colleagues used when they invited parents to their classrooms, and by organizing the 11-page packet of information that she intended to distribute to the parents. Her strategy was to prepare well for the event and present to the parents her positive image as a teacher. On the night of the event Nancy explained to the parents in some detail what she thought was important: curriculum and instruction for each subject area, her approach to teaching, her literature-based reading program, her homework policy, instruction in vocabulary, and journal letters. Moreover, she presented a demonstration lesson in "Read Aloud."

The following day Nancy told us of her impressions of the event:

> I was very nervous last night, but felt that I came out as a very strong personality. I had a stomach upset and was flushed the whole night. My mouth was dry, and I was dwindling. You know what Westville residents are like. They make a lot of money. They were indeed scrutinizing me. They were looking at my outfit and staring at me for the whole night. I am a first-year teacher and insecure. So they scrutinized me. That was that. But I felt I impressed the parents. I do not want to have the same experience in front of 50 people.

Suffice it to suggest that the back-to-school night was an orchestrated but tense and strained experience for Nancy. Because she wanted to earn the parents' respect, she worked especially hard to prepare and concentrated her efforts on impressing them.

Respect was a notion that Nancy cherished. She repeated the word daily in her routine lessons, and it was a criterion against which her students were expected to measure their behavior and performance. Likewise, she applied it to her own performance. She also saw her relationship with the parents in terms of control. For example, a few parents had suggested that more time be devoted to writing, and she responded to the suggestion with the following comment:

> No, I am not going to devote more time. I have writing periods on Tuesdays and Thursdays. Plus, children can do writing during the English lessons. They also do writing in other subject areas. So I am not going to push it further. They are pushy parents and I will not yield to their pressure. Their daughters can do writing during the lunch period if they want, but it is not ethical for me to spend more time on writing because of their pressure.

Nancy's strategy was to build an image of a teacher who sought parents' respect but who would not yield to their pressure. It represented strategic compliance.

We will now briefly explore Ellen's self-image and its influence on her teaching. She had two contrasting influences on her image as a teacher. One can be traced back to her early childhood, during which, as we noted in chapter 2, her kindergarten teacher had an immense impact on her. Ellen vividly recalled the characteristics of her teacher: nurturant, caring, loving, patient, resourceful, generous, and devoted. Her teacher's superior and exceptional quality of devotion to, and fondness of, children impressed her as unique. Ellen developed an unalterable relationship with her, and it remained a constant source of guidance and emotional support until the teacher died when Ellen was a college student. Ellen saw her as a mentor in a broad sense and a friend with whom she sought close bonding. Without fail Ellen visited her to seek her advice every time she had a "major" problem. When Ellen decided to become a kindergarten teacher, it was the image of her teacher, a prominent role model, that influenced the decision. We may point out that her mother's influence on her career choice was comparatively small, although her mother was once a nursery schoolteacher. Ellen's aspiration was indubitably to become a teacher who could reflect the professional and personal attributes that represented her own kindergarten teacher.

Another influence on Ellen's self-image originated in her recent encounters with children. During student teaching in her senior year, she experienced a couple of incidents that she described as traumatic. On one occasion a heavy third-grade boy violently pushed her in anger when she tried to stop him from fighting another boy. As a result, she fell and, overwhelmed by his aggression, burst out crying. She was so embarrassed, humiliated, and angered by his assault that she immediately reported the incident to school authorities. Subsequently, the school district pressed charges against him, and eventually he was placed in a special education class. On another occasion she was equally scared when a boy in her class threw a chair at her. These incidents had a profound impact on her development of attitudes toward children and classroom management, making her less open-handed and more cautious in her interaction with children. When we interviewed her for the first time in early September, she shared her feelings:

> To be frank, classroom management is difficult for me. I
> feel I was too nice to the kids before. Now I have reversed
> my attitudes toward them. I have become too strict in
> handling them, which I am afraid defeats my purposes in
> kindergarten. This is something that I have to work on a
> great deal. It does not come naturally.

Although the extent to which these incidents contributed to
"reversing" her attitudes toward children is unclear, it seems
that the incidents made her guarded in her relationship with
children.

Thus Ellen came to embrace conflicting images of herself
as a teacher. One image stemmed from her positive self-portrait
as a teacher: "I always love children and like to be surrounded
by them. So it is natural for me to become a teacher at the
kindergarten level." These were the qualities of attitudes that she
attributed to her kindergarten teacher. Another image was
revealed in her own admission that authority and power
preceded friendship in teaching and that she was a stickler. This
image was associated with the incidents in her student teaching
and with her strategy to handle children. Ellen held these con-
testing images and exposed her students to them throughout the
first year. Changes in her attitudes toward children were more
often than not extreme, even within a single day. While she
warmly greeted her children, affectionately hugged them in the
morning, and praised them for their orderly behavior, she
abruptly became punitive when they did not meet her
expectations. For example, she chided and often isolated some
children from the class for making noise. Apparently there was a
constant tension in Ellen between these extremes—between the
image of pleasant and caring teacher and the image of stickler
whose concern was order and control. So control often took
precedence over the relationship of love and care that she sought
with children.

In early October, several weeks after Ellen assumed
teaching at Southtown, a shocking incident occurred. A five-
year-old boy in her class was abruptly switched to Susan
Taylor's (her buddy's) class after his parents negotiated a
transfer with the principal, Ellen, and Susan. The boy, who wore
thick glasses, was shy and slow and needed Ellen's patience and

nurturance. Instead of providing that needed support, however, Ellen demanded that he become swifter to learn and her pressure made him unhappy. The boy's transfer stunned Ellen because she felt her competence as a kindergarten teacher was being questioned. The incident affected her for many weeks, and she referred to it whenever she spoke of classroom management. She expressed her anxiety, which was revealed in her comment: "I am afraid I might lose them [the children] along the way." That anxiety was played out in this incident.

Ellen's biographic factors may not adequately account for her concern with control, but at least they illustrate a source of the tension between the two images she held of herself. As we saw in chapter 3, she often developed strategies to resolve the tension in favor of control.

Let us turn to another aspect of practical rationality. Jackson (1990) points out that teachers have a tendency to approach problems "intuitively rather than rationally." His teacher informants suggested to him that their "classroom behavior was based more on impulse and feeling than on reflection and thought" (p. 145). Our research participants were no different from Jackson's informants in their approach to teaching. *Intuition* is a term that was often used to explain their practice; it is a notion that refers to what we earlier called "tacit theory," which beginning teachers applied to solving problems. Derived from patterns of past actions and the immediacy of situations, tacit theory suggests a personal belief that explains how things work and justifies consequences of action. Indeed, the actions of our beginning teachers were guided by their tacit theories. Some tacit theories are personally constructed and unique to particular individuals, whereas other tacit theories are shared by colleagues. We will illuminate how the neophytes' individual theories influenced their teaching.

Nancy's tacit theory of teaching may be best illuminated in the construction of her image of students and her concern with students' work attitudes. It served as a covert rationale, not only for explaining characteristics of her interactive and institutional environments (including work, students, staff, and the district) but also for guiding her instructional approach. As noted earlier, her image of her students was that they were pampered, upper-class children who expected "massive entertainment" in the classroom. She resorted to a metaphor to describe her perception of her students as expecting "a nickelodeon style of learning and teaching" all the time and hoping that she would do all the work for them. Moreover, the students wanted everything to be fun and games, and they expected to be lying on the floor reading books because it would be relaxing. In short, Nancy portrayed her students as displaying passivity and a lack of discipline. In the following passage, her perceptions are depicted well:

> I guess what I am experiencing here is that they kind of expect a nickelodeon style of teaching and learning. Everything has to be fun and games. . . . I don't know whether their expectations are a function of being wealthy, but I am now coming to grips with a very upper-class community. I don't think they appreciate what they have in this room, and they don't appreciate the kind of effort I am putting in. And they don't appreciate what's hard work time.

She commented further:

> There is an absence of control in this school. Anything goes, and every teacher can do her own thing. It's like a free-for-all. Nobody defines what is appropriate.

It appears that she overstated what she saw at Westville Upper Elementary School regarding distinctive characteristics of her students, the school, and the community, district features that she attributed to an upper-class community. Obviously her perception of Westville as an upper-class community represents an overstatement, because it is a typical upper middle class community if judged by standard socioeconomic criteria. As noted in earlier chapters, our observations also suggest that her students generally displayed disciplined attitudes toward learning in the classroom. Further, in her classroom there were few notable indications of the laxity and entertainment that she cited. What also appears to be inconsistent in her portrayal of her students is the fact that Nancy more often than not commented on her students as being diligent and vivacious. It seems that Nancy's image of students stemmed in significant part from her impressions of students in general, her discontent with the liberal atmosphere at Westville, and what she considered to be a schoolwide pattern of laxity in student work. In any event what is relevant here is not the objectivity of her perceptions, but her interpretations of what she saw, her imagery that shaped her strategies of teaching. It is these interpretations that constructed the social reality in which she taught.

To appreciate Nancy's perceptions (that is, her construction of social reality), it is necessary to view her images of the students, the school, and the community against her biography. As we learned before, Nancy grew up in a working-class family and cherished diligence, self-discipline, and self-direction. Her image of her students was that they did not demonstrate these attributes. That led her to become critical of them. She insisted that they had to understand "there are serious work times as well as fun times at school." When her students complained that she was giving them an excessive amount of homework, she reacted strongly to the complaint, asserting that it was "totally inappropriate" because in her view she did not give them much homework. Nancy further asserted that her students had to develop "character," a disciplined orientation, to undertake hard work willingly. She explained her reason for insisting on discipline: "The reason for the discipline from my point of view is just my experience. I was always a good student and an academic type of person because of my self-discipline. I just feel that I should offer my students the quality I personally have." Her comment makes it evident that her pedagogical belief was deeply embedded in her biography, and her interest in motivating her students to build more disciplined attitudes toward work was guided by that belief.

Nancy commented that earlier in her beginning year, she was willing to accept the general trend at the school and went along with her peers. As her confidence in her teaching grew, however, she became critical of what she saw at the school and drew upon her personal beliefs to develop teaching strategies. Unlike other teachers at Westville, of whom she was critical, she deliberately structured her lessons to teach the students requisite skills and knowledge in what she described as a "lecture mode" because she felt "incredible accountability to set them up before they can run free." Consequently her lessons were often pre-

sented in lecture and recitation formats that encouraged only
dyadic interaction between the teacher and students. She suggested, however, that although "for a while they are passively
receiving what I have to say," her eventual goal was to assist
them to study without such a structure of instruction. Her
strategies obviously contradicted her interest in promoting the
independent dispositions of students that we discussed earlier.
She resolved the contradiction by selectively focusing on certain
aspects of the curriculum for self-directed study. All in all, what
we have seen here is that Nancy's biographically based beliefs
became a tacit basis for forging her instructional approach. She
privately redefined the situation that confronted her and
developed teaching strategies that were compatible with her tacit
theory, strategies typified by strategic compliance.

Practical rationality in teaching is multifaceted, and tacit
theory is elusive. Tacit theory encompasses various types of
beliefs and assumptions that are functional in solving problems
that teachers confront. We identified the biographic origin of
Nancy's tacit beliefs, which influenced her construction of the
social reality of teaching and the strategies of teaching that she
used. We could not pinpoint tacit theories for other beginning
teachers at Westville and Southtown that were as distinctive as
Nancy's. What can be gleaned from our field notes about Ellen's
tacit theory is her disposition to incorporate and synthesize
whatever was viewed as practical. We will call it "incorporative
disposition." Whereas Nancy expressed a distinctive pedagogical
view, Ellen did not reveal one, except for her tenacious incli-
nation toward control. Such an incorporative disposition was
revealed in how beginning teachers resolved difficulties that
they encountered.

For example, when Janet and her colleague in fourth
grade, both of whom were Nancy's peers, were told to teach
whole language, they immediately sought assistance from
experienced teachers to implement it, on the assumption that it
was inherently a good method, instead of critically evaluating it
as a method of teaching reading and writing in the light of their
personal beliefs. In contrast, as will be discussed later, Nancy
evaluated it and did not entirely accept it. Gail at Southtown also
displayed an incorporative disposition when she was told to

teach in an open-space classroom. Although she initially felt extreme discomfort with the totally strange structure of an open-space classroom, she was willing to accept it as a given. Beginning teachers' incorporative dispositions maximized adjustment to new situations encountered in the process of learning to teach. All the beginning teachers, including Nancy, displayed incorporative dispositions, but she blended her personal beliefs with incorporative strategies that she selected when she sought tricks of teaching from her buddy and other colleagues. Pivotal to these strategies were informal conversations in which she was engaged.

Both Ellen and Nancy displayed a common belief regarding independent disposition, which is not exclusively attributable to them; rather it is deeply rooted in American culture. They also shared a common belief about control, but Ellen's concern with it became a preoccupation, was intense and compulsive, and caused sustained anxiety, whereas for Nancy, control was a much more generalized, impersonal, pedagogical issue. And Ellen's belief about control measurably affected her classroom management, and in this sense it was quite distinct.

Meanwhile, Ellen exhibited considerable receptivity and willingness to learn from others, a characteristic of beginning teachers. This kind of incorporative disposition is apparently different from Nancy's tacit theory, inherent in her unique biography, but is essential to learning the practical rationality of teaching. It seems that Ellen epitomized that disposition by participating in an array of workshops made available through the Southtown School District. As a substitute teacher, she took part in a whole-language workshop for four afternoons in April 1990 prior to receiving an appointment at Southtown. During the summer of that year she devoured series of workshops, including an early childhood summer lab for four weeks, a classroom management workshop, the integrated workshop offered by the principal, a peer coaching workshop, and a workshop on drug use. She assumed that she would learn something from each of the workshops, and moreover she was paid to participate. Further, she met and sought advice from her principal and assistant principal at least twice a week after being appointed. She approached them to seek practical advice on mundane problems. She disagreed little with the basic premises underlying the concept of whole language, the framework and procedures of the summer lab, classroom management strategies, and the principal's hands-on approach to apprenticeship. Indeed, she regarded what she learned from these workshops as very useful.

Above all, as we saw earlier, the most instrumental source of practical rationality for Ellen was her buddy, Susan Taylor. Susan was not only her mentor but a virtually fixed model who showed Ellen what to teach and how to teach; her total reliance on Susan as the source of guidance was epitomized by Ellen's metaphor: "Susan is my curriculum," the curriculum being handed down to her just like a folktale. Ellen resorted to this mode of learning to teach (that is, practical rationality) when she was unable to construct her own curriculum. Her strategy to fall back on the existing model contradicted her reasons for choosing to teach at Southtown. She told us:

> Southtown does a lot of innovative things (such as whole language, a new math program, a very innovative assessment of student progress) and maintains an innovative atmosphere. In this sense Southtown is unique. This is a district that encourages you to try new teaching materials and projects. They have put a lot of money and energy into new things and professional development, and teachers here are looked at as professionals who have a lot of freedom, while this is not true in some other districts. I chose to teach here for these reasons.

Undoubtedly Ellen liked the freedom given to teachers and desired to be an innovative teacher who could develop new teaching materials and new approaches to teaching. But when she encountered the necessity of creating a curriculum for her class, she chose not to take advantage of the opportunity; instead, she elected to rely on her buddy entirely and follow her "experience." This meant that the practical rationality Ellen sought was characterized by only practical and immediate value and excluded postulated possibilities. In Ellen's case, the immediate need for action called for practical rationality. Within the framework of practical rationality Ellen adopted new methods and a new curriculum (such as whole language and theme-based projects) that had already been tried by her buddy. Ellen's strategy epitomizes what Lacey calls internalized adjustment.

Social Contexualization of Strategies

As noted earlier, there have been two dominant paradigms of research on teacher socialization (Zeichner & Gore 1990). One is a functionalist approach, which focuses on an examination of the correspondence between institutional expectations and an internalization of those expectations (that is, a replication of uniformity) by neophyte teachers. This approach is primarily interested in the reproduction of the occupation of teaching and pays little attention to individual diversity and personally initiated changes evident in the process of socialization. The second is a symbolic-interactionist approach, which views neophytes as creative actors who respond to situational demands with various motivations and strategies. The emphasis is placed on situational learning by individualized teacher-actors and on their creative adaptation to these demands.

Pollard (1982) offers a third approach, which views teachers as creative, constructive, and adaptive strategists in particular social contexts that influence their strategies. His approach gives special attention to the interactive process between teachers and their social contexts. To explore their coping strategies, he proposes three layers to the social contextualization of teachers. Coping strategies refer to various ways in which teachers approach problems in the classroom, as well as the broader setting of the school and community, and constitute definitions of teaching and management. Pollard's model is useful to our analysis because it underscores the social contexts of occupational socialization, that is, the contexts in which learning to teach occurs. Teachers are viewed neither as situation-focused, individualized actors nor as indistinguishable persons under pressure to conform, but as context-bound actors whose coping strategies are linked to their biographies, images of self, and "interests at hand."

The first layer of Pollard's social contexualization is the micro-interactive context of the classroom, the second layer is the

institutional context of the school, and the third is the macro-
context of the community and societal forces impinging upon the
first two layers. The interactive context of the class room involves
interactions between teacher and students. The institutional
context is the broader social, political, and cultural environment
of a school (and a school district) and includes teacher culture
and "institutional bias," which refers to the influence of institutional ideology and power relationships upon individual
teachers. Central to this model are the concepts of self and the
"interests at hand" of an individual teacher, which shape the
nature of social contextualization and provide a linkage between
different levels of contexualization.

We will adopt Pollard's model to explore the social
contextualization of the two beginning teachers, Ellen and
Nancy, and the development of their strategies and perspectives.
Both teachers displayed patterns in learning to teach in the first
year, which revealed roughly three phases of development. The
initial phase was characterized by highly positive expectations
about teaching, which Ryan (1986) calls fantasy. It was short-
lived and was quickly followed by a coping phase distinguished
by the construction of a series of strategies to cope with problems
at different levels of the social contextualization of the beginners'
work. This was the most critical phase, a "survival" stage
in Ryan's terms, that lasted until January or February. It was
then followed by a reflective phase, when beginning teachers
interpreted and integrated their experiences, leading to the
development of personal schemas or perspectives. Although the
beginning teachers we studied displayed diversity in following the path of development, their paths were commonly
progressive.

Ellen took a job at Southtown for its "innovative" programs and the freedom that was afforded to teachers, and she
was quite excited about the prospects of developing such a
program at the kindergarten level. Her euphoric feelings about
the school were revealed in the following comment:

> They [Southtown] are known for taking the initiative in
> introducing new things and piloting whole language and a
> new math program. They do away with books [textbooks]

and indeed do not have books, and learning is based on
life experience. I was attracted to what this school offers.

Both Ellen and her first-year colleague, Gail, were involved
in the institutional context of Southtown Elementary School and
its district from the outset, through their participation in a series
of workshops during the summer. Ellen's participation in the
early childhood summer lab confirmed her interest in the
school's innovative programs. She and her buddy, Susan, were
teamed up to teach a group of 15 children for two weeks,
focusing on "the police station" as the theme; this was an
exploratory topic, which guided all activities in the lab. The
project involved visiting a nearby police station, inviting a
policeman to the class, and understanding what he did. As a
result of the success of this project, they were assigned to teach
another group of kindergarten children for two more weeks. By
the end of the lab Ellen began to feel confident and inspired
about teaching her own children in September.

Likewise, Nancy built an idealized image of the Westville
School District, based on what she had heard about it from
teachers at the school where she did student teaching, and
decided to apply for a job at Westville. In August, when we had
a first interview with her, she attributed fantasized adjectives to
Westville and characterized it as

a very progressive, exciting place, not just a traditional
school district, especially in language arts. They have a
new whole-language teaching approach, which requires
students to take more initiative in reading. The district
encourages an individualized approach to develop a
passion for reading and writing. This is my primary
interest. The school is on the cutting edge and committed
to excellence.

She expressed her eagerness to learn the whole-language
program and its methods from experienced teachers at Westville.
Indeed, Nancy was very proud to be appointed to teach at the
school, which was newly opened, spacious enough to
accommodate 1,200 students, and completely air-conditioned.
Unlike Ellen, however, Nancy's exposure to the institutional
context of the school and district before the start of the academic
year was quite limited. She only participated in a one-day

human relations workshop to which all new teachers in the district were invited during the summer. But her view of the school was so convincing and potent that it became an important point of reference and influenced her initial approach to teaching in her classroom. She planned "prize-winning" lessons at the outset to meet her expectations of students.

As student teachers, the beginners depended on their cooperating teachers, did not have full command of the classroom, and made relatively inconsequential decisions affecting students. Now they gained new status and became "professionals," the term they proudly used to describe their status. Ellen suggested that given her new status, she started to learn for the first time what teaching was all about. Nancy, on the other hand, defined teaching as requiring "every part of me, my brain, and intellectual skills." Their idealized, optimistic outlooks unfolded in these comments.

The positive portraits of the schools that both Ellen and Nancy drew naturally helped to promote their expectations about teaching and their students. The first two weeks were critical for both beginning teachers and their students, for it was during this period that they learned about each other. Both tried to test each other and their limits of expectations and behavior. The initial common concern that occupied both Ellen and Nancy was classroom management: getting acquainted with students, establishing rules, and planning the routinization of activities.

During the early weeks of the academic year major problems quickly surfaced, and the beginning teachers had to cope with them for many succeeding weeks. Ellen began to be preoccupied with control of students, and her obsession with this problem affected her actions in the classroom through the spring. As a result, her coping strategies concentrated on the interactive context of the classroom. As discussed elsewhere, her strategy was to establish a very quiet, orderly classroom. That was her immediate interest at hand, but her conception of a good classroom was constantly challenged by her children, especially several action-seekers whose agenda did not match hers. The action-seekers sought excitement by touching others, playing actively in the block center, and talking when they were expected to be quiet. The majority of the children were internalized adjusters who largely complied with Ellen's expectations, but she was often irritated by action-seekers. As she put it, noise simply disturbed her personally; this led to her frequent anger and frustration. She admitted, "I tend to get very short and angry with them unnecessarily. Because of that I end up taking on everybody else."

In October, Ellen's frustration even led her to send one of the action-seekers to the school's student-assessment team, with the request that the team diagnose what she called the child's lack of control of behavior. Having reviewed the request, the team suggested that the child's problem was not severe. This supported her confession that she was known as a "crier" by the administrators. Ellen used a set of strategies to counter the problem: frequent warnings and reprimands, isolation of disturbing children, and suspension of their participation in centers. But in the interactive situations involving her children, she also employed creative strategies such as praise and "behavioral modification," to which her children responded. Ellen combined punitive strategies with reflective positive-reinforcement strategies, which produced mixed results through the winter but began to yield some positive consequences in the spring. Pollard (1982) aptly points out:

> The children and teachers will approach any interactive situation in the light of particular perspectives and interest-at-hand. When they act they will each adapt their strategies to cope with the specific situation in which they find themselves and by so doing will create new situations to be experienced subsequently. (p. 35)

Although Ellen received instructional support from her buddy and her other peers, she got little help in classroom management because it was considered by her colleagues a domain that she had to learn herself. This individualistic view of classroom management required her to develop her own coping strategies, and classroom management remained Ellen's personal struggle for most of the year.

Ellen's relationships with parents were relatively smooth and were characterized by mutual accommodation. Although parents generally did not pose a major challenge, Ellen was alert in interpreting their attitudes and accommodating to the pressures they exerted on her. She regularly invited one or two volunteer parents to come to her class every week to assist her. For the first month or so, their presence created silent confrontational situations where she had to stop them from pampering children. Initially she had difficulty in asserting herself as the teacher in charge of her classroom when she was confronted by the parents, who were much older than she. Such parental indulgence in the children directly countered Ellen's interest in developing their independent disposition. Her confrontation with parents in the classroom was resolved in October when she asserted the rules of her classroom by announcing them to the parents. They became aware of the fact that the classroom was under Ellen's exclusive supervision. In general, however, Ellen chose to adopt strategies to accommodate parental pressures instead of resisting them.

In contrast to the interactive context of the classroom, Ellen's institutional context required relatively little coping. She accepted the authority of administrators and regularly sought their advice mostly on instructional matters and occasionally on classroom management; she took for granted the principal's evaluation of her class, although she was tense and nervous when he observed her class. She saw the principal as her mentor ever since the summer, when she had participated in the so-called integrated workshop for beginning teachers he had organized and developed. Likewise, Gail, Ellen's colleague, viewed him in the same frame of reference. There was a sharp contrast between these neophytes' views of the principal and those of veteran teachers at the school, who saw him as paternalistic and authoritarian. Ellen accepted Southtown's curriculum and enthusiastically endorsed its innovative programs, such as whole language, the method of student evaluation used at the early grade levels, and the freedom given to individual teachers to construct lesson plans and teaching materials. Moreover, Ellen and Gail characterized Southtown's atmosphere as "very relaxed," and teachers as receptive and open-minded. They saw little territorialism among teachers. The characteristics of the teacher culture made the institutional context of their work adaptable and accommodating. It follows that both Ellen and Gail displayed internalized adjustment in the social context of the institution.

Let us turn to Nancy and probe her contextualization of teaching. Her interactive context of the classroom was a primary setting for everyday coping actions, as for Ellen, but the principal causes of her actions were often located in the institutional contexts and macrocontexts. In contrast to Ellen, Nancy regarded the second and third layers of social contextualization as critically impinging upon what occurred in the classroom. Those contexts included school policy, teacher culture, parents, and the community.

As we saw earlier, rooted in her biography and her definition of herself as teacher, Nancy's interest at hand was to promote self-direction, discipline in work, diligence, and a proper structure for fostering these attitudes toward learning in the interactive context of the classroom setting. Although her control of students was comparatively tight, control was not her burning concern; in fact, she claimed that she disowned such a concern. She was successful in routinizing student activity, so control as a management principle became part of the routinized structure of teaching. This epitomizes what Bullough (1989) calls "environmental simplification" as a coping strategy. We will highlight here distinct features of Nancy's concern at the institutional levels and macrolevels of contextualization and the strategies that she adopted to cope with the situations she encountered.

What concerned Nancy as a beginning teacher throughout her first year was whole language. We should make it clear that we are interested in exploring Nancy's perceptions of, and strategies to deal with, whole language but not the technical problems of whole language per se, such as its definition and the objective nature of the whole-language program at Westville. Although she was inspired by the Westville's reputation of being on the cutting edge and committed to excellence, she was troubled by whole language. Initially she was willing to learn the method, but her receptivity to it was short-lived and eventually replaced by a strategy to circumvent it. Nancy was briefly exposed to the concept of whole language during her student teaching, but never explored its application to instruction. In the first marking period at Westville, she incorporated some elements of whole language into her program by setting up a series of individualized conferences between her and her students and between students to review their drafts of compositions. She experimented with this setup for one story and quickly discovered that many of her students did not have the essential skills to make such review conferences a profitable part of their learning. Dissatisfied with the approach, she became increasingly doubtful of its merits and started to temper her reading program with critical thought.

Nancy's critical attitudes toward whole language were linked to her broad pedagogical and policy concerns contextualized at the intermediate institutional levels and macrolevels. Many teachers at Westville—especially new and beginning teachers who had been chiefly exposed to the basal approach— viewed whole language as a challenge, but reluctantly accepted it as a schoolwide charge without knowing how to teach it. The whole-language approach called for new and beginning teachers' creative ability to make a transition from the basal method with which they had been acquainted. Yet, as pointed out elsewhere, Westville's reading curriculum guides were still based on a basal approach and were in the process of being revised. Nancy's buddy epitomized the difficulties they encountered: "Since we are moving into a wholistic reading and writing program, there is a lot of confusion among many teachers as to how to teach reading and writing. The confusion was further compounded, partly because whole language was a formative concept about which there was little consensus among teachers at Westville, and partly because it was confused with literature-based reading. Because her background in English literature was compatible with the literature-based-reading approach, Nancy felt comfortable with it, but not whole language. As she put it, "The immediate constraint that I am experiencing now is a hidden agenda at this school. That is basically whether you teach whole language or you teach a literature-based program."

However, Nancy did not entirely reject whole language and, in fact, accepted its "abiding philosophy," with an emphasis on participatory and experiential learning. But she became opposed to whole language as it was practiced by teachers at Westville: it was not controlled by a coherent structure and an operationalized framework of instruction. Whole-language practitioners, she argued, based their language program on "dubious and equivocal" research findings. "They teach to the needs as they naturally develop, but I do not teach them as their needs develop." Given a heterogenous classroom of 24 students with a wide range of reading abilities, she believed it was necessary to structure reading and writing instruction so that they could learn basic reading and writing skills. In her view, before they could attempt to edit each other's writing (as they do in whole language), it would be essential for them to acquire adequate skills first. Students, she feared, would fail to acquire basic skills if instructed in the mode of whole language, and the teacher would relinquish her accountability for her students. Nancy admitted:

> The constraint I feel is that I cannot teach in the way whole-language practitioners do. So I would be deemed nonprofessional, not a "catch," not a "hit," not progressive, not in the mainstream of this school. But you just have to be wary about completely embracing any new method that comes down the pike, totally disavowing and abandoning the method that has been effective and successful for years. Whole language is not part of my training.

Nancy adopted a strategy to covertly reject Westville's policy by structuring her methods of reading and writing instruction and by setting aside one period a week to teach grammar. Her method of teaching grammar was not endorsed by the school, but other teachers, including her buddy, were also teaching straight grammar. In short, Nancy adopted the strategic redefinition of teaching to meet what she described as the needs of her students. Her strategy was justified by her beliefs about teacher accountability and the ineffectiveness of whole language.

We turn to a broader institutional and macrolevel context to understand Nancy's frustration and strategy. The Westville School District had begun to adopt literature-based and whole language programs well before Westville Upper Elementary School opened in 1990. Both the district and the principal of the school, who was known as a spokesperson for whole language, were interested in promoting these programs at the new school. A dozen experienced teachers, who were known as reading experts in the district, and one of whom was a reading specialist, were appointed to teach at Westville. It was obvious that this new school was on the verge of completely transforming its reading program. The district supported the reading specialist's initiative to offer a credit-bearing, biweekly seminar at Westville, staffed by a college professor, to promote the new program.

It was in these institutional and macrolevel contexts that beginning teachers at Westville were coping with constraints. Nancy became much more critical of whole language than the other two neophytes because she was more articulate than they in identifying the merits and demerits of the new reading approach. For Nancy whole language represented a set of complex issues: methodological, philosophical, and political problems. She saw these issues confronting her simultaneously and perceived Westville's push for whole language as a "party line" and an "ideological" mandate ardently advocated by a minority of teachers. The majority of teachers at the school, in her opinion, felt uncomfortable with the mandate but made an appearance of support. In Nancy's words, "It's like silent resistance." The fundamental issue that she saw was an absence of linkage between the "pontificating" about whole language by the school administration and its supporters and the implementation of the new approach when whole language became an implicit mandate for all teachers. As she put it, "You were told about it, but you were never taught about it." That individual teachers were expected to devise operational procedures led to their silent resistance to whole language.

The notion of silent resistance is meaningful when it is placed in the context of teacher culture. The district enjoyed a solid reputation and held high expectations of its teachers. Teachers who were hired in the district were expected to be creative, innovative, knowledgeable in designing lessons and curriculum, and highly committed to teaching; they were assumed to be well informed of current trends in teaching. These expectations contributed to the public image that the district was on the cutting edge, and teachers at Westville, including Nancy, saw themselves as promoters of that image. This image put teachers at Westville in a bind when whole language was mandated at the school. They feigned support for it because they were expected to be capable of adopting it, but they resisted it silently. This, in Nancy's view, created a tension between faculty favorably disposed to whole language and faculty who maintained a somewhat essentialist view of teaching.

We dwelt on Nancy's responses to whole language at length for they are pivotal in understanding the development of her coping strategies during her "survival" phase. Nancy viewed whole language as a covert ideological mandate from above. This created uneasiness and led to her eventual rejection of the program. Initially she was receptive to whole language, in the hope that she would live up to the reputation of the school, but became critical of it when she saw a pronounced incompatibility between whole language and the instructional methods with which she was acquainted through her training. She defined her students' needs differently from how whole language practitioners did, and believed that her accountability for the students was based on her competence to meet these needs. Because Nancy was a dedicated teacher and tried to maintain high standards for her students, whole language created a deep and prolonged conflict between her beliefs and institutional and district policy—a conflict that was only privately expressed to her peers. She never openly challenged whole language, but rejected it in her classroom practice. She even withdrew from the seminar organized by the reading specialist in the spring—a bold decision, since she was aware that her withdrawal could affect the administrators' evaluation of her performance in the first year. Nancy concluded that the seminar was nothing more than a pep rally for whole language. But her neophyte colleagues remained in the seminar, though they also failed to see the promised benefits of the seminar.

Let us turn briefly to another problem, the parents with whom Nancy had to deal—a universal concern that beginning teachers address in the institutional level and macrolevel contexts. As pointed out earlier, Nancy's interest at hand was to gain parental respect while refusing to yield to their pressure, and her strategies for interacting with the parents of her students were influenced by this interest. Her initial strategies were directed toward bolstering her image as a teacher. She assiduously tried to transform her image from that of naive neophyte to a positive one of dependable, mature teacher. She was diligent in creating positive relationships with the parents through means of the back-to-school night, parent conferences, and such routinized activities as student progress reports, student homework, and frequent communication with parents. She gave her home phone number to the parents, to encourage them to channel their concerns with their children's performance. Because Nancy held an image of the parents as rich, demanding, and pushy, she was nervous interacting with them throughout the year.

Nancy's diligence paid off when she earned respect from the parents. But she felt she was manipulated by them when they frequently called her at home, especially late at night. Although she initially encouraged such calls, she became exceedingly annoyed by them and began to feel that they invaded her privacy. She complained that the parents crossed private boundaries with teachers and considered her their "servant." Based on the advice that she sought from her buddy and other experienced teachers to stop what she regarded as abusive phone calls by the parents, she decided to request that the parents call her only at school during her official hours. Moreover, Nancy moved to a new apartment in the spring and obtained an unlisted phone number. Some parents continued to challenge her authority in the classroom by raising questions about her teaching in notes they sent to her. Nancy commented in the middle of the spring:

> I love my kids and we are closely connected. It is such an important thing for me. We are having fun. I cannot tell you how much I love what I am doing with the kids. But parents are making me crazy. I don't want to sound harsh, but I hate them. They make so much work for me. I don't know whether it's because of their wealth or because other teachers are obsequious.

These events led to a change in her interaction with the parents, and her refusal to yield to parental pressure took precedence over her strategy to promote close relations with them. In other words, she adopted a coping strategy to protect herself against aggressive parents, and experienced teachers "confirmed and validated" her actions. She became increasingly concerned with the legitimacy of her status as a teacher, as opposed to her image of teacher as reflected in the parents' eyes.

Nancy's concern with the legitimacy of her actions continued to evolve in the spring, when she was confronted by the mother of a student who was upset by one of them. Nancy initiated a "Student Assistance Plan" procedure, to provide the student with special assistance for improving deficiencies in math skills. Before her initiative was to be formally reviewed by a panel that included an administrator, a social worker, a guidance counselor, and herself, the mother protested the initiative by writing to the superintendent of schools and the State Department of Education. It became incumbent upon Nancy to produce documents justifying her initiative at a meeting with the principal—a very arduous event for a beginning teacher. Subsequently, the principal called a meeting with the mother and Nancy, at which all the documents and rationales were presented to the mother. The mother acted as if she had never protested Nancy's initiative, but asked that Nancy withdraw it anyway. The request was granted by the principal, to appease the parent. Through this event Nancy learned how to legitimate her actions and learned the strategies necessary for this.

Perspectives

The beginning teachers' survival phase is followed by a reflective phase, which Ryan calls the phase of "mastery." Late in the spring the neophytes we studied developed the ability to reflect upon themselves and integrate what they had learned. They gained the self-confidence to detach themselves from the problematic situations in which they were emotionally involved, to reflect on their actions, and to construct a coherent view of their experiences. What evolved from the beginning teachers' strategies was a more generalized, long-term idea-system: a perspective.

To begin with Ellen, her outstanding concerns (classroom management and curriculum) persisted throughout the year. Problems in classroom management especially evolved in a recursive pattern. Nonetheless, the strategies (behavior modification and praise) that she learned to cope with these problems resulted in reducing the number of action-seekers to two boys by the end of the winter. She also learned how to manage her own problem, temper and stress, which Ellen admitted to be a major obstacle to classroom management. She became reflective in dealing with these problems, as revealed in her remarks:

> I think that I discovered that children at this age need a lot of freedom. They need you to sit back, and my role, as I realize it, should sometimes be observer rather than teacher obsessed with control. At this age they need to teach themselves to discover. But that is a hard thing for me. Three months ago I used to think, Why don't I do this or that in the sense of trying to get them balanced. Now I realize that if I sit back and watch them, they figure it out themselves. They need to have a lot of direction, but at the same time, they need to have a lot of freedom.

By spring there was a significant change in her perspective on the two action-seekers. Instead of being obsessed with controlling them, Ellen contemplated how to help them understand the rules and expectations of the classroom, although she still harbored the fear that the two children would still cause upsetting situations. Her fear was still rooted in her inability to control her temper; she was afraid that "they can easily make me lose my temper with other children." But she began to think that her children's violation of her expectations was partly her fault.

Earlier, Ellen had floundered and considered quitting teaching kindergarten. But in the spring, she used the word "self-confidence" to refer to her ability to manage her kindergarten classroom; this had not been part of her vocabulary earlier. She was now able to articulate her sense of commitment to teaching, which represented confidence in herself as a teacher, and that she was reaping a degree of satisfaction from her classroom. That commitment was expressed in her desire to teach a kindergarten class the following year.

Ellen's contradictory orientation toward curriculum changed little throughout the year because her competency anxiety still persisted. Her anxiety was by and large related to her lack of confidence in teaching math at the kindergarten level. As late as May, she still wanted to use a math textbook instead of creating a math curriculum herself, but in the absence of a textbook she relied heavily on her buddy for guidance. Her following comment discloses little change in her perspective on teaching math: "My biggest challenge is me. I still do not know what to teach when it comes to math."

Ellen developed a perspective that was characterized by elements of reflection, moderation, and increased confidence. It represented an increased awareness of constraining and constructive forces in the classroom, a forthright recognition of her personal attributes, and a synthesis of her coping strategies. It was not a complete pattern, but was still forming. Her emerging emphasis on understanding rather than control, the importance of which she was beginning to recognize, enabled her to view in a different light her previous obsession with classroom management. Although she failed to develop a long-term perspective on curriculum, she gained the confidence and drive to teach kindergarten again. Her renewed confidence is an attribute of her materializing self-image which embodied part of her perspective.

Turning to Nancy, she was able to routinize teaching by late in the fall, and classroom control was no longer the center of her concern. Through routinization she simplified her tasks and made her actions more efficient. At the same time, Nancy's view of whole language did not change. She became less reactionary about it and was able to critique it in a more detached manner. In other words, she was no longer overwhelmed and emotionally upset by it because her strategy to deal with it was in place. She continued to reject whole language, in the belief that the whole-language approach failed to provide students with, to use her words, the "bottom-line skills that are necessary." Nancy's characterization of whole language as a political issue involving "a prescriptive undercurrent" remained unchanged. In her view, the school administration was contradictory in making whole language a subtle mandate for all teachers while promoting academic freedom for teachers to enjoy independence and a broad range of initiatives in teaching in general. She believed that the administration and its supporters pushed the whole-language campaign just to be on the cutting edge. Likewise, while she continued to suggest that the parents of her students made "crazy" demands on her, Nancy was able to counter their aggressiveness with a combination of strategies supported by her experienced colleagues. She became less interested in seeking parents' approval of her performance and, in turn, sought the legitimacy of her actions and status. She learned how to validate her actions.

The perspective that Nancy developed from her various strategies was a generalizable pattern of attitudes toward constraints. It consisted of several related long-term strategies. First, in dealing with constraints, she learned that to reduce the personal toll, it was essential not to be emotionally involved. To accomplish that, she tried to generalize and objectify the problem she encountered by defining it as an impersonal matter. Her approach was to "get rid of my ego from the whole process" of dealing with, for example, whole language. Second, and related to the first approach, there was a strategy "to play modestly and keep my nose clean." To protect herself in coping with constraints, she found it essential to reduce the possibility of making herself a highly visible personality by "playing modestly and unassumingly." This strategy evolved in dealing with sensitive institutional and macrolevel problems, such as whole language. Third, by the same token it was necessary to project a positive image that she was innovative, creative, and energetic in teaching. This was an indispensable strategy at Westville where teaching staff competed to live up to its reputation. Fourth, Nancy regarded public relations skills as central to occupational knowledge in dealing with parental pressures and institutional politics. These skills were developed through her own experiences and the advice of veteran teachers. This PR strategy was known among her colleagues as "CYA" (cover your ass). Finally, an effective defense of her position, Nancy concluded, was to have adequate documentation of major decisions she made in her classroom and of the policies she developed and to construct defensible rationales to legitimate the actions.

Summary

Both neophytes on whom we have focused in this chapter displayed distinctive patterns in their social strategies. Ellen typically subscribed to internalized adjustment while Nancy's strategies varied from strategic compliance to redefinition. These neophytes, however, followed a trajectory that displays common characteristics. Their levels of expectations toward teaching were very high at the beginning of the year and quickly diminished as they encountered the complexity and intricacy of teaching and classroom management—a common phenomenon among beginning teachers. In a matter of three weeks, Ellen and Nancy faced interactive and institutional constraints and encountered competency anxiety with respect to curriculum, classroom management, and handling parents. Ellen's notable problems were classroom control and curriculum, whereas Nancy's coping strategies were focused on students' motivation, whole language, and parental pressures. Much of the beginning teachers' first year was concentrated on adapting to the constraints they encountered, improving skills to manage teaching, and overcoming competency anxiety. Toward the end of the year Ellen and Nancy became reflective and began enjoying teaching again; they regained their confidence, no matter how formative it might have been.

In the process of learning to teach, the beginning teachers' biographies played a significant role. Their self-images as teachers were in large measure influenced by formative experiences and, in turn, circumscribed to a considerable extent by the parameters of the strategies that they used. As Lortie (1975) points out, the practices that beginning teachers adopt from other teachers pass through the screen of their self-concepts. The practical rationality of teaching was a major source of knowledge that shaped their orientations and practical approaches to teaching. The notion of constraint used in this chapter is definable as either a phenomenological or an objective condition or as both. Our research participants' biographic factors and personal knowledge base did play a role in defining the constraints with which they had to cope. In this sense, the constraints were defined phenomenologically. Ellen's preservice experiences and personal disposition had a notable influence on her definition of classroom control as a major source of constraint. Likewise, Nancy's formative experiences strongly impinged upon the development of her view of whole language. She saw a whole-language approach as antithetical to her personal beliefs about teaching, which emphasized "bottom-line skills"—beliefs grounded in her biography.

The biographical transformation model linking experiences with beginning teachers' behavior and developed by Knowles (1992) epitomizes the link between our beginning teachers' biographies and their teaching practices. According to the model, formative experiences yield immediate, inherent, and assigned meanings. "Inherent" refers to the first-hand meanings of given events, whereas "assigned" refers to the reflected meanings that result from analyzing the experiences. In other words, the assigned meanings are a consequence of interpreting the experiences, which enables one to develop a schema, a "cognitive filter"—a basis for future practice in the classroom. Both Ellen and Nancy drew upon their previous experiences to interpret classroom events. Their interpretations of those experiences constituted their personal knowledge of teaching (that is, their practical rationality of teaching) and helped to shape the strategies that they used to cope with constraints.

CHAPTER 5

How Japanese Teachers Learn to Teach

Introduction

Learning to teach is a complex, intersubjective process that occurs in multiple social settings, including the classroom, hallways, the teachers' room, and other formal and informal places. We have learned that beginning teachers are active participants in this process of constructing the social reality of teaching. Indeed, learning to teach is a sustained process of intense engagement in seeking advice from experienced teachers and developing strategies in response to demands and problems.

We have examined the occupational socialization of beginning American teachers in the preceding three chapters. Turning now to beginning Japanese teachers, we devote the next three chapters to exploring that process on the basis of the ethnographic data we collected in three public elementary schools in Tokyo. We will focus on both the cultural knowledge of teaching that they learned and how they acquired it. In our analysis we will refer to teaching in the United States to offer a comparative perspective. Although we do not intend to make a systematic comparison of teaching and schooling in Japan and the United States, we hope that our recurrent remarks on similarities and differences in teaching in both cultures will enhance the reader's appreciation of teaching.

In this chapter we will discuss how beginning Japanese teachers structure teaching: the ethnographic descriptions that serve as the basis of analysis in chapters 6 and 7. First, we will present biographical data on the two beginning teachers and illuminate how they became elementary schoolteachers. Then we will investigate how they organized their classroom routines and

what they were teaching students. In the last section, we will
provide an overview of how they learned to teach. To understand these dimensions of Japanese teachers' socialization into
teaching, we will focus primarily on two teachers from among
the seven beginning teachers we studied. One is Kenji Yamada at
Komori Elementary School, and the other is Yoko Kato at Taika
Elementary School. Throughout our analysis we may refer to
other beginning teachers when appropriate.

Two Beginning Teachers

Kenji, Yoko, and the other five beginning Japanese teachers had
only bachelor's degrees, in contrast to the American neophytes
in our study, who held master's degrees. But this does not mean
that these Japanese beginners had fewer qualifications than most
Japanese teachers have when they are appointed. Only 1.1
percent of the men and women hired as elementary
schoolteachers in 1989 held master's degrees (*Naigai Kyoiku*, 12
Dec. 1989). Most teachers at the elementary and secondary levels
start teaching as soon as they graduate from their universities.
Yoko was the same: she began as a first-grade teacher in April
1989, only a month after she graduated. Kenji graduated in 1988,
but failed the teacher appointment examinations, so he taught at
a *juku*, a private enrichment school, for a year, during which time
he took the examinations again. He began teaching a fifth-grade
class at Komori in 1989.

For many neophyte teachers, including our research
participants, their own teachers had a measurable influence on
their decision to become teachers. Yoko's first-grade teacher was
a significant factor in her desire to become a teacher, and Kenji's
third-grade, fourth-grade, and ninth-grade teachers influenced
his choice of teaching as a career. He decided to go to a teachers
college when he was a high school senior. As reported by
researchers (Ito & Yamazaki 1986; Kojima & Shinohara 1985),
many research participants identified their role models as
teachers who had influenced them during their childhood. Lortie
(1975) reported the same findings with respect to American

teachers. In other words, regardless of the culture, neophytes' childhood teachers are significant role models.

How did their teachers most strongly influence them in their choice of a career? The affective attributes of their teachers were felt to be more lasting than their cognitive characteristics. For example, Yoko told us that her first-grade teacher often spent a lot of time with his students in the playground and permitted them to sit on his lap. She recalled that her teacher displayed thoughtfulness to his students. She was attracted to this role model and desired to become a teacher like him.

Kenji's teachers in the third and fourth grades were similarly outgoing and devoted a lot of time to their students in a variety of ways. Another beginning teacher was impressed by her teacher's patient efforts to intervene for her in solving a prolonged problem she had in getting along with her classmates.

Thus motivated in their childhood to become teachers, our Japanese beginning teachers went on to universities and took four-year teacher education programs. To become qualified as elementary schoolteachers, they had to attend seminars and classes on school subjects, teaching methods, the social foundation of education, educational psychology, and so on. They also had to do four weeks of student teaching when they were seniors.

After finishing these courses, they took the teacher appointment examinations conducted by the Metropolitan Tokyo Board of Education. The board establishes a hiring plan and conducts appointment examinations for about 1,500 elementary public schools in metropolitan Tokyo every year. In 1989, the year in which both Kenji and Yoko passed the examinations, the board hired 780 elementary schoolteachers. The competition was very keen; only 1 of every 4.2 candidates was successful (*Naigai Kyoiku*, 12 Dec. 1989). The board ordered Kenji and Yoko to begin teaching at their respective elementary schools in April. (The Japanese academic year begins in April and ends in March.)

The reader will recognize some differences between Japan and the United States in the ways teachers are hired and placed. In the United States teachers are hired by local school districts, but in Japan most of them are employed by one of the 47 prefectural boards of education, under which are local, municipal-level boards of education. (A prefecture is equivalent to a state in the United States.)

Another characteristic of Japanese hiring procedures is that the educational authorities in each prefectural board of education assign beginning teachers to particular schools without consultation. Individual candidates therefore, have no choice with respect to the school at which they are to teach. In the United States, our research participants applied for teaching positions at schools of their preference. Not only do the Japanese beginning teachers have no choice, but they also do not know until late in March which school they will be going to. Hence it is not surprising that beginning teachers are initially little aware of the special programs or the particular policies at the schools where they are assigned. In contrast, American beginning teachers make their teaching plans in light of their school's special emphases and special approaches.

Learning to Establish Classroom Routines

All seven teachers we studied were hired by the Metropolitan Tokyo Board of Education in 1989. Kenji was assigned to teach a fifth-grade class in Komori Elementary School in Ota Ward, and Yoko was assigned to teach a first-grade class in Taika Elementary School in Toshima Ward.

For both of them, teaching a large number of students in one class was a big challenge. Their initial priority was to establish routines for daily activities. Routines would enable them to anticipate and monitor effectively what would happen each day. They had to establish such routines not only for the periods in which they were teaching subjects, but also in other situations in which they would be interacting with their students, whether in the classroom or outside. One of the most important tasks for beginning teachers learning to teach in Japan was to know how to set those routines, just as it was for their counterparts in the United States.

First we will describe what the routines were and then point out the features of these routines on the basis of field notes taken as we observed an entire day's activities.

Establishing Routines in First Grade

Let us first review Yoko's activities at Taika on Monday, May 22, a little less than two months after she had begun teaching. At 8:15, when we arrived, we found the principal at the school gate greeting children as they arrived. Unlike American children, Japanese children walk to school. The principal's morning routine revealed a characteristic of Japanese education, the idea that teacher rapport with students through direct contact is important. At Taika, as would be true everywhere in Japan, a schoolwide assembly in the playground was scheduled. During spring this would take the form of a music assembly on Thursdays and a sports assembly on Saturdays, but otherwise, for 15 minutes each Monday morning, all students and teachers gathered in one place to participate in schoolwide events. Yoko's first-grade students regularly participated in these assemblies, as did the older students. During each morning assembly the principal spoke to the students of his various concerns, including school goals, moral subjects, and his expectations of the students.

Yoko had arrived at school shortly before 8:00 A.M. to prepare for the day, and she had not forgotten that there was a morning assembly that Monday. At 8:30, the chimes used to punctuate the start and finish of activities sounded and a *nicchoku* teacher, a teacher assigned to be in charge of supervising the school on that day, instructed the students on the playground to form lines by class. She was followed by the principal, who stepped up onto a podiumlike wooden stand and greeted the assembly. He reported that the Taika sumo team, consisting of boys and girls, won second place in the ward's sumo tournament held the day before. He asked the team members to come forward and reminded the assembly that the goal of the school was to develop both body and mind.

At 8:45, when the assembly ended, music was turned on and students returned to their classrooms, but Yoko's and her senior colleague's first-grade classes remained on the playground to rehearse a Japanese folk dance they were to perform at the athletic festival in June. The boys wore white shirts, white pants, and white sneakers, while the girls wore white blouses, black pants, and red sneakers. The two classes were distinguished by the color of their caps, which was either red or white. With each pupil holding a large lampshade type of hat made of paper, they gathered at one corner of the playground and formed lines. At 9:05, as folk music was turned on, the children began marching toward the center of the field, where they formed two circles to begin the dance. The teachers helped the first-graders keep a proper distance between themselves as they danced and rehearsed their exit. After one more rehearsal, the teachers gathered the pupils around them to give them further instructions. Both teachers concentrated on using the exercise to develop the children's coordination and patterns of movement. When the chimes sounded at 9:30, to signal the end of the first period, the children quickly returned to their classrooms and changed their clothes. Their ability to follow instructions with promptness was quite impressive, given the fact that they had become first-graders only in April.

The classroom was a traditional four-walled classroom in which the teacher's and students' desks faced each other. Each student was assigned a desk, inside which several textbooks and notebooks were kept. Yoko had only 22 students, a relatively small class considering that the average class size is about 30 in Japan. The following school goals, in the form of mottoes, were written in large characters on a poster on the front wall of the classroom: (1) a child who is mentally and physically strong; (2) a child who is cooperative and takes the initiative; (3) a child who has a rich mind and thinks deeply. Next to this was written the school's special goal for the month of May: "Let us clean up thoroughly in accordance with our rules." (Such a display of school goals can be found in all Japanese schools. The principal and nicchoku teachers often remind students of these goals at school assemblies. Throughout Japan, banners with such school mottoes are often displayed in the hallways and at the entrance of the main school building, and a moral importance is attached to them.) Next to the poster Yoko had placed a colorful timetable. An assignment sheet for school lunch duties was posted on one of the side walls. School lunch was to be served by the task group, with assistance from Yoko, in the classroom. She kept her work desk at the front corner of the room, facing the windows.

At 9:40, when a language arts class began, Yoko urged her class to get ready for the lesson. Two nicchoku (duty) students, who were assigned to be in charge of the day's classroom chores, walked to the front of the room and ordered the class to sit up straight. They called out the names of any students who were not paying attention. Yoko took the roll call and checked whether there were any messages from their parents.

The language arts class focused on practicing reading and writing *hiragana* (Japanese cursive characters), the character "mu" in particular. Having handed a work sheet to each student, Yoko wrote "mu" on the board and demonstrated the order of strokes for this character; she then instructed the class to practice the character on their work sheets, and moved around to check their work. When she found children who were not writing the character correctly, she returned to the board to show how to write it.

Although most children appeared relaxed and concentrated on their work, some did not. But even when Yoko saw a boy not practicing hiragana, she only told him, "Now is not the time to play; just practice the character." She also just called another boy's name when he spoke to someone. Moreover, when a boy, Kazu, stood up and left the classroom without her approval, she did not pay attention to him, acting as if she were not bothered by his behavior. (We were told later that a counselor at the Toshima Ward Education Center was studying this boy's antisocial behavior.) Yoko did not impose any punishment or penalty on him for having left the room.

When the chimes sounded to signal the end of the second period, students turned in their work. Normally the day's nicchoku students went to the front of the room to announce the end of the period, but on this day the lesson was finished without that exercise. All the children went out to the playground with Yoko for a 20-minute break. (A 20-minute outdoor break in the company of the teacher was a common practice at Taika and the other schools we studied.) The purpose of playing with the children, Yoko explained, was to develop close relations with them.

At 10:40 the chimes sounded for the third period, and students immediately returned to the classroom. The two nicchoku students stood in front of the class, shouting "Attention!" and calling out the names of those who were still making noise; and then, when everyone was quiet, they announced the beginning of the third period. Yoko began a music lesson. She was not a music specialist, but in Japanese elementary schools music specialists usually teach only upper-grade music classes, while classroom teachers usually teach them at the lower-grade levels. Yoko instructed the class to stand up and sing the school song as she played the organ. This lesson was part of rehearsing for the upcoming athletic festival. Students sang the school song in harmonious and cheerful voices, looking at the words written on a large sheet of paper Yoko had hung over the blackboard. After one round of singing, Yoko removed the sheet of paper and suggested that the class sing the song again. She told the students to sing with more energy. She then explained the meaning of the song line by line, and the class appeared to be enjoying the music lesson. Then they practiced playing a tune on the *pianica* (a kind of musical instrument).

During the lesson, however, there were several students who could not concentrate. Yoshi pushed a child in front of him, while Jiro was jumping around. That prompted Yoko to warn them to be quiet, but her warning did not include the threat of punishment. When Kazu had his legs propped up on his desk, she just called out his name. Subsequently he suddenly moved to the front of the room and banged the organ keys. Told to stop it, he pulled out a white tablecloth for school lunch and wrapped himself in it and left the room. Yoko often admonished him and other misbehaving students by calling out their names, but she never resorted to punishment by isolating them from the group, a method often used by American teachers. In this classroom there were few commonly understood rules for dealing with the consequences of student offenses. But even though Kazu often misbehaved, the class did not seem particularly disturbed by it. At first sight, the class may have given the impression of being completely disordered, but in reality there certainly was order. The third period came to an end with the sound of the chimes at 11:25, and the two nicchoku students announced the end of the class. Some children went out into the corridor to play.

At 11:30 the nicchoku students announced the fourth period. Yoko told her class to open to page 17 of the math textbook, where there was a picture of five children on slides. Holding up the teacher's manual, she asked the class to explain the difference between "three children" and "a third child." A dozen students raised their hands to indicate that they were able to distinguish between them. She then told the class to color the five cars shown in the textbook and walked back and forth through the aisles to inspect the students' work. She placed a large black sheet of paper on the board and asked for volunteers to place five paper cars on it. When Yuki placed the cars on the sheet correctly, the class responded in unison, "That's right." The lesson continued, as did Kazu's deviant behavior. At 12:15 the chimes sounded to signal the end of the fourth period.

The last morning lesson was followed by a lunch period. The lunch task group went with Yoko to the kitchen to fetch meals. Back in the classroom, the children stood in line as the six lunch servers, wearing white caps and aprons just like professional cooks, handed out the meals. After lunch the children were dismissed and went home. A short time later some sixth-graders came to clean their classroom and hallway under Yoko's supervision. This brief depiction of Yoko's class reveals the characteristics of her teaching. First, repetition of routines is a major feature of her activities, which are regulated by the chimes. Students' behavior was also conditioned by the chimes punctuating the start and finish of each lesson. Educational activities in Japanese schools are structured according to a fixed time schedule that allows multiple activities (morning assembly, classes for various subjects, lunch, and the cleaning of the classroom, for example) to occur smoothly. Students had to follow the schedule while in school, and it was Yoko's responsibility to develop this response in her students. To our surprise, Yoko's students had already learned this response to the set routine by the time we observed her class in May. They were able on that Monday to leave their personal belongings and knapsacks in the classroom and go out to the playground to attend the assembly. They had already learned too, that at the sound of the chimes, they were expected to be seated at their own desks for lessons. And they had also internalized the rules that forbade them to walk around in the classroom during lessons. Most of her students could learn the appropriate way of behaving in a few months.

Second, a teacher needs to develop in students an attention pattern conducive to effective teaching. Getting the first-graders' attention and maintaining it for a sustained period is critical for her classroom management. Yoko was working hard to develop an effective attention pattern by issuing what Japanese teachers call *shiji*, instructions or directions that shape student activities. A senior colleague of hers teaching at the same grade level had suggested that developing in the children a habit of listening to the teacher was of utmost importance at this level. This required motivating them and applying shiji properly. A schoolwide activity, such as a sports event, was an especially good opportunity for students to learn how to listen to and follow teachers' directions. With this in view, Taika Elementary School actively promoted group-oriented activities (as most Japanese schools do). During the spring excursion trip for first-graders in another elementary school we studied, several teachers accompanied more than 100 students on a train ride to visit a zoo. Both going to the zoo and on the way back, one of the major purposes of the whole experience seemed to be practicing how to form lines and how to walk in orderly ranks.

Third, her method of teaching was conventional despite her having only 22 students. Although she paid attention to individual students, her instruction was not individualized. Nor did she consider forming small learning groups (commonly called *han* in Japan), a practice often adopted by experienced teachers to promote cooperative learning. Instead, she taught the whole group, following the teacher's manual in the planning and execution of her lessons.

Fourth, the moral goals of schooling were emphasized. Yoko made a conscious display of the school mottoes and stressed the students' sitting posture. Yet, unlike American beginning teachers, she had no operational rules of classroom management. To outward appearance, she was rather incompetent in handling Kazu in the absence of such rules. But she was patient and hoped, as she told us, that her patience and love for him would eventually be repaid. Operating under the assumption that he needed and wanted her attention, she often took pains to speak to him before he went home.

From the preceding description of Yoko's activities it is quite obvious that teaching is an inclusive activity. She taught all subjects (including music and physical education), helped to serve lunch, supervised students when they cleaned the classroom, and provided guidance for a child like Kazu.

Establishing Routines in Fifth Grade

We next turn to Kenji Yamada, who taught a fifth-grade class at Komori Elementary School. His routines of teaching were similar to Yoko's, suggesting that there was a great deal of continuity between the first and fifth grades. We will highlight Kenji's activities by focusing on one typical day.

Kenji arrived at school around 7:50 A.M. on Monday, May 1. Just as at Yoko's elementary school, the first day of the week at this school started with a morning assembly in the playground, and this included the entire student body and faculty. At 8:30, as each class lined up in two rows, the nicchoku teacher directed the assembly. Students began to sing the school song, accompanied by the school brass band set up in front of the assembly, and the school flag was raised. The principal stepped up to the podium to greet the assembly and spoke about the significance of the upcoming national holiday on May 5. He also praised the good results of Komori's track team, which had participated in a track-and-field competition. His speech was brief, but its moral symbolism was important. The principal was followed by the nicchoku teacher, who reminded the students of the school's goal for May, emphasizing that students should prepare for lessons every day. The assembly ended after 15 minutes, and students marched back to their classrooms in time to the music of the brass band. All Kenji's students proceeded in orderly fashion to their classroom.

Kenji's classroom, identical with Yoko's, was a traditional self-contained room. The 32 students were seated at desks arranged in four rows facing the front chalkboard. The school's May goals were clearly posted on the chalkboard, as were the students' objectives (for example, "Study steadily and participate actively in physical exercise"). A wide-screen TV set was also located at the front of the room. On the rear wall was a large poster identifying several student task groups, including those charged with lunchtime, recreation, health and first aid, library, and chalkboard-cleaning duties. At the rear of the room were lockers for knapsacks, gym bags, art materials, and so on. Compared with the average American classroom, Kenji's classroom (like Yoko's) was rather plain.

At 8:50, when Kenji arrived at his classroom as the chimes were sounding, his students were seated at their desks. A nicchoku student shouted to the class, "Stand up," and the students rose. They then bowed to him as he did to them. The first lesson was language arts, focusing on a poem entitled "A Horsefly" found in the thin textbook used by the class. He told the class to open to the proper page and to read the poem to themselves. After they finished reading, he asked a boy to read it to the others. Then students discussed their impressions of it for 10 minutes. While they were talking about which part they liked, some students began to whisper to each other, but he didn't tell them to be quiet.

At 9:13 Kenji started reading the same poem, pausing after he had read a few lines to pose a question about the meaning of a word or phrase. He wrote on the board, "The heart of a horsefly becomes larger than a mountain" and asked what this line meant. No one answered the question. He then directed the class to form han (small groups) to discuss the meanings of the line among themselves.

Dividing students into han, or cooperative learning groups, is a frequent practice at the higher levels of elementary education. It is resorted to when the teacher wants students to solve problems collectively, to be more closely involved in some task at hand, or to carry out classroom duties. It is a popular practice that is used extensively not only in schools but also in industry. In Kenji's class a han consisted of four students, two boys and two girls, who either sat next to one another or sat in front of and behind one another.

The students broke up into their han and began to talk to one another loudly. After a while the groups were asked to respond to the questions posed by Kenji. At 9:35 the chimes sounded and the lesson ended. He told the class to read over the poem three times at home. Then the nicchoku student ordered the class to rise and bow to the teacher to mark the completion of the lesson.

After a five-minute break the class went to the music room for a lesson given by a specialist. Meanwhile, Kenji returned to the staff room to work there. In the staff room teachers' desks were arranged in several rows, with the desks of teachers of the same grade level clustered together to enhance interaction among them. Even the principal had his own desk there, despite the fact that his large office was located next to the staff room. In this staff room a briefing was held every morning, and all staff meetings took place in this room.

A 20-minute break began at 10:25, when the music lesson was completed. This break provided students with opportunities to play outdoors and interact with one another in ways decided by the students themselves. Teachers did not supervise, though some of them often went out to the playground to play and interact with students as equal participants. In American schools, we noted that adults always supervised students when they were at play in their schoolyard.

At 10:45, when the chimes signaled the start of the third period, Kenji's students returned to their classroom promptly, after which he came into the room. The third and fourth periods were devoted to a science lesson in the science lab, taught by Kenji. He asked his students to form a line in the hallway and walk down to the lab, which was located on the same floor. The students formed eight han, each of which sat around one of the 12 large black-top tables in the lab. The class was experimenting on kidney-bean germination under various conditions and with sunlight, air, water, and temperature control. Kidney beans were germinating in the containers brought from the classroom, in a refrigerator, and in a water tank. When Kenji instructed his students to record their observations on germination on a sheet of paper, members of each han recorded the degree of germination of the beans under different conditions. Kenji circulated in the lab to monitor their work and answer their questions. He then drew seven vertical lines on a large chalkboard in the lab to allocate space for each han to record the results of its experiments. The class displayed noticeable interest and involvement. Within five minutes, four of the eight han had written the results of their experiments on the board. When the chimes sounded at the end of the third period, he gave the class a five-minute break, but the four remaining han continued writing their results on the board.

The fourth period resumed at 11:35. The discussion shifted to sharing the results of each han's experiments, and Kenji wrote the findings of the different han on the board. He asked the class how many times the results of their experiments differed from the initial predictions they had made. A girl responded by reporting her (unexpected) finding that the beans planted in a dark box grew faster than those planted in bright sunlight. He pointed out that several of the results written on the board confirmed her finding. He then asked if the findings supported hypotheses that they formulated the previous week regarding the germination of the beans under different conditions. Student participation was high, and there was active interaction between the teacher and students.

As the discussion between Kenji and his students continued, a few students engaged in private conversations, thus distracting the class. He noticed them and asked one of them to explain what conclusion could be drawn from the entire experiment. When the student did not answer, he scolded him by saying, "I figured you were talking too much" and told him and his friends to listen carefully because it was something important. When they began talking again a little while later, Kenji isolated them by making them sit at a table at the rear of the room. This was the first time he imposed a penalty on any of his students.

The discussion lasted for nearly 30 minutes, mainly focused on the reason beans grew faster in the dark. At the end of the discussion students started to copy the findings recorded on the board. At 12:25, when the fourth period ended, Kenji told them to clear the tables and return to their classroom with their textbooks and experiment materials.

Now it was time for lunch. The four students of each han pushed together their desks and spread white tablecloths over them; members on the lunch-duty roster quickly put on white aprons and caps and went to fetch the food and utensils. The food was set out on a large table at the front of the room, and students lined up for their servings, carrying them on a tray to their own places. Kenji joined them. When all were seated, they said in unison "Itadakimasu," a Japanese expression of gratitude for a meal, and began to eat. The meal was a convivial occasion, with students conversing and having a good time as they enjoyed the meal. Kenji also chatted away with several students as he ate. After everyone was finished eating, they expressed thanks for the meal by saying "Gochiso-sama" ("thanks for a good meal"), returning eating utensils and leftovers to the table at the front of the classroom, cleaning their own tables, and folding up the tablecloths.

The chimes sounded at 1:10, and over the loudspeaker a student announced cleanup time to the entire school; the announcement was followed by music. Students went to their assigned cleaning areas. Kenji's class was responsible for not only its own classroom but also the resource room, the library, and the gym. Kenji remained in the classroom to participate in the cleaning. At 1:25 the loudspeaker reminded the entire student body that only five minutes remained for completing the cleaning. Kenji also encouraged his students in the classroom to finish cleaning. After cleanup time, the students spent 20 minutes playing on the playground, while Kenji went to the staff room for a rest.

The fifth period was moral education, starting at 1:50. Local school authorities did not provide textbooks for moral education, something that made Kenji feel uncomfortable in teaching the subject. He used a TV program, "Jump for Tomorrow," designed for moral education in the upper-elementary years; colleagues teaching the same grade were also using it. After he distributed printed materials for their homework, he turned the TV on at 2:00. The program was a drama that lasted 15 minutes and that depicted a moral issue, with emphasis on honesty and integrity. He then went over the general outline of the story, asking the students about their impressions of it and writing their answers on the board. He then recounted an anecdote about something that occurred to one of the children in a neighboring class and showed how it was relevant to the TV story.

Although he planned to devote all the remaining time to a discussion of the program, the students were not concentrating, partly because they had just had lunch and felt sleepy. His questions fell on deaf ears for the rest of the period, perhaps to some degree reflecting Kenji's lack of confidence in moral education. When his students became noisy and restless, he tried to reclaim their attention several times, with little success. At the end of the lesson, he summarized the theme of the lesson by saying, "Be honest and admit it, even when you break something valuable." At 2:35 the chimes announced the end of the fifth period.

Incidentally, moral education, as an independent subject at the elementary level, was incorporated into the new national curriculum in 1961. Although the Ministry of Education has attached great importance to moral education since then, Japanese teachers have vacillated for three decades over how to handle it as a subject. This reflects the tension that exists between the Japan Teachers' Union, which is opposed to it, and the Ministry of Education. It would seem that Kenji echoed the general mode of ambivalence regarding the subject. However, this ambivalent attitude is not shared by all teachers, as was evident among some of the teachers in our study schools.

When all the lessons of the day had ended, Kenji called the two nicchoku students to come forward and asked them to inquire if the task groups or committees had any announcements to make. Noting that there were no student announcements, he reminded the class of their homework. Normally, 15 minutes is allocated as a period during which students reflect on problems encountered during the day. At 2:50 all the students rose, the nicchoku students led the others in loudly saying "Sayonara," and they all bowed to the teacher. They then prepared to walk home.

From the preceding observations we can see several similarities in Yoko's and Kenji's teaching methods, even though they taught grades that were very different in terms of intellectual, social, and biopsychological development. First, Kenji's teaching was as routinized as Yoko's. Both teachers followed the precise punctuation of activities by the chimes: class starting and finishing times and lunch and recess times were clearly differentiated. Most students in Kenji's class were more familiar with the routine set up by the school than were Yoko's first-graders. Kenji's students already knew almost everything they should do on each occasion. The schoolwide events were also common: morning assembly, recess, lunchtime duty, and cleaning (though first-graders were exempt). This shows that regardless of grade, common routines were institutionalized as part and parcel of the school's organization.

Second, in both classes textbooks were the main teaching materials. Yoko and Kenji used textbooks in all their subjects. A veteran teacher in another study school pointed out that the absence of a moral education textbook was the source of the difficulties teachers experienced in teaching the subject. This suggests that Japanese teachers rely heavily on textbooks.

Third, Kenji adopted a conventional lecture method of teaching, just as Yoko did. He frequently issued shiji or directions for developing an attention pattern. Although it is often said that the teaching in Japanese schools should be individualized, most Japanese teachers use shiji and follow the question-and-answer format throughout an entire class period, as the two beginning teachers did. Division into han, which Kenji used to promote learning, was a primary part of the lecture method.

However, it is also true that these small learning groups facilitated interaction and cooperation among students. This feature of his teaching contrasts with the American teachers' mode of teaching, which emphasizes the individualization of learning and encourages dialogue only between students and the instructor, rather than interaction among students.

The fourth similarity between the two beginning teachers' teaching approaches is related to this feature of han. Although Yoko did not use han in her lessons, like Kenji she granted a variety of opportunities for her students to engage in social interaction: in the morning, before school began, and during the recess, the 20-minute break, and the lunch period. During these times students were encouraged to take the initiative in cooperating with one another to carry out their duties and to control themselves by following rules. This reflects the Japanese philosophy of schooling at the elementary level, which puts a priority on social interaction and cooperation among students. In comparison, the American students we observed were granted much less opportunity for social interaction.

Fifth, the patterns of control Kenji and Yoko used to deal with students were similar. Both ordered their students to sit up straight and speak politely during lessons. Permissiveness toward unruly students was also a common feature. In general, neither of them imposed any penalties, but just called out the names of students who could not concentrate on the lessons.

On the basis of these findings, we can conclude that both Kenji and Yoko shared a fundamental pedagogy. The differences we found between the two were differences in the activities they engaged in and the degree of control they issued, and these were mostly related to the different grades they taught.

What Are Beginning Teachers Teaching?

From our observation of the two beginning teachers, we found that Japanese neophytes engaged in a variety of activities and established several kinds of routine. Before we inquire, however, how they learned to teach, we should identify which areas of their activities were defined as teaching. As will be seen shortly, Japanese elementary education has generated its own concept of teaching, one that is significantly different from the American one. In each culture, schooling is organized on the basis of its own concept.

To obtain an overall picture of activities in a Japanese elementary school, we can look at Kenji's weekly timetable (see table 1). It confirms the fact that his teaching was inclusive. In his fifth-grade class, besides 27 academic periods running from Monday through Saturday, there were also club activities,

TABLE 1. Weekly Timetable for Kenji's Class at Komori Elementary School

	Monday	Tuesday	Wednesday	Thursday	Friday	Saturday
8:30–8:45	School assembly		Sports assembly		Student assembly	
8:45–8:50	Short meeting	Short meeting	Short meeting	Short meeting	Short meeting	Short meeting
8:50–9:35	Language arts	Math	Language arts	Math	Language arts	Arts and crafts
9:35–9:40	Break	Break	Break	Break	Break	Break
9:40–10:25	Math	Language arts	Math	Language arts	Language arts	Arts and crafts
10:25–10:45	Recess	Recess	Recess	Recess	Recess	Recess
10:45–11:30	Science	Social studies	Home economics	Social studies	Math	Social studies
11:30–11:35	Break	Break	Break	Break	Break	Break
11:35–12:20	Science	Math	Home economics	Science	Homeroom	Gym
12:20–13:10	Lunch	Lunch	Lunch	Lunch	Lunch	Reflection (12:10–12:30)
13:10–13:30	Cleaning	Cleaning	Cleaning	Cleaning	Cleaning	
13:30–13:50	Recess	Recess	Club activity (13:30–14:15)	Recess	Recess	
13:50–14:35	Moral ed.	Gym		Music	Gym	
14:35–14:50	Reflection	Reflection		Break	Reflection	
		Student committee (14:50–15:35)		Extra period (14:45–15:30)	Reflection (14:35–14:45)	
				Reflection (15:30–15:40)		

TABLE 2. Total Time Spent Weekly for Each Activity in Fifth Grade

	Japan: *Komori Elementary* *School*		*United States:* *Westville Upper* *Elementary School*	
	min.	%	min.	%
Academic classes[1]	1,170	(54.2)	1,200	(64.9)
Nonacademic classes[2]	191	(8.8)	200	(10.8)
Lunch	250	(11.6)	200	(10.8)
Break and recess	315	(14.6)	250	(13.5)
Cleaning	100	(4.6)	0	(0.0)
Assemblies, meetings and reflections	135	(6.2)	0	(0.0)
Total	2,161	(100.0)	1,850	(100.0)

[1] Academic Subjects:
   Japan: Language arts, math, science, social studies, music, arts and crafts, gym, home economics.
   United States: basic reading, language, spelling, activities, social studies, science, health, gym, art, computer, basic math.
[2] Other Activites:
   Japan: moral education, student committee, extra period, club activity, homeroom activity.
   United States: activity period, open time.

homeroom activities, moral education, and morning assemblies. In addition, there were lunch periods and cleanup times (every day except Saturday), in which all the tasks were carried out by his students. Between the second and third periods, as well as after cleanup time, 20-minute recesses were set up for students to play together in the playground.

Table 2 indicates that Kenji's students spent more time on nonacademic activities than American students did. The table shows the number of hours spent by Kenji's students and American fifth graders in Westville Upper Elementary School on each type of activity. Kenji's students spent 2,161 minutes per week in the school, while the American fifth-graders spent 300 minutes less, or 1,850 minutes in total. As to time spent on academic lessons, however, Kenji's class spent as much as the American class. This suggests that Kenji's students were engaged in other types of activities as well: morning assembly, recess, club activities, homeroom activities, lunch, cleaning, and so on. In addition, the Japanese elementary school holds many events during the year, almost one every month: athletic meets, school performance days, art exhibitions, and the like. Fifth- and sixth-graders in most schools also go to summer camps and school trips. A considerable amount of time normally used for academic subjects is used for these activities or preparing for them. One of the significant differences between Japanese and American elementary education is the amount of time spent on these extracurricular activities.

But more important is the fact that Japanese teachers regard all these extra activities as being as much within the scope of teaching as are their academic lessons, while American classroom teachers tend to think that teaching is largely limited to the academic lessons in the classroom. In this connection, it may be interesting to the reader to notice that Japanese teachers commonly use the term "teaching school lunch." A handbook entitled *Introduction to Teaching*, distributed to Kenji and other beginning teachers by the Board of Education of Ota Ward, illuminated the significance of teaching during school lunch as follows: "Teaching during School Lunch: Besides helping students to learn proper dietary habits, it should aim at nurturing desirable human relationships among them through eating together, as well as helping them develop physically and mentally." Because Kenji was expected to assist in accomplishing these aims, he encouraged his students to cooperate with one another in fetching and setting up the meals, and he provided them with the opportunity to chat during lunch by clustering their desks into several groups.

The first-grade teachers were expected to teach students how to serve meals by themselves. We were able to observe a neophyte teacher at Komori spending two periods early in May to teach his first-grade students how to organize lunch service. He told them to push their desks together into three large clusters first, and appointed eight students as members of the lunch task group. He then had each of the eight students put on a white apron and white cap and led them to the wing of the building where meals were prepared. After the task group returned to the classroom with the meals, he showed them how to serve the food out to the others.

Cleaning classrooms and other places in the school is also regarded as part of education in Japan. The handbook published by the Board of Education of Ota Ward stated:

> Teaching during cleaning-up: Not to be taken as a merely utilitarian exercise, the school-cleaning activity needs to be understood as an occasion to provide education; it is a valuable activity that affects the educational efforts of the school as a whole.

The handbook emphasized that cleaning is important for students because it teaches them how to cooperate, as well as to appreciate the importance of a clean environment:

> It is very important for the students to deepen their human relations through experiencing pleasure and hard work together with their classmates. The satisfaction of having done something with others helps a child develop thoughtfulness for others as well as an attitude of working without complaint.

To achieve these educational goals, Kenji worked with his students and urged them on to greater efforts in order to finish the cleanup on time.

Yoko's experience provides another example. As part of her internship program, she attended a summer seminar on recreation planning, including how to run a campfire or an orienteering exercise. The instructor at the recreation center told participants that the educational meaning of making a campfire was to encourage students to cooperate with one another and to allow teachers to integrate their students into a group. While the very fact that she learned how to run a campfire indicated that this is regarded as a relevant teaching activity, the explanation given by the instructor makes it even clearer that such an activity is as important for Japanese teachers as academic lessons. The broad scope of teaching we mentioned here will be explored in detail in the succeeding chapter.

On the basis of this evidence, it may be suggested that all the various activities that take place in an elementary school are defined as "teaching" in Japan. Therefore, every interaction of beginning teachers with students is evaluated from the educational point of view, and teachers themselves have to be careful not to adopt the attitude that their activities are not educational. In the next section we will explore how they learned teaching.

The Process of Learning How to Teach

Preservice Teacher Education

The opportunities for learning how to teach are divided into two stages: preservice education at a university, and the period after one actually becomes a teacher. As pointed out previously, most teachers take only four years of preservice education and only a few obtain master's degrees. During the second stage, informal learning, through interaction with senior colleagues and through personal experiences while teaching, or formal learning, through the official internship program offered in and out of the school, takes place. We will explore what and how the two beginning teachers, Kenji and Yoko, learned to teach in each of these stages.

As for the teacher education program in their universities, both of them were required to do course work on relevant subject matter and on teaching methods. Kenji thought that the lectures he took were not practical enough for him to teach successfully in the classroom. He suggested that his university taught him little about strategies for using materials appropriately. Nor did Yoko feel she learned anything there about how to teach, although she learned a philosophy of education that stressed that teachers should not "scold" children, but should wait patiently until they began to study of their own volition. Likewise, a beginning teacher at Ikeshita Elementary School was not very sure how much she learned about teaching at her university. Kano (1984) reported that very few teachers felt that their preservice education had enabled them to develop the competence needed to teach successfully. In particular, many of them felt they did not learn any practical skills on how to teach in their classrooms or any knowledge of how to develop teaching materials. According to Jinnouchi (1987), one of the reasons universities did not train students effectively was that most professors tended to attach more importance to teaching the academic knowledge in each subject rather than to practical teaching skills.

However, both Kenji and Yoko identified student teaching as an exceptionally valuable preparation for teachers. Imazu (1978 & 1979) and Ito (1980 & 1981) also reported that preservice students generally felt student teaching had a considerable impact on their becoming teachers. As discussed in chapter 2, American neophytes identified a similar impact. Yet student teaching in Japan is condensed into four weeks, a far shorter period than in the United States. No matter how short it is and no matter how it is organized, it seems to have a powerful impact upon most student teachers.

But we also found some characteristics unique to student teaching in Japan. Let us look at Yoko's case, for example. When she student taught for four weeks in her senior year, she went to her assigned school every day without attending any of her university classes at all. During the first week, after she was given a very brief explanation of the way the school operated, she was assigned two hours of classes to teach by herself. From the second week, the number of class hours she taught was gradually increased, so that by the end of the fourth week she had taught a total of 20 hours of classes. She stayed in school long after her students had gone home, to prepare for her next day's classes. Her supervisor also stayed with her, but he did not assist her unless she was up against a difficult problem and sought his advice for a solution. Nor did he plan any specific program for her to follow; instead, he let her teach in her own way through trial and error.

Kenji, on the other hand, did not do as much student teaching as Yoko, although he also stayed at his school for four weeks. In the first and second weeks he observed classes taught by his supervisor; he was assigned several classes of math and language arts only from the third week on. He did not teach the large number of classes that Yoko did; instead, he tried to take advantage of as many opportunities as possible for interacting with students. Through playing with them, he remarked, he came to feel how lovable children were and how rewarding it was to be with them.

Yoko and Kenji's student teaching was completely supervised by cooperating teachers at their assigned schools, and their university instructors gave little guidance and few suggestions during that period. The only time Yoko's university supervisor came to observe her progress was when she conducted a demonstration class in her fourth week. Kenji's student teaching was also supervised solely by the cooperating teacher.

This reveals that there is a weak connection between universities and schools with regard to student teaching. This makes student teaching an occasion for learning the routines of teaching and the patterns of interaction that exist between teachers and pupils, both in the classroom and in other areas of a school. As Yoko commented, considering the fact that during her course work at her university she had hardly any occasion to come into close contact with schoolchildren, student teaching was very helpful for her in learning how to speak and deal with children. Kenji also felt glad that through his student teaching he was able to acquire some knowledge of the inner workings of a school. A senior teacher at Taika Elementary School agreed with both beginners about the effect of student teaching, stating:

> During the period of student teaching, a person can get some notion of how a classroom is managed throughout a whole day and can experience what it is actually like to be standing in front of children. I think these experiences have a great impact on a person's becoming an excellent teacher. . . . Although most student teachers are here only a few weeks, they learn a great deal from interacting with children all day long. They unconsciously internalize an appropriate attitude toward teaching.

In summary, although student teaching is one part of a larger preservice education package offered by universities, students did not find it to be an opportunity for putting into practice the academic knowledge learned from their universities; what they did find, however, was that student teaching confirmed (to their relief) that the actual patterns of teaching were just the same as the ones they had experienced in their childhood.

Learning Teaching on the Job

Formal Internship

We now turn to the stage after the beginning teachers began teaching, to identify the most effective methods for them in learning teaching.

One of the opportunities for learning how to teach made available to them was a one-year internship program for beginning teachers that had been introduced in all public elementary schools by the Ministry of Education in 1989. As discussed in chapter 1, this program resulted from recommendations submitted by the National Council on Educational Reform (NCER), which was established in 1984 by the national legislature. Concerned about the dramatic increase of deviant behavior among students, the NCER pointed out that the Japanese school system was in a "grave state of desolation," a "crisis" caused by pathological social conditions (NCER 1988). Characterizing Japanese education as desolate provided a strong stimulus for introducing some sort of internship (Shimahara & Sakai 1992).

The official purpose of the teacher internship program was for a teacher to develop (1) "practical teaching competence," (2) a "sense of mission" in teaching, and (3) a "broad perspective" as a teacher (NCER 1988). NCER suggested that a "sense of mission" refers to an awareness of purpose in teaching. Although the phrase has not been defined clearly, it has often been repeated and emphasized in government reform reports in the postwar era. The notion of mission is embedded in the time-honored assumption that teachers have a special moral responsibility in teaching (Shimahara 1991). "Broad perspective" refers to a broad social view that teachers are expected to develop "through exposure to business organizations and other institutions, as well as national and international events" (NCER 1988, p. 98).

With high hopes that it would achieve these purposes, the internship program was introduced in our study schools in

April 1989, just as it was introduced in other public elementary schools. For our purposes, what we wished to see was the way this program was put into practice and how effective it might be for the neophytes regarding the content and methods of teaching. A handbook for the 1989 educational program published by the Metropolitan Tokyo Board of Education listed the following four areas of internship training:

1. A training program at the education center in each ward (once a week, 20 times all told during the year)
2. An in-house internship program (twice a week, 60 times)
3. A five-day retreat
4. Seminars on specific themes (three seminars, 15 times all told)

As part of the training program held at the education center, several retired principals, university professors, and experienced teachers lectured on their own experiences in teaching, human rights, home visitation by teachers, classroom management, moral education, and so on. The board of education also held workshops on the use of computers and audiovisual equipment and organized tours to public facilities in the ward. Most of the beginning teachers in our study did not regard these programs as highly useful, however, because they did not feel the programs related closely to their everyday problems.

In contrast, the seminars on specific themes and the five-day retreat, which took place during the summer vacation, were valued. In the seminars, they learned the accepted ways of exchanging greetings in business settings, how to operate a video camera and a computer, and methods of educational counseling. During the retreat, the neophyte teachers learned how to organize recreational activities, for example, "orienteering." They also discussed problems in teaching specific subjects and in student behavior, and supervisors or school administrators from the ward sometimes offered suggestions for attacking these problems. For example, in the retreat planned by the Ota Ward Board of Education, 85 beginning teachers, including Kenji, participated and 20 supervisors or administrators served as their instructors. For the first three days, neophyte teachers were clustered into several groups by the grades they taught, so that they could discuss strategies appropriate to their teaching problems. Kenji felt that this discussion was very useful because he discovered that many other neophytes faced the same problems that he did. Yoko joined Toshima Ward's retreat, which was held for both beginning and second-year teachers. She also felt the retreat was valuable because she had time to talk to other beginning teachers regarding the problems she was experiencing.

But the core of the program was the in-house internship training, which the Ministry of Education required to be completed in 60 days over the course of the year. In each of the three schools we studied, a full-time supervising teacher was assigned to guide the beginning teachers. A memorandum, issued in April 1989 by the superintendent of Ota Ward Board of Education to the principals in the ward, listed the duties of the supervisor as follows:

1. First of all, the supervisor shall guide and advise the beginning teachers or interns.

2. The supervisor shall plan a training program for the interns in which approximately 10 hours per week will be spent training one intern.

3. The supervisor shall observe each intern's classes on a weekly basis and give each intern the opportunity to observe classes taught by "veteran" teachers.

4. The supervisor shall offer assistance to the interns to develop their classroom management plans, to prepare lessons in moral education, to offer educational counseling, and to gain familiarity with the division of duties at the school.

At Komori Elementary School, where three beginning teachers including Kenji were employed, a veteran teacher, Mr. Murai, was appointed as the supervisor. He told us that, as a full-time supervisor, he was aware of his responsibilities, which included observing twice weekly the classes taught by the beginning teachers and coordinating opportunities for them to observe classes taught by senior teachers. But Mr. Murai did not always perform all these responsibilities. He taught Kenji how to fill out report cards, how to handle students during lunch time, and how to deal with emergencies, and he also briefed Kenji on home visitation and the division of work at the school. As for teaching classes and student guidance, Mr. Murai preferred to let him learn through trial and error.

The supervisor in Taika Elementary School was Mr. Ando, who was a bit more active in performing his duties. He reviewed Yoko's weekly plan of lessons and observed her classes periodically. After observing her class, he always offered her general comments such as "You taught well," which greatly encouraged her. However, he did not plan any formal meetings with her to discuss her problems in teaching unless she asked him for his advice. But she was not unhappy that he did not take greater initiative in directing her, because she felt that if he had made any detailed comments on her teaching, she would not have been able to integrate them into her framework. What she hoped he would do was to keep her headed in the right direction, so that she would not make serious mistakes.

Informal Opportunities

Both Kenji and Yoko learned more through other occasions than through the formal internship program: typically, casual opportunities that produced cumulative effects on beginning teachers. One of the occasions in which they learned considerably about teaching was during their actual teaching process. Yoko could not understand why students had difficulty in writing hiragana until she taught it to them herself. On the basis of this experience, she developed and modified her teaching method. She also learned from her colleagues. The most significant influence on her was Mrs. Suzuki, another first-grade teacher, who served as her model teacher. For example, when students were asked to draw a picture of morning glories, during the arts-and-craft class, Mrs. Suzuki drew a model picture on the blackboard, while Yoko simply told them to look at some actual morning glories carefully and then draw them. After the class finished, Yoko found that Mrs. Suzuki's students had drawn the picture much better than her students. She then realized it was important to give them a concrete demonstration of what was wanted. Although until then she had believed it was important to respect children's creativity, she began to realize

that she had to take the initiative and instruct them on how to accomplish the task at hand.

Kenji also learned about deep-seated tenets of teaching from his senior colleagues, as well as through his own trial and error. For instance, when he was concerned about the poor participation of his students in the lessons, a senior colleague gave him some valuable advice. She told him how, when she taught farm mechanization in the social studies class, she was able to make the class discussion more lively by assigning them homework in which they collected information relating to the topic. Taking her advice, Kenji adopted the same strategy for his Japanese language class. On another occasion, when he observed a fourth-grade gym class taught by an experienced teacher, Kenji noticed that the students enjoyed the exercises even though they were rather strenuous. Kenji applied the teaching method of that teacher to his own class after this observation.

In addition, to prepare their lessons better, the beginning teachers often referred to the teacher's manual. In response to the question "What did you do to prepare for the Japanese language class?" Kenji commented, "I use the teacher's manual to get hints." Likewise, Yoko prepared for her lessons by relying upon the teacher's manual, to make sure she did not overlook the essential points in each unit.

Furthermore, Kenji valued informal association with his senior colleagues as a means of obtaining helpful suggestions. Partly for this reason, he made it a point to participate in all the practice sessions for the annual schoolteacher volleyball or baseball competitions in Ota Ward. He also went frequently to restaurants or bars with the other teachers after the practice sessions, because in informal conversations he could get more tips about teaching.

Beginning teachers thus talked to their senior colleagues in informal situations, such as in the staff room or other places during recesses or after-school periods. Through these short chats with their seniors, neophytes were able to learn common ideas on what to teach or how to teach, even though senior teachers did not tell them anything directly. In accordance with the sociology of knowledge of Berger and Luckmann (1966), this learning process of the beginning teachers can be defined as the process of sharing experiences with senior colleagues through interaction with them. The beginning teachers constructed a common frame of reference with their seniors, and acquired the dominant ideas on teaching that were held in their schools. Through this process, beginning teachers were able to learn a typical pattern of teaching and to develop a sensitivity toward teaching so that they could determine which types of teaching were most appropriate.

One of the reasons why both Kenji and Yoko did not attach much importance to the formal internship was a shared belief that beginners had to learn teaching by themselves through trial and error. Senior teachers insisted that beginners had to agonize over their own teaching at first, because that was an essential step to learning the craft of teaching; only through this painful internal process could beginning teachers integrate their practice. A veteran teacher at Komori commented:

> It may be important to observe the teaching of other teachers, but the most important thing is to "practice" on their own. Beginning teachers have to decide which area they would like to concentrate on, and then they should work on it. If it were me, I would write out my own plan for every single lesson in one subject and keep at it at least for one year. This has been found to be a big help to me when I teach the subject the next year.

The supervisors of the beginning teachers in our study supported the view expressed by the veteran teacher. Mr. Murai, who supervised Kenji, suggested, "Beginning teachers learn best by accumulating experiences of teaching in front of children." He went on to say: "Even when they have picked up ideas from other teachers, they have to judge the value of the ideas. There will be no development in them if they just follow the advice of other teachers." Asked what he meant by "no development," he commented:

> Even though he can teach successfully this year by listening to the advice of others, he can't develop his own approach to teaching. Until he listens to others' opinions and then tries to establish his own way of teaching, he won't become a full-fledged teacher.

Mr. Ando, who supervised Yoko, also insisted, "Beginning teachers must make it on their own." In his view, the beginning teachers who were in the internship program that year were being pampered. "It is better to leave them alone," he said.

Another shared tenet is that learning to teach through trial and error would be enhanced through "borrowing" or identifying useful skills and knowledge developed by experienced teachers. But the transmission of the cultural knowledge of teaching would occur incidentally and circuitously. Senior teachers felt that they should not be expected to give specific information to the neophytes. At Komori Elementary School, Kenji was paired with a senior teacher as teacher representatives on the student committee, which discussed how to run assemblies and other schoolwide activities. When we asked the teacher how she, as an experienced teacher, gave advice to Kenji on the committee, she said:

> I do not give any direct guidance to Kenji during the students' committee meeting. However, when I advise the children on a more effective way of holding a discussion or on how to clarify their comments or how to proceed in their assigned work, etc., Kenji can listen to my advice. It is not necessary to guide him in front of the children; if I did, he would lose face, you see. All he has to do is make mental notes on what he might say in certain situations. . . .

As this episode suggests, experienced teachers expected the beginners to "mentally note" their observations and then to establish their approach to the problems with which they were coping.

Beginning teachers internalized the tenet of borrowing. This is evident in Kenji's comment, "Only after I try what I observe do I begin to think." In fact, when he observed classes taught by senior teachers, he did not discuss his "mental notes" with them afterwards but merely speculated on how he could apply the tips he got from the observations. Yoko also went along with the expectations of her senior colleagues and explained that she had to make her own decisions, even though she was always able to obtain advice from these colleagues.

In addition, because the supervisors of Yoko and Kenji also held these expectations, they were reluctant to lead the neophytes actively. They saw their supervisory role as something much more modest than that of "leader." Mr. Murai, for instance, defined his role as that of consultant: "In my case, as a supervisor I am more like a consultant for the beginning teachers. I do not help them as an officially designated mentor, but rather as a big brother ready to listen to their problems." Mr. Ando expressed his role as that of, in his word, *urakata* (stagehand), which is close to Murai's definition of himself. A stagehand, he said, offered assistance from backstage; the stagehandlike supervisor should offer assistance when the beginning teachers come to him with some difficulty. He believed that beginning teachers would gain confidence in their ability to teach, as well as feel at ease about teaching classes and managing their classrooms, if he continued to adopt a stagehand approach.

In a survey that we conducted of all the supervisors of elementary schools in Ota Ward, similar expectations were revealed. Of 40 supervising teachers, 19 defined their role as that of "someone who gives a minimum amount of advice so that the beginning teachers can be free to develop their independence." Furthermore, 7 defined their role a bit more conservatively by saying that they were "the senior teachers who can be consulted when necessary." In comparison, only 14, or one-third of the total response, defined their role as "actively guiding the beginning teachers according to a set plan."

The shared "rationale" for encouraging beginning teachers to learn teaching through informal occasions was that the supervision of beginners conflicted with the culture of teaching. In Japanese schools, teachers, once employed, are all regarded as equal in status; there is a tacit code among them that no teacher tells another teacher what to do to his or her face. This code, which could be termed an "egalitarian ethos," tends to inhibit "direct teaching" of neophytes by senior teachers. When we asked a teacher at Komori how he advised Kenji and the other beginners, he replied promptly, "I don't give any advice unless they ask me." Another teacher in the same school was more candid: "Do you expect me to tell them something without being first asked? Maybe it's wrong of me to hang back . . . but to tell the truth I cannot figure out how much I should say to them." The tacit code made the supervisors reluctant to teach their "charges" directly. Mr. Ando at Taika expressed his reluctance as follows:

> I feel it is rather insulting to lead them by the hand step by step. They have learned about teaching in their universities already. And the principal also told me not to stand over them. At any rate, they are already to some extent mature adults. Whether a beginning teacher or an experienced teacher, he is a teacher in any case. It does not matter whether his teaching is as good as that of the others. I have no intention of tutoring them in detail just because of the introduction of the internship program. I urge them to use their own initiative.

The supervisor's orientation toward beginning teachers and full-fledged teachers, embedded in the culture of teaching, did not apply, however, to student teachers in the process of initiation into the culture:

> Ishida, you see, is a student teacher, not a beginning teacher. So I will do more teaching as far as he is concerned. In other words, it is easy for me to teach him because he is not a full-fledged teacher yet. Also, that's the purpose of student teaching, to be trained.

> Should an accident or something happen in the class of a student teacher, it is not the student teacher but Mr. Yasuoka, the supervisor, who is responsible for it. A student teacher teaches a class under the supervision of his supervising teacher, which means that the supervisor could stop the student teacher and take over the class in an extreme case, though we try not to do such a thing.

> Such a course of action is allowed in the case of a student teacher because we are the ones responsible. But we do not do the same when beginners teach a class. Because they have a teaching certificate and are assigned to a class, we just cannot say to them, "Step aside. I will teach for you." It is easier to supervise a student teacher.

This supervisor's comment marks a characteristic of the Japanese culture of teaching. He felt that it was all right to lead a student teacher step by step because the person had not become a full-fledged teacher yet. But he did not feel he could take the same position toward Kenji, because Kenji had already obtained a teaching certificate and was responsible for his class.

We may add that at Komori an agreement had been reached among the principal, the supervising teacher, and the leader of the teachers union not to force an excessive burden on the beginning teachers during the internship program (Shimahara & Sakai 1990). The Japan Teachers Union, which is the largest teachers union in Japan, criticized the internship program as a "top-down" rather than a "bottom-up" program for molding beginning teachers into a stereotyped teacher image (Miwa, 1988). Reflecting this union's policy, teachers affiliated with the union at Komori expressed reservations about the internship program.

Another feature in the learning process of the beginning teachers was that they developed an image of experienced teachers, especially dedicated and respected ones, as role models. The development of such an image eventuated through continual interaction with senior colleagues teaching the same grade. As mentioned earlier, through continued interaction with more experienced teachers of the same grade, both Kenji and Yoko learned hints that enhanced their teaching. It suffices to point out that experienced teachers' influence on the beginners was reinforced through the interaction.

Active interaction between teachers was a characteristic inherent in the organizational arrangements of the elementary schools we studied. For instance, special concerns and the rate of progress of classes were often discussed at the weekly grade-level meeting. Because most school events, such as excursions, were planned and implemented by the teachers in charge of the same grade level, they had to cooperate with one another. Through these occasions, beginning teachers engaged in recurrent face-to-face dialogue with experienced teachers.

The architectural structure of these schools also encouraged interaction among teachers teaching the same grade. For one thing, in the staff room, the desks for teachers were grouped by the grade they taught. The first thing teachers did every morning was to gather in the room to hold a short meeting, and during the recess some of them came back there to have tea or talk with their colleagues. Further, the classrooms for the same grade were located side by side on the same floor of the school building. Thus, even during a five-minute break, they were able to talk to one another.

On the other hand, as one supervisor pointed out, close-knit associations among teachers sometimes led to territorialism, so that experienced teachers had more influence over beginners than supervisors did. Partly because of this territorialism, one supervisor hesitated to supervise his intern actively, though he was responsible for her progress. His comment on the influence of himself versus that of colleagues who taught the same grade as the intern elucidates his concern:

> It's not only me, but Mrs. X and Mr. Y are also supervising her. They are keeping pace with one another. As for how much homework they should give to the students, they sometimes decide to give the same kind of homework. I didn't give her any suggestions about homework. The teachers at the same grade may have their own policy in regard to pacing teaching. It is a little bit difficult for me to decide how much I should intervene, because there is a head teacher for each grade who has an influence on the intern.

The learning process of Japanese beginning teachers described above parallels the traditional apprenticeship system in Japan. An apprentice enters a workplace where, without formal training, he learns the trade through observing his master. This modeling is based on intimate identification with the master, as the apprentice pays attention to his skills, knowledge, and attitudes. Likewise, the two beginning teachers, Kenji and Yoko, learned teaching not through direct instruction but by observing their senior teachers, as well as listening to them on informal occasions. Their identification with particular senior colleagues was by and large achieved through this process and reinforced by recurrent interaction with them.

What should be noted here is the fundamentally conservative nature of the apprenticeship system. Although most senior teachers insisted that beginning teachers should develop their own approach to teaching, they also expected them to draw upon the cultural knowledge of teaching they possessed. They saw beginning teachers in a positive light when their teaching was in line with what they thought appropriate. Recall what the teacher who was on the students' committee with Kenji expected of him. She wanted him to observe her approach to handling the committee, so that he could make mental notes of what was important. Mr. Ando expected Yoko and the other neophytes at Taika to seek advice from their seniors, even though he thought it was not prudent to give them much advice or to supervise them closely. Both supervisors and senior teachers thus expected the beginners to develop their teaching competence on the basis of what they could observe. In line with these expectations, both Kenji and Yoko largely developed their perspectives on teaching. This process of learning to teach thus contributed to maintaining the continuities of the dominant pattern of teaching among teachers.

Summary

We offered a descriptive account of the routines that beginning teachers developed, followed by an analysis of both their definition of teaching and their mode of learning to teach. Because teaching at the elementary level is inclusive, learning to teach is highly challenging. The inclusiveness of teaching has evolved gradually since the Meiji Era, nearly 120 years ago, when Japan established the modern school system to contribute to the country's modernization. Because teaching initially encompassed mainly the transmission of academic knowledge, the meaning of teaching has been transformed significantly. One good example is the change in the meaning of the classroom cleanup. The regulations for elementary schoolteachers, issued by the Ministry of Education in 1881, stipulated that cleanup was necessary to maintain the classroom in a sanitary condition. At that time, the teachers were responsible for keeping the classroom clean (Ishii 1978). The educational significance of cleaning to promote cooperation was ascribed later.

Our study of beginning teachers in Tokyo suggests that the culture of teaching distinctly influenced both the process and outcomes of learning to teach. Its influence was enhanced by the patterns of intense teacher interaction facilitated by the programs of the school, a stress on cooperation among teachers, and the physical structure of the school. The influence of experienced teachers on beginners figured potently in this context. Beginners gained hints through casual conversations with and observations of experienced teachers, and this enhanced their teaching competence. Although the process of learning to teach was believed to be governed by an egalitarian ethos, the cultural knowledge of teaching that experienced teachers possessed was considered the primary source of guidance for neophytes, which granted higher status to experienced teachers. It was that cultural knowledge that contributed to the development of neophytes' teaching competence.

This pattern of developing teaching competence had a more significant effect on interns than did the government-initiated internship program, at least during the first year of its implementation.

CHAPTER 6

Japanese Pedagogy and Teachers' Expectations of Students

Japanese beginning teachers learned to teach through their enculturation into teaching. What they learned ranged from how to teach specific subjects to what general goals of teaching they should pursue. Our findings suggest that beginning teachers in Japan and the United States shared the goals of teaching embedded in the culture of teaching.

Japanese neophytes held beliefs that were isomorphic to those of their senior colleagues regarding expectations for students, classroom management, and control of students. This reveals that these pedagogical beliefs are part and parcel of the culture of teaching, often tacitly transmitted through occupational socialization. As Weick (1982) and Tyler (1988) point out, school organizations do not always fit the hypothesis that formal organizations are rationally organized to accomplish their goals. They saw, rather, that schools were more loosely organized than other formal organizations and needed other attributes besides rules in order to bind up all the parts of the school. Weick argues that schools need "symbol management to tie the system together." He further suggests: "People need to be part of sensitive projects. Their action becomes richer, more confident, and more satisfying when it is linked with important underlying themes, values, and movements" (p. 675). Tyler, on the other hand, maintains that symbols alone do not suffice and that "knowledge of the background and shared assumptions of the staff becomes more important, as does their socialization into a common imagery and terminology" (pp. 88-89). Our ethnographic findings reveal that these symbols and assumptions were built up into what may be called a Japanese theory of pedagogy, and that the beginning teachers learned the theory, including the purposes of teaching. Evidently the effectiveness of Japanese elementary education is grounded on the application of this pedagogy. It seems that it is indispensable for the versatile management of school activities, including teaching academic matters and running a variety of school events. In this chapter we will inquire into the themes, assumptions, and ethos of Japanese teaching that beginning teachers learned: the explicit and implicit purposes of teaching and the pedagogical ethos that underscores classroom management and student control.

The Themes of Teaching in Japanese Elementary Schools

What teachers expect of students is closely connected to some of the explicit, official goals of their schools, which are shared assumptions on which schooling is organized. The meaning and content of these goals in Japan, however, and how far they might extend, are quite different in some respects from those in the United States. We noted earlier that American classroom teachers are mainly concerned with the students' development of cognitive skills, and pay relatively little attention to other aspects of schooling, which are addressed by specialists. It is no overstatement to suggest that elementary schooling in the United States heavily leans toward cognitive instruction. Suppose one envisages a continuum of orientation in schooling in which one end of this continuum stresses cognitive content and the other, expressivity and morality. It is obvious that on this continuum American schools lean toward the cognitive end while Japanese schools can be said to strike a balance. Japanese elementary teachers view cognitive, expressive, moral, and aesthetic content as equally vital. Thus, in terms of the cognitive aspect of instruction, Japanese teachers put in considerable time and effort to teach cognitive skills and knowledge. Still, as briefly discussed in chapter 3, contrary to American classroom teachers, Japanese classroom teachers regard the other areas to be highly relevant, too.

Every elementary school in Japan publishes a school handbook in which the goals of schooling are ritualistically stated. But the relevance of these goals for our discussion is that they are not simply perfunctory official statements but reveal major themes that guide teaching. Let us take a brief look at the goals of schooling as presented in three handbooks:

1. Komori Elementary School:

    "To nurture healthy children with an outgoing disposition who are able to be self-motivated. [We shall nurture:]

    - healthy and cheerful children;
    - children who take the initiative in doing their work;
    - children who get along well and help one another."

2. Taika Elementary School:

    "To achieve the educational goals for elementary schools, we shall make an effort to nurture children who:

    - are healthy in body and mind;
    - are cooperative and diligent;
    - think deeply and are generously outgoing."

3. Ikeshita Elementary School:

    "On the basis of a spirit of respect for human rights and dignity, we shall nurture children who have richly humane hearts and shall motivate them to be able to study by themselves. [We shall nurture:]

    - children who think deeply and take the initiative;
    - children who follow the rules and are cooperative;
    - children who are cheerful and healthy."

The main themes, which are readily identifiable in these excerpts, encompass the cognitive, moral, expressive, and social dimensions of students' development. The goals of schooling enunciated by our study schools commonly place a priority on cooperation, a healthy body and mind, and initiative, in addition to cognitive skills. The responsibilities assumed by classroom teachers are aimed at embodying these broad goals. Cooperation and group-focused human relations are promoted through a variety of programs involving classroom teachers. We have already referred to these programs in the previous chapter.

Reflecting these broad goals, the Japanese elementary school curriculum consists of three components: the subject matter area, moral education, and *tokubetsu katsudo*, or special activities. The subject matter area was referred to in chapter 5, but the other areas demand further attention here. The Japanese want moral education to pervade all aspects of schooling. Hence, the course of study stipulates that moral education be provided "throughout all the educational activities of the school." It stresses that moral education is involved in all dimensions of teaching and learning, especially "special activities." There are 28 moral education themes at the elementary level and 16 at the lower-secondary level. Every year our study schools planned to cover these themes in all grades during a 35-week period (34 weeks in the first grade). Notice that this is in addition to the hours of informal moral education included in special activities to be discussed shortly.

The 28 themes roughly fall under six categories. The first involves the importance of order, regularity, cooperation, thoughtfulness, participation, manners, and respect for public property. The second stresses endurance, hard work, character development, and high aspirations. Such moral attributes of human life as freedom, justice, fairness, duty, trust, and conviction are central concerns in the third category. The fourth examines the individual's place in groups, such as the family, the school, and the nation, and the world. The fifth category focuses on harmony with and appreciation of nature and the essential need for rational, scientific attitudes toward human life, and the sixth emphasizes originality.

Each school annually identified central goals in moral education. Individual teachers, too, developed their own goals for their classes. For example, Komori stressed cooperation and respect for each other as the moral theme for the school. All the teachers, including Kenji, were expected to establish common emphases and were responsible for organizing instructional materials. Unlike other subjects, no textbooks were used in moral education. Teachers often used educational television programs, expressly developed for moral education, and commercially available materials to promote students' discussion of moral issues.

Turning to special activities, our study schools delineated them in some detail. They were designed to enhance the "harmonious development of body and mind," individual students' awareness that they are members of a group, and cooperation. The special activities include a variety of formally organized programs as part of "classroom activities," *jidokai*, (student self-governing activities), and club activities, for which 54 to 85 periods are allocated each year, depending on the grade level. The special activities also included what are commonly identified as *gakko gyoji*, or school events, which refer to such school rituals as commencements; popular art and sports festivals that involve parents, excursions and retreats (such as study trips, nature classrooms, and "mountain school"), and volunteer work. The principal at Komori said that school events were significant because they provided students with a sense of belonging and community. His description is fitting because school events often involve all students, the entire teaching staff, administrators, and even parents in the acheivement of common objectives. The reader is reminded that special activities are mentioned elsewhere, to suggest the inclusiveness of teaching in Japanese schools.

Let us further illuminate how the ethos of cooperation is conceived and embodied in other activities. Kenji worked alongside his students in cleaning the classroom and encouraged them to work cooperatively to finish it. The repeated rehearsal by Yoko's students of a Japanese folk dance for the athletic festival provided a good opportunity for them to learn how to achieve an educational objective together. Reinforcing the prominence of cooperation in Japanese schooling, a senior teacher at Ikeshita pointed out that she considered the way students interacted with their peers to be a special concern. She told us how she evaluated students:

> I evaluate them in terms of both academic and nonaca-
> demic, or life, aspects. In the nonacademic area I attach

importance to how well my students are relating with each other. In their school life they function as a group, so how well they interact with peers is important. In other words, I try to determine how well they do in a group learning situation and how they can work cooperatively in the performance of group tasks in and outside the classroom.

We observed an incident where a teacher was noticeably disenchanted with what he regarded as students' lack of cooperation. All fifth-graders at Komori, including Kenji's students, were expected to get ready for a softball game on the playground. The following note, which we made during our observations, shows how Mr. Furukawa, the fifth-grade head teacher who supervised the students with Kenji, reprimanded them for being tardy and showing little cooperation during the period. Mr. Furukawa lectured them for nearly 10 minutes to emphasize how essential it was to behave properly and cooperate among themselves:

> 11:30 A.M. The chimes sounded. Students were scattered around the playground. Only a few students were preparing for a softball game while others were running around aimlessly. Mr. Furukawa, a female teacher, and Kenji stood by the podium and watched them for a while. Noticing that the teachers stood by the podium saying not a word, students realized that they had to form lines in front of the podium. Several students in charge came forward to direct the others to line up. Mr. Furukawa kept watching them, leaning against the podium and waited until the students formed lines. He then had the students squat down, and he started to talk. He told the students who did not take part in the preparation to stand up, and he reproved them. He sternly questioned why they did not help out so that they could start the game earlier. He told them he was extremely disappointed with their evident lack of cooperation. As he told them to shape up, they listened in silence.

This incident is significant because it clearly demonstrates that cooperation is a very important part of teachers' shared vocabulary and that Mr. Furukawa expected the students to display it actively.

To accomplish these broad goals of schooling, both beginning and experienced teachers at our study schools were expected to participate in a gamut of programs. This is why beginning Japanese classroom teachers' responsibilities differed from those of beginning American classroom teachers. The division of work among Japanese teachers is deliberately diffuse, so that classroom teachers may broadly share common responsibilities. Whether or not this is an effective structure of schooling is not relevant to our discussion here; suffice it to say that this diffuse division of work is an expression of the long-standing ethos of schooling in Japan.

The cultural expectation of inclusiveness in teaching at the elementary level is justified by the broad goals of teaching. As a foreign observer (Cummings 1980) points out, Japanese parents expect elementary schools to develop the noncognitive aspects of human development, as well as to impart cognitive skills. Cummings goes on to suggest that this is not because Japanese parents leave all the educational responsibilities to schools, but because, in Japan, both parents and teachers are expected to share these responsibilities. His observation is quite pertinent in view of our preceding discussion.

Azuma, Kashiwagi, and Hess (1981) elucidate this cultural notion of shared responsibilities in their study of mothers' attitudes toward the education of their children in Japan and the United States. American mothers of preschool children believed in a clear distinction between the responsibilities of mothers and those of teachers. American mothers assumed that the development of children's social attitudes is their domain of duty while teachers should assume the responsibility of teaching the cognitive domain of children's experience. In contrast, Japanese mothers presumed that both mothers and teachers should collectively assume responsibility for developing both domains. White (1987) aptly calls Japanese mothers' attitudes toward schooling "the heightened sense of collective responsibility."

Ethnopedagogy: Japanese Cultural Theory of Teaching

We have illuminated the orientation underscoring teaching at the elementary level in Japan. Now we will discuss how this same orientation informs beginning teachers relative to the motivational enhancement of students, focusing on time-honored collective beliefs embedded in the culture of teaching. Japanese teachers have resorted to these beliefs to encourage, inspire, and exhort students to meet their expectations. These pedagogical beliefs are considered elemental to schooling in general, although they are more often enunciated at the elementary level and they are less prominent at the secondary level as teaching becomes more focused on academic subjects.

These beliefs comprise part and parcel of what may be called ethnopedagogy, a cultural theory of teaching shared among Japanese teachers as a frame of orientation. Ethno-pedagogy is not identified as a scientific concept or as a field of study in teacher education or in scholarly circles. Instead, it is intrinsic to the craft of teaching invented by practitioners and reproduced through self-discovery, casual conversations, and in-service education. The significance of ethnopedagogy resonates among supervisors of beginning teachers, administrators, and officials of boards of education and the Ministry of Education. This suggests that it is a cultural concept widely accepted throughout Japan and learned independently of the teacher education offered at college. Japanese teachers' cultural knowledge, identified here as ethnopedagogy, is a widely accepted principle of schooling in our study schools. Teachers are a fiduciary agent of ethnopedagogy and interpret teaching competence in terms of its application to the motivation of children.

Ethnopedagogy concentrates on ligature, close inter-personal relations, as the primary condition for effective teaching and learning. Elsewhere, we briefly referred to the concept of ligature, and we will elaborate on it here, discussing how it is incorporated into teaching. This central concept of ethnopedagogy is often alluded to as *kizuna* or *kakawari*. Intense ligature, one of the two chief constructs introduced in

Dahrendorf's (1978) interpretation of life chances in the process of modernization, is in contrast to the concept of option. *Kizuna* is believed to foster empathy and what is characterized as the "touching of the hearts." It is social "attachment" in Rohlen's (1989) term, a notion that is universally stressed in Japanese culture. It is said to be a paramount principle for promoting effective classroom management. To cultivate it, both supervisors and experienced teachers encouraged interns to promote intrinsic, unpretentious, interpersonal experiences that engaged children.

According to Yoko:

> *Kizuna* is a primary condition for teaching and for children to learn from the teacher. If it is not developed, teaching becomes a matter of mechanical process. Kizuna means to me developing trust. Without it, discipline would not be effective and children would not listen to me. Teaching is based on the relationship of trust. Classroom management is impossible without trustful relationships.

An experienced teacher elaborated on her comment: "Teaching is a kind of art. Emphasis should be placed on the relationship of hearts, the nurturing of bonding between the teacher's and children's hearts." Mr. Furukawa added:

> It is important to understand children as human beings whose characteristics are expressed in their activities. It is my belief that all children can do their best and concentrate on work. But it depends on the teacher's approach and desire. I am not concerned with how to teach children; rather, I try to understand them first, by developing personal relations, *kakawari*. When I get a new class, I do not teach subject matter immediately. Instead, I play with the children intensely for a week to gain a good understanding of them. Then I will begin to know what kinds of children they are and gradually direct them toward the goals of learning on the basis of happy and trustful *kakawari* with them.

The starting point of ethnopedagogy is the teachers' appreciation of the feelings that shape children's lives—the emotional commitment by teachers to children, which leads to fostering the bond between teachers and children. The attachment that evolves from this bond is marked by shared feelings of inclusiveness and trust. Beginning teachers came to learn that effective teaching is governed by the ligature and that developing it takes precedence over technical competence in teaching. Because the ligature creates an environment where children can trust teachers, it enables the teachers to inspire the children to meet their expectations. A small handbook titled *An Introduction to Teaching for Beginning Teachers*, prepared by the Ota Board of Education (whose district includes Kenji's school), highlighted the prominence of teachers' personal knowledge of students in teaching:

> To become a classroom teacher trusted by the students, he/she must fully know the fears, worries, and aspirations of each child and deliberately and effectively plan ways to deal with the problems children have. By doing it, the teacher will promote their confidence in him/her and positive attitudes toward themselves.

It is evident that Japanese teachers, including our beginning teachers, unfailingly try to cultivate students' dependency on them, which is inherent in kizuna, and this, in turn, fosters a sense of security and self-confidence. When Kenji attended a workshop for beginning teachers in the summer, he made the following entry in his notebook: "I must build trustful relationships between my students and myself and among students. Such relationships would make them feel they could come to school without worries." Kenji also suggested in an interview:

> In order to gain my students' confidence in me, I have to sweat with them. I think that trustful relationships will develop when I, as a teacher, let my children see me do all I can in my encounters with them, joining them in what they are doing.

Kenji made sustained efforts to gain a personal knowledge of his students. For example, as is common practice in Japanese elementary schools, he visited each student' home to familiarize himself with his students from the perspective of their parents. He also often talked with his students during lunch time, when they were relaxed, and encouraged them to write journals and share them with him.

Yoko recognized that personal knowledge was critical in creating ligature with children, but for her it involved the notion of love. She commented:

> Although I am still groping, I feel that as long as I love my students, whether I am reprimanding them or playing with them, I can communicate with them. If I ever feel that my students are bothersome or annoying, whatever I say to them will be of no use. Telling them to be quiet out of annoyance would be just a waste of time.

Yoko patiently approached Kazu, the deviant boy in her class who was described in the previous chapter, believing that her love for him would eventually make him feel secure and stop acting up. She noted that when the trustful relationships between her and her children began to develop in the late spring, the children responded more enthusiastically to her expectations. Given this development though fragile ligature, she said, "When I am doing my best, they know it. When I am serious about what I do, they understand my intention." She told us that kizuna is a relationship that reinforces the reciprocity of the emotional commitment to one another. She related one episode to illuminate it. When she told seven-year-olds to enjoy their holidays in the spring, but to be careful to avoid accidents, one of them came up to her and said, "I will be careful because I like you and want to see you again after the holidays. If I got injured I could not see you again." Even such a seemingly insignificant encounter with her children made her euphoric, because she felt she had finally begun to receive a positive emotional response from them.

It may be suggested here that in the following respects, Japanese ethnopedagogy can be differentiated from the American emphasis on emotional involvement in teacher-student interaction. First, the authority of Japanese teachers is assumed to emerge in the context of interaction with students, especially at the elementary level. Beginning teachers were encouraged to "mingle with students without disguise and pretense"—an expression often used by teachers. In contrast, our data suggest that American student teachers, as well as beginning teachers, were expected to assert their authority *a priori*. As White reports, cooperating teachers "universally tell" their charges, "Don't make the mistake of trying to be friends with the kids" (1989, p. 183). Second, the Japanese emphasis on kizuna is a cultural attribute, not fundamentally a means to an end. It differs from what Jackson (1990) characterizes as the "intensity of emotional involvement" by teachers, which is guided by the explicitly instrumental purpose of developing students' individuality. In contrast to Japanese beginning teachers, American beginning teachers expected their students to be independent and self-disciplined.

Classroom Management: An Interpersonal Approach

In chapter 3 we explored the cognitive approach to classroom management dominant in American schools. It highlights procedures—rules and policy—as a framework for management, and the degree that students internalize and adhere to the rules manifests a measure of success in classroom management. The emphasis is put on each student's cognitive organization of rules, so that it may become a guiding principle. In sharp contrast to the cognitive approach, Japanese teachers have developed what may be called an interpersonal or affective approach to classroom management. It is embedded in ethno-pedagogy and applies ethnopedagogy's tenets to management. In this approach interpersonal relations are viewed as para-mount in promoting effective management of students and their activities within and outside the classroom.

Japanese teachers define classroom management as a broad, rather diffuse domain, as American teachers do. It includes a plan for teaching and strategies for improving students' work and enhancing the classroom environment, con-structing a comprehensive plan for relevant activities (such as picnics, sports festivals, and a swimming program), demon-stration classes for parents, and what Japanese teachers call *seikatsu shido*, "guidance for living." Consistent with this descrip-tion of classroom management, the Japan Society of Education-al Sociology (1986) defines it as "the function of maintaining conditions for enhancing effective classroom teaching and learning through involving all aspects of a classroom" (p. 99). In any event, central to the effective implementation of such activities is thought to be the Japanese teachers' belief that interpersonal relations characterized by trust and cooperation are fundamental.

Through their "apprenticeship of observation" for a number of years as students, beginning teachers became partially acquainted with their teachers' approach to classroom management. That observation is a primary source of the latent culture of teaching that influenced the formation of beginning teachers' disposition toward teaching. As neophyte teachers they become keenly aware of the need to construct and apply it effectively. The beginning teachers we studied were invariably tense and nervous in the first month or so, and they became frustrated and sometimes depressed when they were not able to handle children. In fact, it was no accident that three of the six beginners who participated in our research stayed home for a couple of days in the first month because they had a fever resulting from the tension and fatigue that they experienced in the classroom. Yoko and Kenji were understandably nervous, and both struggled at the beginning of the year. Their problem was what they perceived to be their inability to relate themselves to children, resulting in children's inattention to lessons. Their common expression of the problem was "I cannot handle children."

Supervisors unvaryingly saw this problem as a classroom management issue. Yoko's supervisor suggested, "Classroom management is key to teaching effectively. Its purpose is to develop *shudan* [a group] and an environment where children can express their problems openly." Kenji's supervisor concurred with him, suggesting the need to create an environment to foster the "touching of the hearts" between the teacher and students. Supervisors believed that classroom management is a craft that teachers learn through their encounters with students, not an abstract plan that can be given to beginners, although such a plan is suggested in handbooks for teachers and experienced teachers have such a plan.

Our beginning teachers gradually learned to adopt the interpersonal approach to classroom management in more focused fashion. Yoko, for one, suggested that bonding between students and herself was fundamental to building a well-managed classroom, as is clear in her remark "Unless there is kizuna, classroom management will not be effective." Kenji also felt that to create an effective classroom, a relationship of trust must be created between himself and his students. Bonding among students, he added, is a basis on which they can get along well and develop a sense of cohesion as a group. During an interview he mentioned his plan for moving his classroom in "a good direction":

> [Good direction is when] the class becomes a cohesive group and my students come to be on good terms with one another. When this occurs, students feel relaxed, spontaneous, and active as members of the class. There will be uninhibited communication and a sense of connectedness between students and myself. To build a classroom of this nature is my ultimate goal.

Understandably, beginning teachers' views regarding classroom management are an epitome of ethnopedagogy because they saw classroom management as an application of that pedagogy.

"Good direction," however, represented Kenji's aspirations only, not what he could realistically hope to achieve soon. In what ways, then, did the beginning teachers actually try to manage their classrooms? Let us explore this question, beginning with Kenji, who had been considerably concerned about his inability to form his students into a harmonious group. When he taught at a juku, a tutoring school, as a part-time teacher, he had to deal with only a small number of students attending to their academic work only, but at Komori he realized that teaching meant not only teaching academic subjects but also guiding some 30 students in how to conduct themselves in a group. Here he experienced immense difficulty.

To overcome this problem, Kenji followed a commonly used classroom management pattern that he learned from various sources, including experienced teachers. He created han, small groups that could work together closely. Earlier, we saw Kenji form his class into several han during a lesson in the Japanese language, during a science project, and during the lunch period. To develop cooperation among students, he also created *kakari*, groups for performing classroom chores, including attending to pets, managing the library, posting notices, serving lunches, distributing handouts, and promoting recreational activities.

Meanwhile, Kenji expected that his students would participate in various schoolwide programs because their peers in other classrooms were involved in the programs. One of these programs was an excursion to Nikko, a famous national park, to which the entire fifth grade went for three days during the summer. Kenji hoped that this event would provide an opportunity for his class to achieve an identity:

> Staying overnight and working together, they would bond closely and become cohesive as a class. They would also display a sense of cooperation through an experience like this. Moreover, they would always remember this trip as a happy, shared event of their elementary school days.

Also, at Komori students assembled every Friday morning to join in special programs planned and coordinated by teachers in the fourth grade and up. Games and music performances were planned so that all students could participate in one way or another. During the second semester, Kenji volunteered his class to perform a music concert, at which his students led the entire school in singing and dancing. Through these experiences, his students were thought to develop appreciation for participation, cooperation, and group work.

However, despite these programs, all Kenji's diligent efforts, and all the expectations he harbored, problems more often than not arose among his students, his class failed to become a cohesive, cooperating group, and this affected individual students' morale and work in the classroom. He discovered that there were latent conflicts among students, which were revealed to him during his visits to their homes in May. He then learned that not only his students but also their parents were concerned about the conflicts. Kenji entertained the thought that he might discuss the problem with the students actively involved, but his senior colleague, Mr. Furukawa, advised him to discuss it openly with the entire class. Kenji cancelled a class period to bring it to the attention of the whole class:

> I was scared because I had never done this before. No experience whatsoever. At the beginning I told my students, "I myself have no idea where this discussion might take us, but I will try my best to find a solution to this problem, so let us discuss it openly."

Thereafter, however, interpersonal conflicts still lingered among his students, with added hostility between boys and girls. During the summer vacation Kenji told us that this problem took precedence over any other matters, because he thought group harmony to be an elemental condition for effective teaching and student work in the classroom. Still convinced that the interpersonal approach to classroom management would eventually work, he decided to spend more time with his students, playing with them outdoors and engaging in casual conversations with them as often as he could. He believed that this active interpersonal strategy would enable him to know his students' problems better and gain their confidence.

Turning to Yoko, she became aware of several problems of classroom management. Unlike Kenji, she did not have to deal with interpersonal conflicts, notwithstanding the constant behavior problem of one boy, which concerned her deeply. She perceived her primary problem as managing her class as a group. Although she had only 22 first-graders, an ideal number of children for individualized instruction, she never attempted to individualize their work—an idea that she did not entertain. Her challenge was in how to teach the whole group, bringing every child to the performance level of the group regardless of individual differences. To accomplish this, she organized her classroom in the most conventional fashion with all students seated in several rows facing her. She typically taught her class standing in front of the chalkboard. Her problem was how to attract the attention of these six-year-olds for a sustained period without many distractions. She was fully aware that these students would not pay attention to uninteresting lessons and could be easily distracted by little things. So she devised lesson plans as attractively as possible, mixing difficult lessons with music, gym, and exercises for school events such as athletic festivals.

In any case, her primary concern remained how to deal with the group. Realizing that students' cooperation with her and other students and their active participation in the class would contribute to effective teaching, she began to concentrate on interpersonal relations. She felt it was imperative to focus on developing students' adaptive dispositions to the classroom environment, so that they could be distinguished by diligence, cooperation, and participation.

Like Kenji, Yoko became familiar with how the Japanese classroom was typically managed, and tried to adopt it to foster these dispositions. She recalled the relevance of kakawari, personal connectedness, which was accentuated by a lecturer at a retreat for beginning teachers she attended in the spring. She organized task groups to promote cooperation and made herself available to play and talk with her students. She used the nicchoku setup, in which two students were assigned to maintain classroom order on a rotating basis—a student self-governing system created to facilitate classroom activities. Yoko noticed that what her supervisor called "naked *tsukiai*," unpretentious engagement with students, slowly began to produce some positive results shortly before the summer vacation. Students became more attentive, showing interest in her initiatives, and, moreover, tolerant of and even cooperative with the deviant boy.

In summary, the strategies of classroom management that Japanese teachers typically employ are part of the Japanese culture of teaching. The fact that official and practitioners' views on classroom management are remarkably compatible suggests that the Japanese classroom management ethos is widely accepted throughout Japan. Seikatsu shido, guidance for living, to which we referred earlier, is part of Japanese classroom management, and the teachers' network movement to develop guidance for living has been supported by both the Ministry of Education and the Japan Teachers Union, although the union's and the ministry's interpretations of it were often at variance. What is common is the belief that interpersonal relations are fundamental to good classroom management. Our beginning teachers were also committed to this belief, although they met with only limited success in adopting it in their first year.

The Pattern of Control

In chapter 3 we pointed out some salient differences between American and Japanese patterns of control. We noted that beginning American teachers exerted a high degree of control over activity, space, and time and affirmed the legitimacy of institutional authority entrusted to them as the source of their control. We noted the comparatively low profile of the Japanese teacher as a control agent. Control of students, however, is a ubiquitous, dominant concern of teachers in American and Japanese schools; it demands considerable attention from both American and Japanese teachers.

Ethnopedagogy, classroom management, and control strategies are closely related and cannot be arbitrarily separated, because the underlying principle governing these domains is inherent in what the Japanese perceive to be the management of ligature in students' behavior. While American teachers celebrate individualism and self-reliance as the core of American culture, which accounts for people's behavior in not only education but also economic, political, and social spheres (Bellah et al. 1985; Hsu 1963), Japanese teachers embrace group orientation and interdependence as the central cultural tenet that influences behavior in these spheres (Hsu 1975; Nakane 1970; Shimahara 1979). These contrasting creeds epitomize two distinct cultural ideologies to which people in each nation by and large conform. Inevitably, individuals adhere to the cultural ideologies to varying degrees in both cultures, especially in the United States, because it is made up of multiethnic and racial groups. Yet, as we saw, there is a remarkable uniformity in American schools in their adherence to cultural tenets. The same is true of Japanese schools.

In this section we will look at the strategies of control that Japanese teachers employed. Control is a mechanism to establish order and to accomplish students' compliance with rules and expectations, and therefore it involves the use of power, authority, punishment, and rewards. Let us now turn to the control strategies used in Japanese schools.

Both beginning and experienced Japanese teachers believed that order is established not so much by the stipulation of rules and authority as by the development of basic habits of everyday life. They had broadly framed rules in the form of slogans, mottoes, and weekly objectives, such as "Let us keep the classroom clean" or "Let us observe the traffic laws." The expectations of the school and teachers are not codified to the extent that they are in American schools. Instead, they are communicated to students through institutionalized activities in which teachers use authority to enforce their expectations. In this regard, the teachers' creed is remarkably consistent with the policy on basic habits promoted by the Ministry of Education. The teachers assume that children's orientation toward order and control result from practice, just as the Japanese in general believe that character formation is grounded in practice. Speaking of preschool education, Peak (1991) illuminates the point:

> The term "basic habits of daily life" and its ubiquity as a goal of character training in preschool education stem from Japanese assumptions about the nature of ethical behavior. Good character and morality are driven by a person's beliefs and attitudes, and these are formed from the habitual residue of the personal habits and customs of daily life. (p. 65)

The same assumptions apply to the formation of children's attitudes toward order.

In teachers' handbooks published by the local board of education and the Ministry of Education, the notion of basic habits is spelled out in relation to moral education and special activities in the course of study and as a basis for moral behavior as well as academic work. Likewise, school handbooks unfailingly refer to it as fundamental in schooling.

Both Komori and Taika Elementary Schools offered a variety of programs to develop students' basic habits; these programs ran the gamut from cleaning the classroom to outdoor activities. Likewise, the habits that Yoko's first-graders were expected to develop ranged from elementary to highly complex. The former included such customs as greeting people and neatly placing sneakers in a shoe box located in the entrance where students took off their outdoor sneakers and put on indoor ones.

Japanese schools always emphasize greetings and changing shoes to keep the floors clean.

A more complex behavior that her children learned from the first month of their enrollment in school was to join the entire body of students on the playground for a regular Monday morning assembly. At 8:30 A.M., when the chimes signaled the start of the assembly, all students were expected to line up promptly in several rows, grade by grade, on the school playground in less than two minutes. The nicchoku teacher (monitor) directed them from the podium to line up in precise lines, with a proper distance between individual students. Every child was expected to stand straight, and no talking was allowed during this process. When all students lined up in front of their teachers, the principal went up to the podium to greet them and gave a speech, which was followed by an announcement by a nicchoku teacher and a message by a student government representative. The whole event took less than 15 minutes, during which first-graders stood still and paid attention to the speakers.

What is marked as relevant in a meeting like this is not only the morally inclined messages communicated to the children, but also their attitudes and behavior in a large collective setting. When it was completed, music was turned on, and all students proceeded to their classrooms. This whole complex behavior required Yoko's first-graders to respond to the chimes promptly, form lines by responding to authority, develop the self-discipline needed to stand still and listen to the speakers, and return to their classroom in an orderly way. What is described here is how six-year-olds are expected to learn a rather complex practice of group behavior, coordination, concentration, self-discipline, and compliance with authority. This practice, in addition to other collective events, is repeated every week throughout the year.

Teachers at Taika and Komori articulated the important habits developed through practice, such as the Monday morning assembly, and also regarded special activities (referred to as gakko gyoji earlier) as highly relevant for training students and teaching them the values and norms that underscore the activities. These norms always become pronounced during the group-oriented activities that are regularly organized at these schools.

Cleaning is another familiar example. Performed every afternoon by all students, including first-graders, it demands diligence, coordination, cooperation, and promptness. Tardy students are singled out during the reflection meeting held before students return home. One of the big schoolwide events aimed at developing these behavioral attributes at our study schools was a sports festival held in the spring. This all-day program was carefully planned by students themselves in consultation with teacher advisors. The festival required nearly three weeks' preparation. The program consisted of several events for each class and required several rehearsals during gym periods. Incidentally, the reader may recall the rehearsal that Yoko's children were engaged in. The execution of the program was coordinated by teachers and students. The festival attracted several hundred parents and influential community leaders, such as members of the board of education. We observed athletic festivals at both schools and were impressed with the six-year-olds, who displayed extraordinary coordination and precision in movement, and ability to respond to their teachers' directions. Students who rejected or deviated from these norms were reprimanded by their teachers and were under pressure to conform by their peers as well. We rarely saw such students during the festival, and even the deviant boy in Yoko's class was participating in the events.

In brief, a variety of schoolwide special activities was used to teach relevant norms, and peer pressure was effectively brought to bear in this type of teaching. Teachers significantly accomplished their control over students by developing their habits through the use of the school as a community or through an outside environment, such as "mountain school" or excursions. These strategies for control employed by our study school and other schools in Japan represent a sharp contrast to the pattern of control we saw in American schools.

We will turn to the pattern of control at the classroom level. We commented on beginning American teachers' high level of control over students with respect to time, space, and activity. They did not invent a high profile of control, but it reflected the collective pattern of control manifested at the school level. From our descriptions of teaching in the preceding chapter and elsewhere, it is evident that both Yoko and Kenji displayed a relatively low profile of control with respect to time, space, and activity. Put differently, Japanese students displayed a higher degree of control over these aspects of schooling than did American students.

When Yoko and Kenji's students came to school, they controlled use of the school playground for 10 minutes before the first class began. They had a brief morning meeting, which was their space and time, and they were free to use recess time, including a 20-minute break between the second and third periods. Most students went outdoors to play, often accompanied by teachers during the long break—one of the most animated scenes we observed at the study schools. Students managed the entire lunchtime (including serving lunch and cleaning tables), the classroom cleaning period, and the brief recess following the cleaning. In addition, students had a couple of special-activity periods each week.

Student self-governing routines are popular in Japanese schools, and their success is contingent upon the classroom teacher's competence to engage students effectively in the routines. Both Yoko and Kenji established these routines, just as experienced teachers did. The student self-governing setup included rotated nicchoku duties to maintain classroom order; task groups, including lunch-servicing groups; and jidokai, or a formal classroom period in which children's interests and concerns were discussed. While some activities designed to promote student self-management were marked by tokenism, others, such as the task force for lunch duty and nicchoku duty, were functional parts of life in the classroom. The symbolic meaning of student self-governing routines lies in Japanese teachers' assumption that part of the control of a classroom is shared with students.

But this does not suggest that Yoko and Kenji did not exercise enough control over students during the class. Because both adopted largely conventional methods of teaching (except when they organized han, small discussion groups), they taught the whole class and demanded the simultaneous attention of all the students. This required a considerable degree of control in directing students to their tasks, namely, listening to the teacher, answering his/her questions, and doing work at their desks. In our beginning teachers' classrooms, students were expected to sit upright, follow directions in minute detail, and speak only when they were granted permission. Teachers reminded them if they did not display expected classroom manners and occasionally blasted admonitions if they were too noisy.

Beginning teachers undeviatingly accepted the time-honored assumption that sitting upright at one's desk and keeping a proper distance between the eyes and the book on the desk are morally correct. This posture, according to them, suggests diligent and disciplined engagement in study, and intimates the importance of self-discipline. When we questioned Yoko's supervisor about the educational significance of this posture, he suggested that a disciplined attitude toward learning was an essential habit for a child, although he was not sure of the relationship between the child's sitting position and his or her ability to learn. He attributed the customary emphasis on correct posture to Japanese tradition. Another supervisor used a Japanese calligraphy lesson to emphasize correct posture; in the lesson he first taught students the appropriate way of holding the writing brush and the appropriate posture for writing as an elementary skill. In short, Japanese teachers often remind students to adjust their posture if it is not considered proper. We saw it as a control strategy to induce students to pay attention to the teacher.

All in all, our field notes reveal that Japanese beginning teachers were relatively patient toward students when they were noisy or even failed to observe classroom manners. Yoko never isolated her deviant boy, largely appealing to his sense of guilt, although she occasionally fired stern warnings at him. The noise and occasional rule breaking notwithstanding, beginning teachers generally did not attempt to keep a constant control over students' behavior and activities. It was evident in our observations that Japanese classrooms were relatively noisy, while American classrooms were distinctly quiet and orderly.

Relative to our study, the sociologist Tsuneyoshi, in her comparison of Japanese and American elementary schools (1992), points out a contrast in behavior control: in the United States teachers resort to their authority to control students, while in Japan teachers tend to appeal to students' sense of guilt. Cross-cultural findings by the psychologists Azuma, Kashiwagi and Hess (1981) suggest a similar marked difference in the ways mothers in the two countries disciplined their children. American mothers tended to issue clear and concrete directions in a firm voice, while Japanese mothers were inclined to suggest indirectly what they expected their children to do (p. 74). These contrasts paralleled the Japanese and American teachers' different control strategies: a low and a high profile of control, respectively.

Summary

We have explored themes, assumptions, and domains of teaching in Japanese schools. Broadly defined, teaching in Japan is characterized by the inclusiveness at the elementary level of the cognitive, moral, expressive, and social dimensions of children's development. This definition of teaching is reflected within three interrelated categories (subject matter, moral education, and special activities) of each school's programs. It is expected that elementary teachers actively and inclusively address these aspects of schooling because of Japanese schools' emphasis on holistic education. Therefore, the diffuseness in the division of work in elementary schools is dictated by the Japanese ethos of schooling. It seems to take precedence over the technical efficiency that might stem from a well-defined division of work among teachers, as seen in the United States.

Ethnopedagogy, classroom management, and student control are closely connected in Japan. Ethnopedagogy has been developed on the Japanese assumption that ligature is basic to the enhancement of children's orientation toward schooling. It is evident from the preceding discussion that ethnopedagogy is the foundation of the Japanese style of classroom management, with its emphasis on interpersonal relations and group harmony. Japanese teachers believe that control over students can be achieved by developing students' proper habits, putting a priority on practice over the codification of rules.

The concept of inclusive teaching, ethnopedagogy, class-room management, and student control are part and parcel of the culture of teaching in Japan. They are shared and reproduced by practitioners without the mediation of teacher educators. The beginning teachers who participated in our study partly learned them as students during their apprenticeship of observation and mainly learned them as teachers through their enculturation into teaching.

In its emphasis on human bonding, ethnopedagogy is an expression of Japanese culture. Hamaguchi (1988), a cultural anthropologist, maintains that for the Japanese the self is identified in relationships with others. He suggests that the self, as conceived by the Japanese, is analogous to the Japanese mother, who perceives herself as a mother through the insep-arable bond with her child. He characterizes the Japanese notion of self as "contextual," the attributes of the self being inter-dependence and mutual trust. Hamaguchi's contextual view of self is comparable to what Lebra (1976) calls "interactional relativism":

> If the actor is primarily concerned with a social object, as the Japanese are, his actions will be governed by something far removed from unilateral determinism. The Japanese Ego acts upon or toward Alter with the awareness or anticipation of Alter's response, and Alter in turn, by responding according to or against Ego's expec-tation, influences Ego's further action. If Ego talks, Alter is likely to talk back, and thus they will alternate in a chain of interaction until a conversational trajectory is felt completed. Activation of the chain cannot be attributed to either Ego or Alter exclusively but to both or to the relationship between the two. The actor is unable to locate the prime mover and is likely to be indifferent to its existence. Instead, he is more aware of influence flowing both ways between himself and his object. (p. 7)

Ethnopedagogy is closely grounded in the contextual view of self and interactional relativism. Bonding between the teacher and students is cemented in a relative social context in which students' selves are defined.

CHAPTER 7

Occupational Socialization
of Beginning Teachers in Japan

Introduction

It is evident from the preceding discussion that Japanese beginning teachers learn to teach in a context of schooling that is in sharp contrast to the context of schooling in the United States. They were expected to achieve much broader teaching goals than those in American schools. In other words, the definition of teaching embedded in the Japanese culture of teaching is broad, and this makes teaching an inclusive engagement. Moreover, Japanese pedagogy is distinguished by its emphasis on the ligature, or bonding, between the teacher and students as the fulcrum for creating a conducive learning environment. Beginning teachers' success in teaching measurably depends on nurturing kizuna with their students.

In this chapter we will turn to other significant, related dimensions of the occupational socialization of beginning teachers. Our exploration will focus on the perspectives on teaching that beginning teachers developed, including their thoughts on the transition from college to elementary school and their approaches to problems in teaching, collegial relationships, and relationships with parents and the community.

Until recently, the functionalist model dominated the discussion of occupational socialization. Brim (1969), for example, defines socialization as the process of transforming "the raw material of society into good working members" (p. 5). His view embodies the functionalist model of socialization, which assumes a given social structure to be stable and unitary. At the same time, it tends to portray the socialized person as a completely passive entity (LeCompte & Ginsburg 1987).

As Lacey (1977) points out in his critique of functionalism, a human being is nothing but "an empty vessel to be filled with the basic value orientations and customs of the society of which he will become a part" (p. 18). The functionalist model has thus omitted any analysis of how teachers react given their own perspectives vis-à-vis the expectations or influences being exerted on them from the outside.

In response to these criticisms, a new approach began to attract scholarly attention in the 1970s and 1980s. It includes different paradigms concerning the process of occupational socialization, all of which examine the process of socialization from the point of view that has been neglected by the functionalist model. These paradigms are usually lumped together as the "interpretative approach," but strictly speaking, they should be divided into two theoretically separate models of socialization.

One is based on symbolic interactionism. Stressing the autonomy of individuals, this model assumes that they construct their own frame of reference in response to the situation in which they are. As Reid (1986) maintains, those who adhere to this model argue that "in a social situation a person is capable of deciding what his/her needs are and how these can be satisfied, review[ing] the possible ways of achieving them, decid[ing] on the most appropriate action, undertak[ing] it and change[ing] course if [his/her] predictions prove incorrect" (p. 31). The best-known work based on this socialization model is that of Becker et al. (1961). The authors offer an account of the occupational socialization of medical students and define the students' socialization as a process of developing their own perspectives in response to the expectations and demands of their professors. Lacey (1977) modifies this position by emphasizing individual strategies for highlighting the goals that they embody in actions to cope with problems. His emphasis on strategies, he maintains, would make it possible to capture more clearly the aims or needs of actors in the actual situations they are in.

The second model within the interpretative approach is derived from the field of phenomenology. Reid (1986) summarizes it as follows: "Phenomenologists are concerned, after Schutz, with how reality is constructed through social process and how the individuals involved acquire ways of thinking" (p. 32). Representing this approach as the foundation of the sociology of knowledge, Berger and Luckmann (1966) explain how reality is socially constructed and maintained. According to this approach, occupational socialization can be seen as the process wherein individuals construct their own reality by sharing knowledge unique to the occupation through interaction with other members of the occupation. Applying this model of socialization, we (1990) offered an account of how beginning Japanese teachers constructed their social reality of teaching. We defined teacher socialization as the process whereby beginning teachers acquired knowledge of teaching and sensitivity toward it by typifying their experiences through interaction with experienced teachers.

Comparing these two models, it is suggested that the former, the symbolic interactionist model, regards the conscious judgments of a person made from his/her own perspective to be critical, while the latter, Berger and Luckmann's model, focuses on the fact that the reality on which the person's judgment is based is itself socially constructed. In other words, Lacey attaches great importance to the intentional choice of the actor, while Berger and Luckmann shed light on the nature of the perspective by which the actor makes a choice, stressing that the perspective reflects a reality, or a commonsense assumption regarding the reality, constructed through the intersubjective process.

Symbolic interactionism has been attracting more attention in the study of teacher socialization than has the Berger and Luckmann approach. Taking teachers' autonomy as a primary concern, recent studies have focused on such issues as the interests of teachers and the ways in which they cope with problematic situations, and these studies have analyzed the variety of strategies that teachers adopt to deal with these situations. But it is our view that if we take the approach advanced by Berger and Luckmann, the social reality of teaching that is constructed through the intersubjective process meaningfully defines what teachers are concerned about. Especially in Japan, whose culture is significantly different from American culture, a clear grasp of the ways the social reality of teaching is constructed by Japanese teachers is essential if we are to understand the process of their occupational socialization. Without insight into this process of the construction of reality, it would be difficult to explain why some matters are regarded as problematic by Japanese beginning teachers and others are not. Furthermore, Japanese beginning teachers naturally look for the grounds of their problems, and the strategies they use to deal with the problems are also influenced by their own perceptions of the reality of teaching. They thus develop long-term perspectives on teaching through this process of reality construction, coping with specific problems as they face them.

To probe how the beginning Japanese teachers we studied constructed their own perspectives on teaching, we will first explore the extent to which the preservice training programs offered by their universities had an impact on them and how they experienced the transition from their universities to their schools.

The Transition from University to School

Studies have been conducted both in Europe and in the United States on how beginning teachers experience the process of the transition from their universities to the schools where they began teaching. Veenman (1984), who reviewed the English and German literature on this subject, comments that "the transition from teacher training to the first teaching job could be a dramatic and traumatic one" (p. 143) and that this transition was often referred to as "reality shock," "transition shock," "Praxisschock," or "Reinwascheffekt." He suggests that these terms characterize "the collapse of the missionary ideals formed during teacher training by the harsh and rude reality of everyday classroom life" (p. 143). He further points out that many beginning teachers learned an idealistic view of teaching from the professors in their universities, but soon after they began teaching in the schools, they were disappointed to find that it was extremely difficult to realize their ideals in the schools. As we saw earlier, Nancy, who was one of the American beginning teachers in our study, displayed a somewhat similar experience. When she was at her university, she took classes involving discussions on William Blake, Maxine Green, and so forth, and believed in the value of independence, a questing spirit, and the pursuit of excellence. But after she began teaching, she realized how demanding it was to instil these ideals in her students.

Japanese beginning teachers, however, underwent the transition from their universities to schools differently from how the students reported in Veenman's article did. Japanese beginning teachers maintained a significant degree of continuity by retaining in some important measure the image of teaching that they formed from their actual childhood experience of schooling. Kenji displayed that continuity: his image of former teachers was a latent force that influenced his orientation toward teaching, and as a beginning teacher at Komori, he espoused an ethos of teaching that was compatible with that latent image. Because such an image was related to the pedagogical beliefs underlying ethnopedagogy, Japanese beginning teachers were inclined to weigh the teacher preparation program in terms of how effective it was in passing on that ethnopedagogy. Kenji remarked that the program at his university was not useful for learning teaching skills or for enhancing competency in understanding children, an essential part of teaching in Japan. The exceptions were the classes on educational psychology and on educational counseling, because both of them contributed to some degree to building a personal knowledge of children.

In an interview conducted before he began teaching, Kenji stated that he had chosen a suitable occupation, one to which he would be able to devote his life, even though he had encountered some difficulties during his student teaching. He gained confidence and renewed his desire to become a teacher as a result of his student teaching. In response to our question "What areas of student teaching were useful to you?" he stated:

> The fact that I became acquainted with students was very valuable. Up till that time, I was not sure about what teaching was like and whether I could perform it. I was not confident until then, but through student teaching I came to feel I really wanted to become a teacher. I learned that knowing children and developing good rapport with

them is key to teaching them effectively. The children
were so sweet and I felt like staying with them all the time.

Even before he had taken up a teaching position, he was
exposed to some of the dominant teaching tenets shared among
experienced teachers in the school and to the actual methods of
teaching organization based on them. His problem, when he
assumed teaching at Komori, however, was his unfamiliarity
with the complexity and multiplicity of teaching. For instance,
though he had some experience of teaching in front of a group of
children in a private enrichment school, he had never taught
more than 30 students at one time prior to assuming his teaching
position. He found it exceedingly challenging to teach such a
large number of students, because he not only had to teach
academic subjects but also had to deal with the moral and
expressive dimensions of students' development.

But even with this difficulty, he was able to maintain a
level of motivation toward teaching. After a month at his new
job, he commented: "I am so glad to be with children. It is hard
to teach, but I feel like seeing them even during the weekend."
After another month passed, he had this to say about teaching:
"I've wanted to be a teacher since my high school days. I am
quite satisfied now that I have started my teaching. It was a good
choice for me, I believe." Yoko, on the other hand, may be
distinguished as one who changed her views about teaching as
she moved from her university to teaching in school. However,
she did not experience the reality shock that Veenman speaks of.
She was interested in the educational philosophy she studied at
her university, with its emphasis on children's spontaneity and
education without punishment. Before she began to teach, she
believed that these pedagogical beliefs should be an underlying
principle of teaching, and she wanted to teach in accordance
with that principle. Standing in front of a group of children,
however, she realized that controlling children was critical in
effectively managing her class. She felt she was compelled to
adopt some control strategy when dealing with her entire class.
During the four weeks of her student teaching she became aware
of the need for control. She suggested that although it was not
necessary to exercise overt control over children when she
taught a small number of students, it was unavoidable when she

taught a large group. After she finished her student teaching, she and her friend admitted to each other, "I can hardly teach without scolding children." "Scolding" suggested a gamut of control.

After she started her job, she recognized that there were gaps between theory and practice. Two months after she began teaching she revealed:

> I have been taught not to scold a child, but sometimes children won't understand unless they are scolded. I cannot allow them to do dangerous or harmful things to others, so I have to scold them. When I came here, I told them not to make me angry. But when they do something wrong, it's wrong. They would understand if I went up and patted them on the head, too, but it is more important to tell them outright not to do certain things. Especially in the case of first-graders, a larger part of teaching is devoted to developing their social habits rather than to teaching them academic things. In such a situation, rather than explaining, I need to tell them simply, "You must not do this." As for the academic subjects, since they are learning simple matters, they can learn as long as I go over the things repeatedly. But in terms of their school life, I think I have to make them understand clearly what is allowed and what is not, even if I have to use such a control strategy as scolding.

The change in her view could be seen as a transformation from a progressive orientation to a conventional attitude toward teaching. In his research Tanaka (1974) finds a similar change in the attitudes of Japanese beginning teachers. But it is not quite right to attribute her change to a loss of idealism, as Veenman put it. When she began teaching at Taika, Yoko learned the imperative of maintaining order in her classroom and shaping six-year-olds' expected behavior. And she legitimated the use of control strategies when they were properly applied in the context of ethnopedagogy. As discussed in the previous chapter, Yoko was exposed to that ethnopedagogy at Taika, which attaches great importance to the ligature between teachers and students and to cooperation among students. It may be suggested that she learned a different teaching "ideal," one that is more congruent with the culture of teaching, rather than implied that she lost her original idealistic view and became authoritarian. When we asked her how she viewed her experience as a beginning teacher after two months of teaching, she responded:

> I must say I had a hard time in April. Partly because of Kazu's presence in my class, I felt, "What a job!" Time passed very slowly, and I was depressed. Because I was obsessed with the idea that I had to perform my duties successfully, I was often disheartened. In May, however, after the Golden Week holidays, I began to feel that time was passing more quickly. I got used to my job and started to embrace my children as lovable and gentle.

She further commented:

> I began to feel that the children liked me, though maybe I might have been flattering myself a bit. They would come around and call me "Kato-sensei [Teacher Kato], Kato-sensei." And I noticed that my students were kind to Kazu, even though he is such a difficult child. Seeing such an attitude on their part makes me feel very gratified. In the month or so since I have gotten to know them better, I already feel, "How wonderful it is to be assigned to this class!" It was the right choice to be a teacher.

As Yoko put it, it was because she had not adjusted to the daily routines in the school that she was depressed during the first month of her teaching. But after she developed familiarity with them a couple of months later, she started to feel glad about choosing teaching as her career. It is evident that Yoko did not experience a reality shock, and she diligently learned shared tenets of teaching, which became a framework of her orientation toward teaching. Against this framework, she reflected on her university course work.

Other beginning teachers in our study experienced variable degrees of stress when they encountered the pressures of teaching. But their experiences did not lead to a loss of idealism about teaching. For example, one beginning teacher at Ikeshita compared what he had imagined about teaching prior to assuming teaching with what teaching actually entailed:

> I sometimes feel sorry for having made light of teaching
> when I was a college student. Now I realize how heavy the
> responsibility of a teacher is, and sometimes I worry about
> whether I can handle it or not. I become embarrassed
> when I think of it. "Why can't I be more confident?" I ask
> myself.

He was overwhelmed when he realized the importance of his role as a teacher, because he had begun the job without an articulated image of teaching. Another beginning teacher at Taika agreed:

> When I am teaching, I feel that every minute the children
> spend at school is very important and I, as a teacher
> entrusted with their education, have an awesome respon-
> sibility to them. I can't cut corners. If I do, the effects show
> up right away.

Although this beginning teacher felt that knowing his students was important for effective teaching, in the first month or so he was ambivalent about how to enhance his personal knowledge of students. Moreover, he was pressed by a large amount of paperwork at school and various special activities, to which we referred earlier. Before he assumed teaching, he was unaware of the inclusiveness of the teacher's role in a Japanese elementary school.

From the preceding discussion, we can suggest that most of the challenges that beginning teachers encountered did not result in disillusionment with teaching, but resulted in a keener awareness of the responsibility and duties expected of them; in other words, their image of teaching in an elementary school was not defined well until they became classroom teachers. Soon after they began teaching, they came to share the ethnopedagogy dominant in their schools, and from this pedagogy they derived educational beliefs different from the theories taught at their universities. It is probable that the reason few Japanese beginning teachers experienced a shock lies mostly in the fact that ethnopedagogy became a frame of orientation and aspiration in teaching.

In a similar vein, Lortie (1975) comments, "Training is not a dramatic watershed separating the perceptions of naive laymen from later judgments by knowing professionals" (p. 66).

Japanese beginning teachers' transition from the universities to the classroom supports his observation. Zeichner and Tabachnick (1981), who reviewed the literature on teacher education both in the United States and in the United Kingdom, speak of the two different types of impact of professional education on teaching. One is "the liberal impact of professional education and a progressive-traditional shift in teaching perspectives" (p. 7), and the other is "the low impact of professional training and the maintenance of traditional teaching perspectives throughout professional education" (p. 8). It seems that the second type by and large reflects Japanese beginning teachers' transition from training to teaching.

Having accepted the basic cultural premises of teaching, beginning teachers gained confidence in their teaching while losing confidence in the programs offered by their universities. Jinnouchi's (1987) finding suggests that classroom teachers generally tended to distance themselves from professors, because they felt that the professors were out of touch with the actual teaching scene. Kenji's comments reflect Jinnouchi's finding:

> Well, I think it is not connected with, or—shall we say it?—is remote from, actual teaching. All I know is that we were told, "There is this theory," but we did not learn how, and in what situation, we could use the theory. We were only given a brief explanation of the theory. And that was the end of it.

We suggest several reasons for the fact that Japanese teacher education programs do not have much influence on the socialization of beginning teachers. First, most teachers in Japan obtain teaching positions immediately after four years of undergraduate education. In comparison with teachers in the United States, where 37 percent of the elementary public schoolteachers hold a master's degree, the period of teacher education is not long enough for Japanese teachers to become acquainted with theories in teaching and reflect on them in connection with classroom practice. However, as may be recalled, we note that American beginning teachers with master's degrees did not actively draw upon theory in classroom teaching.

The second reason may be found in their personal biographies. As Lortie (1975) argues, we should not overlook the apprenticeship of observation that teachers undergo as students. He maintains that their school experiences encourage them to identify with the teaching occupation, and this surely can be applied, in large measure, to Japanese beginning teachers. As may be recalled, the reason Yoko held her own childhood classroom teacher up as a model was that he played with children and permitted them to sit on his lap. Kenji was also deeply impressed by his own teachers, who were devoted to their students in a variety of ways. Their former teachers remained a source of guidance and inspiration for both beginners when they taught.

Third, it may be suggested that university preservice programs do not offer an effective alternative to the time-honored, indigenous pedagogy shared among practitioners. Elementary teacher candidates have also been receptive to that pedagogy for the following reason. Because the number of universities that offer elementary certification programs is limited, the admissions requirements for elementary certification candidates to these universities are very competitive. In 1990, for example, to be admitted to the universities at which Kenji and Yoko studied, applicants had to be in the top 30 percent of all university applicants that year (Nippon Nyushi Center, 1991). When both Kenji and Yoko sought admission to their universities in 1985, they had to study just as hard. It is apparent that most college students who want to be elementary schoolteachers must have ranked relatively high in their elementary and secondary schools and must have adapted well to the dominant pedagogy when they were children.

Coping and Adaptation

Although they did not experience a "reality shock" that caused them to lose their teaching ideals, these beginning teachers did encounter many difficult problems. In which aspects of teaching did they find difficulties, and how did they cope with them? We also want to explore those aspects of teaching they did not regard as problematic. By inquiring into these questions, we will discover that their interests and concerns were oriented toward certain aspects of teaching.

Relationships with Students

For beginning Japanese teachers, their relationships with students were a focal concern. This is quite understandable in view of the fact that they regarded bonding with their students as crucial in teaching and felt that the bonding was fostered through close interaction with students and a deep personal knowledge of students. But managing one entire class demanded use of authority and power: control of them. The beginning teachers' dilemma was how to maintain a proper balance between the centripetal forces of bonding and the control of students exercised by the teacher as an agent of socialization who is endowed with the status of authority. Beginning American teachers resolved this dilemma by putting authority over friendship with students; friendship was encouraged on the condition that students respected the authority of the teacher. In contrast, beginning Japanese teachers believed that their authority evolved in the context of intense interactions with their students. Their belief made control problematic, although they recognized that it was necessary and indispensable, especially in managing a group.

One of the main anxieties that commonly plagued the Japanese beginning teachers was how to control students' behavior in a group setting. In Japanese elementary schools, teachers interact with students in a variety of formal and informal situations both inside and outside the classroom. Their concern with control is omnipresent in such situations. The problem of control loomed large for Yoko. When we asked her what was the most serious problem she experienced during the first marking period, she responded:

> On the whole, I would say, that of controlling a group of students. It was easy for me to deal with them individually, but I found it most difficult to manage a group of students, whether in the classroom or other places. I guess I can handle individual students without

> problems, but in many situations I have to deal with them as a group. I am not as yet competent enough to manage a group. This is the hardest thing for me.

Obviously, her problem was not that she could not control her students. As her following remark suggests, her dilemma was that she more often than not resorted to reprimands to control students in a group setting.

> In the beginning, I was pressing my students more than necessary to meet my expectations by issuing warnings at them. I shouted typical warnings such as, "Be quiet," "Stop it," and "Shape up." I don't like to use those words. But there were times when I was using them, even though I hated to do so.

It seems that from her point of view, the problem was that she had to rely on the control strategies that conflicted with her desire to develop close relationships with her students. Therefore, her main concern at that time was to create an environment compatible with her own expectations. As elucidated in Yoko's case, the problem of control beginning teachers encounter is perceived in relation to the expectations toward teaching they form on the premises of ethnopedagogy.

The beginning teachers' related difficulties were revealed in their admission that they were unable to understand children well. In our interviews with beginning teachers and their supervisors, they often used the phrase "understand children." "Understand children" conveyed several overlapping meanings in the context of schooling in Japan, three of which will be mentioned here. First, it meant building a personal knowledge of students based on kizuna that is formed through unpretentious association with children. Second, it meant broad familiarity with students' personal lives and with the motivations underpinning their behavior in school and at home. Third, it meant knowing and appreciating children's feelings, which would enhance communication with them. In everyday conversation the phrase was used to refer to any of these meanings, depending on the topic of the conversation.

On the assumption that teachers must develop bonding with students for effective management of their work, beginning teachers were expected to know their students. In the first few months the beginners were commonly plagued by their difficulties in understanding children. For example, in the absence of personal knowledge of them, a beginning teacher at Taika did not know how to handle his students when they became confrontational toward him. A beginning teacher in Komori commented that she did not have a large enough *utsuwa*, (translated as a receptacle or a capacity), to be able to understand the feelings of her students. Likewise, Kenji's salient concern was that he was not competent at getting to know them. He first spoke of this problem about two months after the school year had begun. He characterized his inability to understand his students as "not being able to see my students": "I cannot figure out what they are thinking about. During lessons, I am not sure if they are actually concentrating or not; they may be just pretending to do so. I still do not understand what they are really thinking." To know them better, he strove to develop personal ties with his students through close association with them in the classroom and outside. As referred to in the previous chapter, his strategy for coping with this problem was to encourage each student to write a diary and share it with him daily. He explained the aim of the diary:

> I do not know what my students are doing after they go home. I can understand the children who come up to me frequently, but not the others. I wonder how they get along at home or how they spend their time after school. I want to know more about their lives through their diaries, which would reveal their private feelings.

Encouraging students to write diaries is a well-established, common practice in Japan. Senior teachers at Komori told us that diaries offered a vital communications channel between them and their students. One teacher encouraged his students to create what he called a "home-study notebook," which included reviews of lessons and preparations as well as personal notes about themselves. Students handed home-study notebooks to him every morning, and in turn, he wrote comments on them before returning them to the students before they went home. The diary entry could be just three sentences or a paragraph, but through it the teacher was able to understand his children and communicate his own feelings to them as well. One of the students he had taught from first to fourth grade had gone through 27 notebooks by the end of the fourth year.

Socialization into Interpersonal Relations

In Japanese schools, managing interpersonal relations among colleagues is as important as managing them among students. This is especially so in Japanese elementary schools, where teachers closely associate with each other for both instrumental and expressive purposes. In contrast, in the United States, as Lortie (1975) observes, the "single cell of instruction has played a key role in the development of the American public school" (p. 15), and "schools were organized around teacher separation rather than teacher interdependence" (p. 14).

As previously mentioned, Japanese elementary school classes are not run as independently as those in the United States, because school programs, especially special activities, require teachers to cooperate closely at the grade as well as the schoolwide levels. Teachers at the same grade level meet weekly to coordinate curricular matters, such as the pace of instruction and other common activities. The entire teaching staff meets at least once a day in the faculty room. The physical and social structure of the faculty room in Japanese schools is designed to encourage beginning teachers to meet experienced teachers daily and interact with them to ensure cooperation in implementing a variety of programs. All teachers, including the head teacher, have their personal desks in the staff room, and they are arranged to promote interaction among teachers. This room is used for staff meetings, work, and relaxation. The structure of the Japanese elementary school contributes to faculty interaction in the staff room, on the playground, and in the specific floors where classrooms are clustered by grade. Moreover, in-service education and recreational activities, which are organized regularly, provide teachers with opportunities for interaction at all levels. In short, there is extensive face-to-face interaction among teachers, making interpersonal relations a pivotal factor in everyday school life. Although intense interaction can create a sense of community, it can also lead to uneasiness because it exerts a pressure toward conformity, leading to veiled judgments of each other's behavior. In any event, it is sufficient to suggest that these relations can have a significant effect on teachers' morale and effectiveness as faculty members.

Adaptation to a close-knit community was an important part of the beginning teachers' occupational socialization. Our beginning teachers displayed differential adaptation to this dimension of their induction. Here we will comment on how Kenji and Yoko responded to it. Although they were equally sensitive to interpersonal relations, they differed in their adaptation.

Concerned with interpersonal relations, Kenji actively availed himself of opportunities for association with his colleagues. He was a diligent participant in all officially announced meetings and activities, as well as after-school recreational events. Moreover, he made a conscientious effort to accompany his colleagues to bars or restaurants after such recreational activities as baseball and volleyball practice. In his school there were several informal groups where special relationships among members of the groups developed, providing a sense of belonging and support. Kenji became a member of a group that included the head teacher, three beginning teachers, and a few other teachers. This group often met after school and socialized, sharing personal concerns. He was quite deliberate in his efforts to avoid conflicts with colleagues in his formal and informal associations with them.

Kenji also went out of his way to avoid being evaluated poorly by his colleagues—part of the covert judgment resulting from collegial interaction. A couple of examples can shed light on his strategies. He was assigned to give a "demonstration" gym class in December as part of his school's in-service education program; his colleagues, as well as the principal, were to observe this class and give him feedback afterwards. In preparing for this lesson, he devised a plan for making it especially appealing to the observers. To impress the observers, he intentionally chose a lesson that his students could plunge into with enthusiasm. On another occasion, he decided to cancel an academic class in order to play with his students, as part of his plan to improve his management of students. He used the gym, where he and his students could not be readily seen by other teachers, rather than the playground. He was afraid that if other teachers saw him and his class out in the playground, they might not have thought that his cancellation of the class was legitimate. Therefore, to avoid veiled criticism by his colleagues, he chose to be inconspicuous when playing with his students.

His sensitivity to his colleagues was quite obvious when he displayed embarrassment about his failure to control his students during a trip to a concert hall. He commented:

> I was so ashamed at the recent concert. We walked to the Komori Station to take a train and, after the train ride, had to walk again to reach the concert hall. The other two classes were walking in neat lines, whereas my students made a poor show, even though I reminded them several times. I felt so bad I could have cried then. It was only a ten-to-fifteen-minute walk, but my class couldn't keep straight lines and were so disorganized. It looked really disgraceful.

Kenji was concerned that his class might be compared with other classes: "Yes, especially in a situation like that, it bothers me. I felt that my students' behavior reflected on my poor teaching. I was really embarrassed."

What Kenji was concerned about as he interacted with other teachers was "impression management," of which Goffman (1959) speaks. For an actor, acquiring and playing a certain role means employing and maintaining an expected "front," that is, "the expressive equipment of a standard kind intentionally or unwittingly employed by the individual during his performance" (p. 22). In other words, "whether his acquisition of the role was primarily motivated by a desire to perform the given task or by a desire to maintain the corresponding front, the actor will find that he must do both" (p. 27). In the process of learning his role, Kenji realized that he must maintain a proper front as a teacher in addition to acquiring the necessary skills to perform the role. Impression management was important for Kenji, especially when intense interaction and the pressure for conformity were present.

Kenji's anxiety about his colleagues and his front, however, is in part inherent in a special occupational feature of teaching. According to D. H. Hargreaves (1980), teachers find it difficult to acquire feedback on their performances to help them evaluate their competence, because their teaching roles tend to be so multifaceted and the goals of teaching tend to be so manifold and indefinite. As we pointed out elsewhere, in Japanese elementary schools, where the egalitarian ethos is strong, others teachers do not offer explicit advice to a beginning teacher directly. Hargreaves suggests that such an absence of feedback in the teaching profession brings about feelings of uneasiness among teachers about their own competence. Kenji's anxiety about his own competence as a teacher seemed to reflect these feelings of uneasiness.

In contrast, although Yoko regarded interpersonal relations as pivotal in her work, she displayed much less anxiety about her colleagues' evaluation of her behavior than the other beginning teachers we studied. Like Kenji, she was a conscientious participant in formal and informal activities organized by her school's faculty. She also joined after-school social events. But she was much more confident with respect to teaching than the other beginning teachers and declared:

> I think the most important thing for teachers is the relationship between teachers and the children. I think you asked me about how I get along with my colleagues teaching next door, but I don't have to be so anxious about it. It may depend on who it is, but at present I am not worried about it. As long as I am able to manage my class successfully, my colleagues will support me. I'm sure the principal and vice-principal will do the same.

She gained more confidence in managing her class and teaching academic subjects during the first marking period than did Kenji. It pointed out that the difference between Kenji and Yoko with respect to their sensitivity toward their colleagues is partly linked to their different levels of anxiety about teaching. All in all, however, beginning teachers were sensitized toward interpersonal relations among colleagues during the course of the first year of teaching.

Orientation toward Educational Goals and Teacher Roles

We have pointed out that one of the salient differences in schooling between Japan and the United States is the fact that Japan has a national curriculum; this has been a feature of Japanese education since the late nineteenth century, when the nation began modernizing. Compiled by the Ministry of Education, the national course of study serves as the binding framework for curriculum construction. Textbooks are written in compliance with the course of study and are adopted for use in schools after they have been authorized by the Ministry of Education. Given legitimacy by the ministry, the textbook constitutes the official curriculum, which is supplemented by relevant materials chosen by individual teachers. Given this definition of curriculum, beginning teachers as well as experienced teachers assumed the role of transmitter of officially legitimate knowledge to students.

Berlak and Berlak (1981) speak of "dilemmas" in teaching. They point out that there is a dilemma between treating knowledge as given and treating it as problematic. If knowledge is treated as given, teachers define it as truth, universal and objective, though if it is seen as problematic, they view it as something constructed, provisional, tentative, and subject to political, cultural, and social influences. For beginning Japanese teachers, knowledge is given and objective, and they invariably take the official curriculum for granted and have few personal conflicts about teaching it. Put differently, in their view textbook knowledge is legitimate and indisputable. They define their role as one primarily concentrated on imparting legitimate knowledge to students. There is a sharp contrast between their definition of their role as an instructor and Nancy's definition of her role. As may be recalled, Nancy constructed her curriculum for reading and writing following her district's guidelines, but firmly challenged school policy on whole-language instruction.

The lessons we observed in Japanese schools were unambiguously aimed at transmitting to students the knowledge delineated in the textbooks. For example, in Kenji's science class, which we described in chapter 5, he instructed his students to experiment on kidney bean germination under a variety of conditions. The content of the lesson, the method of conducting the experiment, and the conclusions that his students were expected to derive from it were outlined in the textbook. But because the science textbook was condensed and compact, Kenji had to consult the teacher's manual to teach the unit and devise some details of the experiment. Given this perspective on teaching, it is understandable that Yoko also heavily relied on the teachers' manual as the source of guidance. She referred frequently to it to "stay on the right track," as she put it, and infrequently to other sources. Unambiguously, one of the beginning teachers' focal concerns was to teach the textbook to their students regardless of the grade level. Because the curriculum was assumed to be indisputable, they concentrated on ensuring that students learned the material in the lessons. They resorted to a variety of strategies, some of which were common to those used by beginning American teachers: recitation, seatwork, small-group discussion, drill, frequent tests, and some homework.

With respect to their more inclusive teaching responsibilities, which we discussed earlier, beginning teachers accept them wholeheartedly. Although they were more often than not overwhelmed by the range of teaching, they found the broad goals of teaching to be legitimate. Indeed, they were committed to "whole person" education, involving cognitive, moral, expressive, and social aspects of schooling. These goals were not only mandated by the course of study but also supported by teachers as the raison d'être of their school. In short, the preceding discussion reveals that beginning teachers were socialized into the role of teaching mandated by the course of study and broad educational goals.

Beginning Teachers' Accountability

Japanese teachers' accountability is broad, since their roles are diffuse and inclusive. Their accountability is defined in the Fundamental Law of Education (promulgated in 1947) and other statutes. For example, the Fundamental Law of Education reads: "Teachers of the schools prescribed by law shall be servants of the whole community. They shall be conscious of their mission and endeavor to discharge their duties. For this purpose, the status of teachers shall be respected and their fair and appropriate treatment shall be secured." As already mentioned in chapter 6, one of the purposes of the nationally mandated internship program was to promote *shimeikan*, a sense of mission. However, because such a legal definition of accountability is abstract, general, and out of context, it did not serve as a practical guide for beginning teachers. Perhaps few beginning teachers, if any, would read it. Instead, their sense of accountability seemed to evolve in the broad context of teaching as they were enculturated into teaching.

Our beginning teachers' views of accountability were affected by the Japanese practice of hiring teachers and by the national curriculum. As referred to earlier, teachers were hired as employees of the Tokyo metropolitan government (and thus designated as prefectural employees nationwide; a prefecture is equivalent to a state in the United States), not by a local ward or a community. Fifty percent of their salaries were drawn from national funding and the remaining, from the metropolitan government. Moreover, it was the national certification law that determined their qualifications as teachers. The law is the basic, binding framework that specifies the requirements in teacher education programs. What distinguishes Japanese beginning teachers from American beginning teachers is that the former are prefectural employees and the latter are employees of local communities. From a legal point of view, Japanese teachers are directly accountable to their prefectural board of education, whereas American teachers are accountable to their local board of education.

As was discussed earlier, the national curriculum is another factor that circumscribes the beginning Japanese teacher's role. Unlike beginning American teachers, our beginning Japanese teachers were not expected to construct curricula suitable to the needs of children in their school districts. They used nationally authorized textbooks as the primary teaching materials, and they were little concerned with what they had to teach. Thus, the hiring practice and the national curriculum made beginning Japanese teachers considerably less accountable to their local districts than were their American counterparts. In other words, Japanese teachers identified their accountability in terms of their responsibility to fulfill national mandates—common national educational goals and materials stipulated in the course of study. Holistic education was part and parcel of these mandates, and the inclusiveness of teaching we discussed stemmed from them, not from local needs.

Further, parents were not as strong a source of external pressure for Japanese teachers as they were for American teachers. Parents were much more accommodating to teachers, emphasizing their children's ability to adapt to the school environments. This evidently reflects Hess and Azuma's (1991) assertion that Japanese teachers and parents emphasize children's adaptive dispositions. Parents of Yoko's class expressed more concern with how their children were getting along with peers and how diligent they were at school. When another beginning teacher at Taika visited his children's homes in the spring, he was surprised to hear many mothers ask him to be "strict" with their children so they would develop disciplined attitudes toward study at school. During our study we rarely heard that parents were a source of concern for beginning teachers. In late June Kenji told us: "I was afraid I would be under pressure from conflicts with colleagues and parents. But as it is, I feel hardly any pressure from parents at all in this school." His feelings were shared by other beginning teachers. Our research supports Hess and Azuma's observation: "Adults in Japan are particularly eager to prepare the child to be diligent and to cooperate with the teacher. In the United States, more concern is focused on acquiring academic (especially verbal) skills, independence, and self-reliance" (p. 3).

However, the preceding discussion does not suggest that Japanese teachers were insensitive to parents. On the contrary, our observations reveal that they were considerably sensitive to the parents and actively participated in parent initiatives. In the spring, as part of the schoolwide program, beginning teachers and experienced teachers devoted five afternoons to visiting parents to gain familiarity with them and their students. Prior to the home visitation, beginners received advice from their supervisors on how to conduct it and also had a practice session at the education center as part of the internship program. Three *hogo-shakai* ("parent schools"), similar to "back-to-school" night in

United States, were organized so that parents could observe classes and consult with the teachers. The beginning teachers were extremely nervous at the first parent school held in the middle of the spring, imitating the anxiousness shown by Nancy. It represented their first formal face-to-face encounter with parents; our beginning teachers invariably admitted that they were quite unconfident in communicating with the parents at the first parent school. In addition, parents were invited to several school programs, including sports festivals (the most popular school events), theatrical and arts festivals, and commencements. Parental volunteers were also invited to participate in "mountain schools" and "nature classrooms," which were retreats for upper-level students that lasted two to three days. Moreover, parents were well informed of school events through newsletters and other forms of communication frequently sent to them.

Despite their emphasis on holistic programs, elementary public schoolteachers in Tokyo, including our beginning teachers, did not have sole responsibility for teaching children. Parents' concerns regarding their children's education were mitigated by the existence of competitive private schools and juku, privately organized, very popular after-school institutions. There are more than 35,000 academic juku throughout the country (U.S. Department of Education, 1987). Beginning teachers in the fifth and sixth grades, including Kenji, informed us that more than two-thirds of their students attended juku after school two to six times each week. Juku are of various types: drilling (exam-oriented drills), enrichment (for example, piano, calligraphy, and abacus), and remedial. As a result, a first-year colleague of Yoko's who taught sixth-grade students assigned students little homework because there was little time left for them to study at home after school. Kenji's internship supervisor also told us that faculty at his school agreed to give minimum homework to students to allow them some private space and time after school.

In urban areas like Tokyo and its environs, many parents aspire to send their children to competitive national or private junior high schools, because this would ensure that they would have a smooth transition to competitive high schools and then to college, despite intense entrance examinations. According to a study by Hida (1989), which included a survey of the parents of sixth-graders living in Tokyo, about a third of the parents expected their children to take entrance exams for private junior high schools, and 93 percent of these parents placed their children in juku. The widespread existence of juku in Japan epitomizes the pervasiveness of parents' concerns with the intense competition during high school and with the university entrance examinations. Effects of juku on schooling at the secondary level are greater as university entrance examinations draw closer.

In concluding this section, we reiterate that beginning teachers' developing perspectives on accountability reflected the culture of teaching at their respective schools.

Summary

It is our thesis in this chapter that beginning Japanese teachers learned how to teach by participating in the social construction of teaching. Our ethnographic analysis supports this thesis. It is evident that the neophytes were actively involved in the reproduction of teaching, incorporating the culture of teaching into their personal frame of reference. Reproduction of teaching was possible through an intersubjective process in which beginning teachers interpreted the relevance of the knowledge of teaching to which they were exposed to the problems that they encountered. The beginning teachers' occupational socialization was not merely a process of situational adaptation, but also a process in which the transmission of the cultural knowledge of teaching played an important role in individual teachers' decisions on teaching strategies.

For Japanese beginning teachers, the latent culture of teaching they acquired through exposure to their former teachers was an important factor in their transition from university to school. It remained as a cathected image, which was potent in creating a linkage between their biographies and the pedagogy to which they were exposed as teachers. In contrast to the preservice education they received, ethnopedagogy was an efficacious framework that guided beginners learning to teach. It was compatible with the cathected image of teaching that they developed. And that compatibility contributed to their relatively smooth transition to the schools where they taught.

These beginning teachers displayed little personal conflict with, and experienced few dilemmas in their commitment to, the goals of holistic education. This broad support for holistic teaching stemmed from ethnopedagogy, which they identified as a foundation of teaching and of the culture of teaching at their respective schools. It was in that context that beginners strove to become effective in attending to the cognitive, expressive, moral, and social dimensions of their students' experience.

The Japanese culture of teaching involved frequent interaction among teachers, which resulted from a broad range of both formally and informally organized activities. This led to close-knit interpersonal relations, which became a source of concern for beginners. Beginners were sensitive to such interpersonal relations because they were conducive to the expression of veiled judgments about peers. While the emphasis on a centripetal orientation toward human relations is expected in Japanese culture, it could become personally constraining and restrict individual diversity and freedom in the interests of conformity.

The accountability of Japanese teachers is circumscribed broadly. Our beginning teachers were accountable for implementing the national curriculum, holistic teaching, and close communication with parents. They did not feel that parents and the district exerted significant pressure on them. The centralized control of schooling is not designed to reflect the district's voice with respect to curriculum and school policy. In this respect, the beginning teachers were somewhat immune to such pressures, if, indeed, they experienced any.

All in all, the beginning teachers adapted well to the culture of teaching. Their active interest in learning the cultural knowledge of teaching through the process of interaction with experienced teachers contributed to that adaption.

CHAPTER 8

Learning to Teach
in the United States and Japan
Contrasts and Conclusions

In the preceding six chapters we have discussed how beginning elementary teachers in the United States and Japan learned to teach. While we have noted a considerable degree of isomorphism in how teachers from these two countries were enculturated into teaching, we have seen a significant divergence in their pedagogical approaches to teaching. Put differently, while all teachers we studied regarded a shared practical knowledge of teaching, or the cultural knowledge of teaching, to be most critical to learning to teach in the first year, American teachers significantly differed from Japanese teachers in other respects. For example, the former emphasized students' development of an independent orientation or an independent disposition toward study as a major factor in learning, while the latter regarded creating a close ligature, kizuna, with students, and encouraging them to develop adaptive dispositions as central to motivating students to study. Teaching, we learned, also had different meanings for beginning American and Japanese teachers. For American teachers, it largely referred to improving cognitive skills, and for Japanese teachers, it included a broad scope of cognitive and noncognitive activities.

These contrasts are grounded in the different definitions of schooling in both cultures. Schooling mirrors the culture in which it is organized, and the process of inducting teachers into the teaching profession reflects that culture as well. Cultures do not dictate what teachers do, but teachers draw upon their culture as a normative framework of values and goals for guidance. Nonetheless, teaching is an occupation that has shared characteristics in the two culturally distinct countries.

This concluding chapter presents a comparison of teaching in the United States and Japan with a focus on shared attributes, patterns of teacher interaction, and definitions of schooling. It is followed by a brief consideration of teacher education and of its problems in both countries.

Practical Knowledge of Teaching: Shared Attributes

Despite the fact that Japanese teaching and American teaching are each deeply embedded in a sharply contrasting culture, they have salient common characteristics in how beginning teachers learn to teach. Learning how to teach has universal characteristics that transcend cultural boundaries. In the following section we will review these common attributes, and follow with a discussion of the contrasts in teaching between the two cultures.

Both American and Japanese beginning teachers viewed learning to teach as an apprenticeship mediated by conversations with experienced teachers and adaptation according to individual needs. Despite the general emphasis on mastery and application of theoretical knowledge during preservice education in the United States, beginning American teachers drew little from that knowledge base during their first year of teaching. Instead, in their endeavor to enhance teaching strategies, they leaned heavily on practical knowledge grounded in both individual biographies and the culture of teaching. In essence, a large part of learning to teach is gaining the acquaintance of what teachers commonly call procedures or "rules of practice" (Elbaz 1983), which enable them to establish classroom routines.

Teachers' reliance on practical knowledge as a foundation for developing coping strategies and for improving teaching is ubiquitous in the United States and Japan. Nearly two decades ago, Lortie (1975) reported his findings:

> Respondents were asked to select the most important
> source of "ideas and insight on my work," from a list

> including in-service courses, reading, college courses, meetings in the system and elsewhere, their immediate superior, and "informal conversations with colleagues and friends,". . . The last was clearly the modal choice from this mixed list. . . . Informal channels are preferred to the institutional means, and the peer group rather than administrators (or, indeed, college professors) is seen as the most salient source of classroom ideas. (pp. 75-76)

From our study of beginning teachers it is obvious that this mode of learning to teach remains pervasive and is still considered efficacious.

Practical knowledge is broad and multidimensional. Elbaz (1983) identifies practical knowledge as involving several domains: self, milieu of teaching, subject matter, curriculum development, and instruction. Schon (1983) focuses on reflection-in-action as the epistemology of practice that yields nonpropositional knowledge. Other researchers look at teachers' use of metaphors to guide their teaching (Munby 1986, 1989; Russell 1989; Bullough & Knowles 1991) and their use of personal knowledge to manage classroom dilemmas (Lambert 1985). As Jackson (1990) points out, teachers' interest in "immediacy" calls for an application of practical knowledge to evaluate on-going classroom events. Suffice it to suggest that practical knowledge is part and parcel of teachers' repertoire of teaching knowledge, which is invented, shared, and regenerated by themselves. As we saw in the chapters that focused on beginning American teachers, informal conversation played a chief role in sharing, regenerating, and transmitting practical knowledge.

In Japanese schools, informal conversation is often referred to as *zatsudan* and is also stressed as an effective means for beginners to learn the ropes from experienced teachers. This casual interaction enabled the beginners we studied to seek ready suggestions for dealing with problems that they encountered. As a matter of fact, both beginning teachers and experienced teachers assumed that the theoretical knowledge of teaching was of little help in providing a framework for improving the practice. As one experienced teacher suggested: "Teachers must constantly cope with problems that arise from emerging situations. Theory plays little role in solving problems in these situations. . . . What is important is not a theory but skills learned from practice." This teacher's view echoes the importance that American teachers attach to practical knowledge and their concern with immediacy. Elsewhere we have conceptualized shared practical knowledge of teaching as part of the cultural knowledge of teaching (Shimahara & Sakai 1992). It is the cultural knowledge of teaching that our beginning teachers focused on when learning to become effective teachers. There is a widely shared assumption in Japan, as well as in the United States, that the cultural knowledge of teaching can better improve the process of learning to teach than can theoretical knowledge. This explains the pervasive absence of partnerships between schools and universities in Japan. Teachers regard university professors, whose primary interest is research and theoretical knowledge, as unfamiliar with practice and hardly draw upon them as practical resources for improving teaching (Shimahara 1991).

The following comments by beginning teachers succinctly illustrate how they tried to gain practical knowledge in teaching:

- "I watch and listen to other teachers. This is quite useful. But I cannot yet make an overall plan to improve the classroom environment. . . . I am just too busy to work on it. To test any suggestion I get, I just have to practice it."

- "My biggest problem is to make children listen to me. . . . I spoke with my senior colleagues about this problem. They were very helpful to me in identifying characteristics of children."

- "My senior colleagues tell me about their experiences regarding how they handled children, especially problem children. When I have a problem, I just walk over to the next classroom to ask for suggestions. The important thing is that I can talk to her at any time when I have a problem."

- "I have learned much more from informal situations where I asked questions and got feedback from veteran teachers and children. I learned much more from interactions with my senior colleagues and children than from the internship program at the center."

Beginning Japanese teachers suggested that they were under *minarai*, an apprenticeship of observation. But as one beginner put it, "I do not imitate everything. I imitate only the things that are relevant to my concerns." Beginners tried to develop their own style of teaching and classroom management through repeated trial and error, which they called *jissen* (practice). Above all, the beginners' concentration on events in the classroom was believed to be critical for gaining competence as teachers. In short, the Japanese teachers' process of learning to teach concentrated on adapting experienced teachers' practices to their needs, just as American teachers did.

It is evident that there are clear parallels in learning to teach between American and Japanese teachers. Emphasis is placed on learning practical knowledge and the cultural knowledge of teaching, and little attention is paid to theoretical knowledge. Learning to teach involves conversation and observation, a social apparatus used ubiquitously for the social construction and maintenance of teaching.

A Comparison of American and Japanese Schools

Differences in teaching between the two countries result, in part, from dissimilarities in school governance and finance. How a teacher applicant is assigned to a position is a useful example. Having obtained certification, American teachers take the initiative in applying for a position in a district of their preference. The selection of applicants is ordinarily based on a careful review of their applications and on interviews by district administrators. Applicants' strengths and weaknesses are usually identified during the interviews. In short, American hiring procedures are consistent with market principles. As we noted earlier, the Japanese procedures of appointment significantly differ from the American approach. After Japanese teacher applicants pass appointment examinations administered by the prefectural board of education, they become eligible for appointments. In consultation with local superintendents of schools, and the principals who make requests for new appointments, the prefectural board of education makes the decision to appoint the applicants at schools where they are needed. This entire hiring process is confidential and does not involve consultation with the applicants. They cannot negotiate about the school of their preference with the decision makers, although they can indicate their preference in their application.

Japanese public schoolteachers are prefectural employees, with half their salaries funded by the central government, whereas American public schoolteachers are employees of local communities. This accounts for a difference between American teachers and Japanese teachers with respect to their identification with community interests and sensitivity toward the parents of schoolchildren. As we saw earlier, American teachers are invariably concerned with the parents' demands and are held accountable to them directly, but Japanese teachers generally do not have a sense of immediate accountability to the parents. Instead, Japanese teachers display a distinct sense of accountability for teaching the curriculum required by the school authorities. Because what Japanese teachers teach is the national curriculum mandated by the Ministry of Education, education essentially is a national affair, the standards of which are maintained by the ministry through the administrative apparatus at the prefectural level.

Another way of comparing American and Japanese schools is to review how American and Japanese students spend their time in school. In chapter 5 we presented a table of weekly time allocations, comparing the fifth-grade levels at Westville and Komori Elementary Schools (see table 2). At Westville, Nancy's fifth-grade students spent 1,850 minutes in school and 1,200 minutes on lessons (64.9 percent), in contrast to Kenji's fifth graders at Komori, who spent 2,161 minutes in school and 1,170 minutes on lessons (54 percent). Further, the American students spent 10.8 percent of their time at lunch, and although 13.5 percent of the time was allocated for recess, it was not usually granted to them. In contrast, Kenji's students spent 11.6 percent of the time at lunch and 14.6 percent at recess, which was unfailingly given them. Moreover, his students spent 4.6 percent cleaning and 6.2 percent in various kinds of engagements with express moral purposes, including the morning assembly, brief morning meetings, and reflection meetings at the end of school. Nancy allocated 10.8 percent for "open house," "family meeting," and current events, which were often devoted to reading. In Kenji's class 8.8 percent was assigned to club activities, classroom assembly, student guidance, committee activities, and moral education.

Students in both schools came to school around 8:10 A.M. and went home between 3:00 and 3:30 P.M. As soon as the American students arrived at school by bus, they proceeded to their classroom in a remarkably orderly manner to get ready for the first lesson. While attending to household business before school started at 8:30, classroom teachers urged students to take their seats to read or do other work, an activity that contributed to the development of academic skills. Once they arrived at school, they were not permitted to stay outdoors or even in the hall without their teacher's permission. In comparison, Japanese students walked to school, and as soon as they left their belongings in the classroom, most of them went out to the playground at their own initiative to play for 15 minutes if it was not raining. This was a time for them to engage in interaction and release energy, as was the 20-minute break. And an observer could not fail to notice the action-centered behavior of these students on the playground and the level of noise they made. Students controlled their time and activities themselves, and teachers provided no supervision over them. On Mondays there were regularly scheduled outdoor school assemblies from 8:30 to 8:45, and on Wednesdays all students participated in gymnastics during the same period. On other days of the week students returned to their classrooms at the sound of the chimes at 8:30. From 8:45 to 8:50 student monitors conducted a brief meeting, called *asanokai*, to announce events of the day or remind the class of the goals of the week. Students' activities were precisely regulated by the chimes, to which they were trained to respond from first grade.

What is striking about the above description is the fact that American students were confined to their classrooms all day except for the lunch period, while Japanese students extensively participated in nonclassroom activities. Moreover, Japanese students participated in other schoolwide events, some of which required sustained preparation: sports festivals, theatrical performance days, art festivals, and excursions. American teachers organized similar activities on a classroom or grade-level basis, but not to the same extent as the Japanese teachers, nor on a schoolwide level. This striking difference between the American and Japanese schools unambiguously marks the diversity of educational purposes.

Turning to another difference, the division of work was clearly defined at Westville and Southtown Elementary Schools, whereas the teachers' work at Komori, Ikeshita, and Taika Elementary Schools in Tokyo was diffuse. The American teachers' chief responsibility was to teach a few academic subjects, and they were not to be interrupted by other assignments, because specialists were in charge of the other areas of responsibility, such as art, music, computer, physical education, counseling, cleaning, and lunch duties. Japanese teachers, on the other hand, handled most of these duties, except arts and crafts, home economics, and music. Further, they were obligated to perform committee work. From a standpoint of the division of work, it seems that American classroom teachers had an advantage over Japanese teachers in specializing in academic subjects. Nonetheless, part of the reason why Japanese school authorities have not differentiated elementary teachers' responsibilities as much as is found in American schools is the Japanese pedagogical belief that teaching is an inclusive engagement at the elementary level. Hence, Japanese classroom teachers are generally expected to address all aspects of students' life at school. We referred to the notion of whole-person education to suggest the significance of that inclusive teaching.

This brings us to another related contrast. We pointed out that beginning American classroom teachers were primarily concerned with the child's development of cognitive competence, especially skills in the areas of reading and writing. We noted extraordinary consistency between the kindergarten and fifth-grade levels in terms of the emphasis that these teachers placed on cognitive skills. Beginning teachers were concerned with *how* to develop cognitive competence, and stressed that their students' independent orientation was essential to successful learning. At Westville and Southtown the beginning teachers' major challenge was to construct appropriate reading and writing curricula. We will later shed further light on this theme from a historical perspective.

In comparison, beginning Japanese teachers were not so much concerned with the instructional medium through which students' cognitive development occurred as with how to teach both cognitive and noncognitive skills broadly, because the medium was the national curriculum determined by the Ministry of Education. Japanese teachers concentrated on what we called Japanese ethnopedagogy, which focuses on ligature and interpersonal relations as intrinsic and instrumental values. Consistent with the national course of study, Japanese educators at all levels invariably underscore learning "group life" as one of the primary objectives of teaching (Duke 1986; Levine & White 1986; U.S. Department of Education 1987). In this regard, for Japanese teachers ethnopedagogy is important in and of itself. It is also instrumental in motivating and encouraging students to learn. The close ligature that teachers develop with their students serves as the basis for exhorting students to work hard. In short, ethnopedagogy represents an expressive approach to teaching.

Patterns of Teacher Interaction

One of the striking differences in learning to teach between the two cultures is the pattern of interaction among teachers. Researchers (for example, Lortie 1975; Goodlad 1984 & 1990) have unfailingly pointed out that American teachers work in isolation, intellectually and physically separated from their colleagues. Their findings have been accepted as a general characteristic of teaching in the United States. It is further suggested that American teachers' isolation is perceived in part as a reflection of the American cultural ideology of individualism. Notwithstanding this general attribute of teaching, we must pay attention to a diversity of teacher interaction among schools. The two American schools we studied, for example, differed in the degree of teacher isolation and interdependence. Teacher isolation is created and reproduced by a number of factors, including the cultural knowledge of teaching shared by teachers, instructional strategies, the size of the school, and the organization and allocation of space.

Lortie (1975) describes the physical organization of the school as consisting of a series of "cells." Westville Upper Elementary School, opened in 1989, typified his depiction of school organization. A Westville veteran teacher's metaphoric suggestion that teachers at the school were "islands" to themselves epitomized the relative absence of social and intellectual interaction among teachers. Teachers had their own cells, and a close social link between the cells was generally missing. Typically, when teachers came to school in the morning, they went straight to their classrooms and confined themselves to the classrooms all day until they left school, except for lunch time. Beginning teachers' informal interactions occurred almost exclusively with colleagues at the same grade level and of comparable age. Such formalized activities as grade-level and staff meetings, which were designed to address administrative issues, did not encourage much interaction among teachers. Perhaps the only exception was an in-service meeting for beginners that met once a month.

Southtown Elementary School did not entirely reflect Lortie's observation. It was less than half the size of Westville in terms of space, student enrollment, and the number of teachers. It was a school that, by economic necessity, housed students in two separate buildings connected by a corridor: one consisting of old, cellular classrooms, and the other, relatively new open-space classrooms. In the conventional building, teachers interacted with their colleagues much less frequently and were more often in isolation than teachers in the open-space building. The two beginning teachers we studied taught in the open-space area and closely interacted with their colleagues at the same grade levels. Their interdependence was promoted by the close relationship between the beginner and her buddy and by team teaching. They were essentially peers of comparable age who differed in teaching experience by only two or three years. Moreover, both of the beginners often consulted with administrators, unlike the beginners at Westville, who had little contact with administrators. But it is important to note that they rarely interacted with their more experienced counterparts in the traditional area or with teachers at other grade levels. The two differential patterns of interaction observed at Southtown may be partly viewed as functions of the organization of space and the instructional strategies in the two buildings. But the cooperation that developed between the beginners and their colleagues was restricted to their unit of four teachers. And in much the same way as the beginners at Westville did, these beginning teachers also isolated themselves in their classroom areas all day. Thus the general pattern of teacher isolation applies to an appreciable extent to beginners and their colleagues who taught in the open-space area.

By contrast, Japanese elementary schools commonly place an emphasis on promoting interdependence and cooperation among teachers. Teacher cooperation is a function of the programs that schools organize formally and informally. Japanese schools consist of classroom cells just as most American schools do, and teachers spend the majority of their time within the isolated classroom. Yet every school invariably provides teachers with common space and activities that enhance interaction and cooperation among teachers. Teachers commonly converge in the staff room several times a day, where they have assigned desks. Beginning teachers are usually seated next to veteran teachers, to promote consultation. It is in this common space where informal conversation often takes place and the entire staff meets every day. They do their work and relax in the staff room. The beginning teachers we studied at the three Tokyo schools had their desks in the staff room and had opportunities to interact with other teachers. They participated in a short staff meeting every morning before first period, returned to the staff room during the 20-minute break between second and third periods, and converged there again after school was over. Every Wednesday they also participated in a long staff meeting.

Moreover, every school has a rich program of schoolwide events, identified as gakko gyoji, an area stressed in the course of study and requiring teachers' continual cooperation and participation. Gakko gyoji include ceremonial events, sports and arts festivals, excursions and retreats, interschool contests in sports and music, nature-study programs, and the like. The course of study states: "Under gakko gyoji each school must promote participatory group activities to develop school order, students' sense of belonging, and the enrichment of school life." The Japanese elementary curriculum is divided into three closely related domains: the subject-matter area, moral education, and "special activities," of which gakko gyoji is part. The last domain includes "classroom activities" designed to enhance classroom cooperation and life skills, programs organized by the student council (such as schoolwide sports festivals), and club activities.

Promotion of special activities is predicated upon the sharing of common goals and necessitates teachers' cooperation. Each of the events under gakko gyoji demands preparation by a group of teachers or the entire staff, as well as collaborative implementation. At the study schools each major event was planned by a committee and presented to the full staff for discussion. Some events, such as sports festivals, required careful planning by the entire staff and the student council and cooperation in implementing the plan.

Each of our study schools, as do most Japanese schools, also had a faculty study committee that articulated schoolwide study goals and organized study groups and a series of demonstration lessons. Such activities involved both veteran and beginning teachers. These schools also organized recreational and social activities that involved most of the staff. Our beginning teachers also frequently participated in practices for intraschool and interschool competitions (such as baseball, volleyball, and basketball), as well as in the games and subsequent social hours. Those sports activities helped to enculturate beginning teachers into their schools.

During our research, we noticed that there was a sharp contrast between beginning Japanese and American teachers relative to their participation in schoolwide events and programs. Japanese schools organized rich collective activities as part of their broad curriculum, whereas American schools had noticeably fewer shared schoolwide activities. It became evident that schoolwide events promoted by teachers did not have as much weight in the American curriculum as they had in the

Japanese curriculum and, as a consequence, were not as extensively organized in American schools as in Japanese schools. Viewed from this perspective, teacher isolation in the American school or teacher interdependence in the Japanese school is a consequence of school programs.

Definitions of Schooling

As referred to earlier, another striking contrast relates to how schooling is defined. We pointed out that the purposes of Japanese education are broader and more inclusive than those of American education. These different definitions of education have significant implications for the roles that teachers play. Public expectations of the teacher's role in Japan have not radically changed since the modern education system was established in the nineteenth century. Traditionally, Japanese society has relied on formal education to develop character, to cultivate moral and cultural sensitivity, and to advance industrialization and modernization. The Japanese belief that teachers should inclusively enhance the instrumental, moral, social, and expressive aspects of their children's education has become so deeply entrenched in that tradition that it has become a virtual cultural expectation (Shimahara 1991; U.S. Department of Education 1987; National Council on Educational Reform 1988).

In the period after World War II, when that cultural expectation was undermined by rapid social change, educational reform initiatives were launched to affirm that expectation. In 1958, as part of the new national curriculum, Japan reinstated moral education as a subject. This highly controversial ideological decision was made in response to the prevailing perception that postwar education reforms initiated during the American occupation undermined Japanese moral education. The latest education reform movement, which occurred in the 1980s, epitomized the nation's concern with the roles of teachers at a time when traditional institutions were declining in the context of unsurpassed economic affluence and evolving centrifugal social forces. There was a widespread public perception that the cultural and moral fabric of Japanese life was being eroded by urbanization, social mobility, and economic and technological advancements. In other words, the educational reform movement initiated by the government was stimulated by these social concerns, along with the economic concerns articulated by business and political leaders (Shimahara 1986; U.S. Department of Education 1987). These concerns stemmed from the public outcry that education was in a state of "desolation" resulting from the deterioration of culturally expected student behavior and attitudes, which was manifested in instances of school violence and bullying and in children's refusal to attend school (Schoppa 1991; Shimahara 1986; National Council on Educational Reform 1988). Immediate public attention was focused on public schoolteachers, because it was believed that their incompetence in performing culturally expected roles contributed to the state of deterioration.

Consequently, educational reform initiatives in the 1980s led to a reaffirmation of the broad purposes of education and a strengthening of traditional teacher roles, as well as a definition of Japanese education in the twenty-first century, with an emphasis on internationalization and adaptability to rapid changes in employment and industrial infrastructures (Ministry of Education 1989a). A comprehensive curricular reform (Ministry of Education 1989b) was undertaken to strengthen moral education, student guidance, special activities, basic education, and international studies. Changes in teacher certification (to be discussed shortly) were made, especially to improve teacher competence in these areas. In short, the cultural concept of schooling in Japan has been altered relatively little by social change. National efforts have been made to articulate the holistic nature of schooling, since economic and technological developments in Japan have created unprecedented changes in lifestyles, an acceleration of the globalization of the Japanese economic sector, and differentiation of the workplace.

It follows that our beginning Japanese teachers were expected to address the purposes of education, including the cognitive, expressive, moral, social, and aesthetic dimensions of schooling. As discussed in previous chapters, the beginning teachers assumed an array of responsibilities, including classroom instruction, student guidance, gakko gyoji, and extra-curricular activities, among others. To promote their competence in achieving these purposes, the government passed legislation instituting one-year mandatory internships for all beginning public schoolteachers, which will be discussed in greater detail below.

By comparison, as we briefly mentioned in this chapter, the two schools we studied in the United States focused on cognitive processes in the classroom. We observed that teaching cognitive skills outweighed instruction in other skills, even at the kindergarten level, whereas in Japan attention is concentrated on teaching social skills at this level (Lewis 1989). That emphasis on the cognitive process in the classroom is embedded in the history of American education. Cuban's (1984) study reveals that in the United States, the teaching of cognitive skills has generally been a predominant concern of elementary teachers throughout most of the twentieth century. The following strategies for effective teaching identified by contemporary researchers, he suggests, echo "the staple core of teaching practices" in elementary class-rooms that has persisted since the beginning of the century:

- Teacher focuses clearly on academic goals;
- Teacher concentrates on tasks, allotting the instructional period to instructional tasks rather than socializing;
- Teacher presents information clearly, organizing instruc-tion by explaining, outlining, and reviewing, and covers subject matter extensively (p. 266).

Notice that effective teaching has been defined in terms of academic instruction and how academic goals are achieved. In this connection Waller's (1967) account of high school classrooms in the 1920s is relevant, though his study is primarily focused on high schools and high schoolteachers: "In the mental universe of teacherdom, academic learning is the supreme value, and life evolves around it" (p. 357).

The decline of progressive education in the 1940s gave rise to essentialist education, which enunciated that the chief function of schooling was transmission of knowledge. Bester's *Educational Wastelands* (1953) and *The Restoration of Learning* (1955) epitomized continued attacks on progressive education through the first half of the 1950s. Subsequently, in the late 1950s "teacher-proof curricula" began to gain popularity, in response to critics like Bester and the prevailing national obsession with Russian superiority in science and technology (Johnson 1989). The academic community was called upon to provide public schools with ideas and methods from the academic disciplines, to construct new curricula and methods of teaching in science, mathematics, and foreign languages. The teacher-proof curriculum consisted of the prepackaged materials and defined the teacher as a mediator between subject and student. This curriculum became an immediate precursor to the accountability approach, which was launched in the 1960s and flourished in the 1970s (Johnson 1989). To put it succinctly, the approach was a business management method that rewarded teachers for results. It was grounded precisely in a mechanical view of the teacher's role in the classroom, just as the teacher-proof curriculum was. Leon Lessinger (1970), then the U.S. Associate Commissioner of Education, promoted a performance contract approach, according to which outside educational consulting firms were paid if they achieved the objectives of their contract, when measured by outside evaluators.

In the 1980s, *A Nation at Risk*, a reform report by the National Commission on Excellence in Education (1983), dramatized the urgent need for raising academic standards to improve America's competitive position. States across the nation initiated legislative action to impose state mandates on school districts, including such regulations as high school graduation requirements, student testing keyed to K–12 standards of learning, detailed and sequential learning objectives for K–12 students in various subjects, a provision for a statewide basic curriculum and competency standards, and a school readiness test (U.S. Department of Education 1984; Furhman et al. 1988). Suffice it to note that the nation became obsessed with academic standards and the strategies to achieve them. Evidently, the reform movement in the 1980s helped to provide a focus for, and refine the cognitive emphasis of, schooling.

It is difficult to ascertain the extent to which the historical development of American education was reflected in Southtown and Westville Elementary Schools. But it is clear that the weight given to cognitive skills in these schools corresponds to the common orientation of schooling briefly reviewed here.

Education Reforms and Teacher Education

Japan's post-World War II school system was established in 1947, based on the recommendations made to Japan by the United States Mission on Education. The prewar multitrack school system was replaced by an egalitarian, single-track system with six years of elementary, three years of lower secondary (middle), three years of upper secondary (high school), and four years of higher education. Only the first nine years of schooling are compulsory, although over 94 percent of eligible youths currently attend high school. This 6-3-3-4 structure remains relatively popular and has remained unchanged throughout the postwar period despite several proposals to alter it. Because this postwar model of schooling in Japan is of American origin, there are considerable similarities between the Japanese and American structures of schooling.

Nevertheless, as we noted, there are also notable differences between the two nations relative to control of education and the political structure of decision making in education. Following the Mission's recommendations, decentralization was initially accomplished by having elected school boards as governing bodies, reflecting the ideal of lay control as in the United States; however, in the 1950s the Japanese orientation toward school governance diverged from the American pattern. Through a tumultuous succession of administrative and legislative measures that the conservative central government began to introduce shortly after Japan's independence from the Allied Powers in 1952, local control was replaced by a new system of centralized control. By 1958 the government took total control of school governance and the curriculum throughout the nation. Elected school boards were superseded by appointed boards, and the courses of study, issued by the Ministry of Education as advisory curriculum guidelines for teachers and textbook writers prior to 1958, became the binding curriculum framework. What is known as Japan's postwar national curriculum was established in that process. In short, the progressive education transplanted to Japan by the American Occupation in the late 1940s eroded quickly in the 1950s, as the "Japanization" of schooling was undertaken by the conservative Japanese government.

Thereafter, the Ministry of Education has assumed entire responsibility for developing and revising the nation's school curriculum. Textbook authors are required to comply with the national courses of study, and the Ministry of Education authorizes all the textbooks that are adopted at the elementary and secondary levels. And teachers throughout the nation are expected to follow the courses of study uniformly. Japan's centralized control of curriculum reinforces uniformity in schooling across the country and permits relatively little variation, regardless of local diversity. Our beginning Japanese teachers viewed their curriculum as a given from the Ministry of Education, whereas one of the primary concerns of the beginning American teachers in this study was how to construct a curriculum.

In contrast to Japan, local school districts in the United States, needless to say, play two pivotal roles: formulating curriculum guidelines that follow state policy and financing schools. The beginning American teachers we studied were required to follow a set of district curriculum guidelines. They used textbooks only in such subjects as math, social studies, and science, and they were expected to develop their own curricula in such areas as reading and writing. Though they had the freedom to choose available materials for adoption, they were expected to assume responsibility for constructing their curriculum, an onerous task for them. These differences between Japan and the United States had an important bearing on the neophytes' process of learning to teach.

Turning to teacher education, another interesting contrast is that American teachers have far more credentials than do Japanese teachers. At the elementary level, for example, 37 percent of American public schoolteachers have at least a master's degree whereas only 0.4 percent of Japanese public schoolteachers hold such a degree (National Center for Educational Statistics 1993; Ministry of Education 1989a). This striking difference in credentials between United States and Japanese teachers was evident for the beginning teachers in our study. Three of the four beginning American teachers who participated in our study held master's degrees, and in contrast, none of the beginning Japanese teachers studied had graduate degrees. The United States emphasizes graduate education for teachers to improve teaching competence and qualifications, whereas Japan emphasizes in-service education to enhance the quality of teachers. That contrast stems from differences in the educational policies of the two countries. In the United States educational credentials are a critical factor for mobility within the educational establishment.

By comparison, in Japan credentials do not play a significant role in appointments and promotions; teachers must only possess uniformly required qualifications. The Japanese policy of an equal footing for the teaching work force has, instead, led to the encouragement of participation in in-service education programs extensively developed by teacher education centers, organizations for in-service education under the control of either prefectural or municipal boards of education; and teacher networks, including voluntary study associations and circles (Otsuki 1982). As part of its education reform initiatives in the 1980s, however, Japan is calling for more formal graduate education across the nation and graduate education for full-time teachers has been gaining in popularity in recent years (Shimahara 1993).

With respect to preservice teacher education at the undergraduate level, Japanese and American practices correspond considerably. As in the United States, Japan's preservice teacher education consists of three areas: general education, a concentration in the subject area, and professional studies. In postwar Japan, normal schools that trained teachers under the exclusive and strict control of the Ministry of Education were replaced by colleges of education and various teacher certification programs offered by universities to emphasize broad general education and to strengthen specialized studies. Japan adopted the so-called open system of teacher certification, which enables any institution of higher education to offer an approved certification program. In 1949 new teacher education programs were started by the education faculties of only 45 universities and 7 teachers colleges with liberal arts programs. But the open-certification system opened the floodgates to certification programs in numerous private institutions. Consequently, by the end of the 1970s nearly 85 percent of the nation's 444 colleges and universities and 84 percent of the 518 junior colleges were participating in teacher education. Currently, more than 800 institutions are graduating nearly 180,000 students with teaching certificates, accounting for 32 percent of the total college and university graduates in the nation (Shimahara 1991). Yet only one-fourth of these graduates receive teaching appointments.

In contrast to the United States, teaching is more popular, and entry into teaching is more competitive, in Japan partly because teachers are comparatively better paid than other public employees (U.S. Department of Education 1987). All applicants for teaching must pass highly competitive appointment examinations administered by the prefectural board of education, and only one out of four applicants wins an appointment (Shimahara 1991). Unlike the National Teacher Examination in the United States which measures the requisite competence for teaching, Japan's appointment examinations are used by and large for the selection of applicants.

There are also parallels in terms of problems in Japanese and U.S. teacher education programs. Teacher education in both countries has long been charged with an array of shortcomings. Both countries simultaneously launched nationwide campaigns to reform schools in the 1980s, and teacher education reforms were a pivotal part of the campaigns (Shimahara 1986, 1991). American colleges and universities were repeatedly indicted for their mediocre academic preparation of teachers and poor screening of teacher applicants. For example, the National Commission on Excellence in Education (1983) depicted teaching in the following words:

> Too many teachers are being drawn from the bottom
> quarter of graduating high school and college students. . . .
> [Moreover], the teacher preparation curriculum is weight-
> ed heavily with courses in "educational methods" at the
> expense of courses in subjects to be taught. (p. 22)

A Nation at Risk, the commission's 1983 report, started a barrage of reports pointing out weaknesses in schooling and teacher preparation. In the same year, at least a half-dozen other nationally publicized reports focused on public education (Sikula 1990). These included *Making the Grade* (Twentieth Century Fund Task Force on Federal Elementary and Secondary Education Policy 1983), *Action for Excellence: Comprehensive Plan to Improve Our Nation's Schools* (Education Commission of the States, Task Force on Education for Economic Growth 1983), and *Educating Americans for the 21st Century: A Report to the American People and the National Science Board* (National Science Foundation 1983). These reports mainly concentrated on overhauling public education, but several reports issued in the latter half of the 1980s focused on reforming teacher education. Among them are two influential manifestoes: *Tomorrow's Teachers* by the Holmes Group (1986), an organization that started with 126 research universities as charter members; and *A Nation Prepared: Teachers for the 21st Century* by the Carnegie Forum on Education and the Economy, Task Force on Teaching as a Profession (1986), a forum of 14 members including business, political, and educational leaders.

The latter two reports advocated the creation and professional control of higher standards for entry into the teaching profession, a solid intellectual education grounded in the arts and sciences at the undergraduate level, and a differentiation of the teaching force based on qualifications and competence. These reports called for extended programs of teacher education at the graduate level, leading to a master's degree as a standard requirement. The recommendations by the National Commission on Excellence in Education, the Holmes Group, and the Carnegie Task Force stimulated a national trend toward solid and coherent academic preparation, and the emphasis on academic preparation has led to a move from four-year integrated programs in teacher education to five-year programs involving extensive clinical experience (Fullan & Stiegelbauer 1991).

In Japan, the Ministry of Education confirmed that teacher education had been deteriorating throughout the postwar period and that the ministry had been attempting to reform it since the late 1950s (Shimahara & Sakai 1992). However, the Ministry of Education, whose primary role is to maintain regulations regarding teacher education, could not amend those regulations without political support and the backing of various interest groups, including the Japan Teachers Union and the associations of national and private universities and colleges. As pointed out previously, these institutions widely participate in the open system of certification. For nearly three decades, to improve teachers' practical competence, the Ministry of Education tried, without much success, to introduce teacher internships. As early as 1958, "re-education" of teachers was first recommended by the Central Council of Education, an advisory body to the Minister of Education (Tsuchiya 1989). And in 1962 the Council on Teacher Education, another advisory body, proposed internships. Though these recommendations were opposed by various interest groups and did not materialize, the government's pursuit of internships was set in motion (Shimahara & Sakai 1992).

The flaw of postwar teacher preparation was evident especially in the certification requirements at the secondary level that were in force until 1990: merely 14 credits of professional studies, including two credits in student teaching, equivalent to two weeks of clinical experience. Students seeking teacher certification at institutions whose primary mission was not teacher education tended to meet only the minimum requirements. These were the students who, of late, filled two-thirds of the lower-secondary positions and nine-tenths of the upper-secondary positions in the public school system. Undoubtedly, these graduates had much greater depth in their special subject areas than the graduates of the colleges of education, but the adequacy of their professional studies was highly questionable. In contrast, a little more than 30 credits in professional studies were requisite for elementary majors, and these studies included a minimum of four weeks of teaching (Shimahara 1991).

These problems were intensely debated by reformers during the 1980s. As in the past, the government took the initiative in directing the nation's education reform movement in the 1980s. The national legislature passed a law to establish the National Council on Educational Reform in 1984, a comprehensive task force with four divisions: education for the twenty-first century, educational functions of society, elementary and secondary education, and higher education. The council took three years to produce recommendations, which were presented in four reports (National Council on Educational Reform 1988; Shimahara 1986).

Reformers recommended a one-year internship for all beginning public schoolteachers as part of a comprehensive in-service education (this would involve not only first-year teachers but also experienced teachers at different stages in their careers) and they recommended reforms of the certification system. Both reform initiatives received legislative approval by the end of the last decade. Teacher internship, approved in 1988, took effect in 1989, the time we observed beginning teachers in Tokyo. They were the first participants in the internship program. New certification standards, approved in 1989, took effect in 1990.

The internship program is a wide-reaching and costly undertaking by the government. It compensates for the inadequacy of student teaching, which had been a long-standing concern of the Ministry of Education. For 1989 the Ministry of Education allocated a large sum, nearly $200 million (20.7 billion yen), for the internship program, which included 14,505 beginning teachers employed at public elementary schools throughout the nation. The ministry's funding increased thereafter with the participation of beginning public secondary teachers. At schools where there are more than one beginning teacher, a full-time mentor for interns is appointed from among experienced teachers by the superintendent of schools.

Higher standards are required by the new certification system, with an emphasis on professional studies. These standards include slightly improved guidelines for student teaching, as well as specialist certification, a new class of certification for teachers who complete a master's degree program. With the establishment of the new certification system, more emphasis is now placed on graduate-level education for teachers. Until recently there were only three national institutions established in the late 1970s and early 1980s that offered master's programs for full-time teachers on leave from their schools. But there are now at least 43 institutions with master's degree programs for teachers, a notable increase in the number of universities committed to graduate teacher education (Ministry of Education 1992).

In the United States, teacher induction programs for beginning teachers have gained support in the past decade. Unlike the Japanese internship program, American induction programs vary from state to state in terms of their content and duration. However, the goals of these programs typically include improving the teaching performance of first-year teachers, retaining beginning teachers, satisfying state-mandated requirements for induction and certification, promoting professional support to beginning teachers, and transmitting the culture of teaching to beginning teachers (Hurling-Austin 1990). Prior to 1980 only a few programs initiated either by local districts or schools existed (Hurling-Austin 1990), but the education reform movement prompted the development of induction programs. By the end of the 1980s, at least 31 states had either implemented or were planning teacher induction programs (Hurling-Austin 1990). School systems that do not have an induction program (such as the ones we studied) participate instead in a series of professional-development in-service workshops. Looking at the trends in the two countries, it then appears that Japan is moving closer to the American model of advanced formal training for teachers in universities. In contrast, school systems in the United States are moving closer to the Japanese model, where responsibilities for improvements in teaching are placed in the hands of other teachers in the schools where beginning teachers work.

A Concluding Remark

We conducted an ethnographic study focusing on several beginning elementary teachers in two very different countries. One of the merits of our ethnographic research is that it can provide depth of findings and rich details of the context in which teaching took place. Our informants also included many teachers who interacted with the beginning teachers. Although we are aware that we cannot project our generalizations regarding the process of learning to teach beyond our research schools, we believe that our study helps to stimulate our readers to reflect upon teaching and sensitize them to problems in the induction process. Given this as a premise, we want to share our final thoughts.

Learning to teach is a prolonged, tense, complex process. The most striking characteristic of this process is beginning teachers' invariable reliance on the practical knowledge of teaching. For the beginning teachers we studied in the United States and Japan, the practical knowledge of teaching far outweighed the theoretical knowledge. Teachers' practical knowledge is grounded in both personal and shared resources, including their biographies and the shared practical rationality of teaching, part of the culture of teaching. Beginning American and Japanese teachers' strategies for teaching were by and large influenced by practical knowledge.

In contrast, the theoretical knowledge of teaching evidently played only a small role in the process of learning to teach. This is hardly a new finding, but what is significant is the fact that this learning is perpetually guided by an array of time-honored practices, which involve the informal conversations and imparting of sacred wisdom inherent in apprenticeships. Both American and Japanese teachers had difficulty in connecting practice with their preservice course work or drawing upon the theoretical foundations of the course work as a source of practical direction. The graduate-level preparation that American teachers had did not seem to offer them a well-defined advantage, at least in their first year, over the Japanese teachers, who had no course work at the graduate level. Moreover, the American teachers who had far more extensive student teaching experience than the Japanese teachers apparently did not benefit enough from the experience. Yet both groups of teachers valued student teaching. We point out here that the amount of preservice preparation does not appear to make a significant difference in teaching in the first year. The primary reason for this, we believe, is that preservice education does not coherently connect course work in universities and clinical experience to complex classroom practice.

The United States is taking the lead in innovating and augmenting graduate-level preparation for teachers, with an emphasis on solid and coherent intellectual content and clinical experience. Japan is following suit. Whether this trend will empower men and women at the preservice and in-service stages of teaching to utilize the knowledge base of teaching remains to be seen. More course work is not necessarily better. What our study suggests, however, is that clinical experience must be improved if beginning teachers are to acquire the ability to connect practice with their course work in a meaningful way. Although our research participants acknowledged that student teaching had a much greater relevance to their in-service education than did their course work, their student teaching experience was limited to those areas with which cooperating teachers were familiar. While exposing student teachers to the culture of teaching and classroom routines is immensely important, clinical training should aim to bridge the gap between teaching practice and the knowledge base of teaching. Clinical training needs to be designed to sensitize student teachers to both the practical and theoretical rationalities of teaching. This requires the creation and enhancement of a meaningful partnership between institutions of teacher education and cooperating schools, so that university supervisors and cooperating teachers may actively collaborate to improve student teachers' clinical experience.

References

Atkinson, P. & Delamont, S. (1985). Socialisation into teaching: The research which lost its way. *British Journal of Sociology of Education* 6: 307–322.

Azuma, H., Kashiwagi, K. & Hess, R. (1981). *Attitude and behavior of mothers and the intellectual development of children: A comparative study between Japan and the United States.* Tokyo: Tokyo University Press.

Bagley, W. C. (1907). *Classroom management: Its principles and techniques.* New York: Macmillan.

Becker, H. S., Geer, B., Hughes, E., & Strauss, A. L. (1961). *Boys in white: Student culture in medical school.* Chicago: University of Chicago Press.

Bellah, R. N., Madsen, R., Sullivan, W. M., Swidler, A., & Tipton, S. M. (1985). *Habits of the heart: Individualism and commitment in American life.* New York: Harper & Row.

Bennett, J. W. (1988). *American education: Making it work.* Washington, D.C.: U.S. Government Printing Office.

Berger, P. & Luckmann, T. (1966). *The social construction of reality.* Garden City, N.Y.: Doubleday.

Berlak, A. & Berlak, H. (1981). *Dilemmas of schooling: teaching and social change.* London: Methuen.

Bester, A. (1953). *Educational wastelands: The retreat from learning in our public schools.* Urbana: University of Illinois Press.

———. (1955). *The restoration of learning.* New York: Alfred Knopf.

Blumer, H. (1966). Sociological implications of the thought of George Herbert Mead. *American Journal of Sociology* 71 (5): 535–544.

————. (1969). *Symbolic interaction: Perspective and method.* Englewood Cliffs, N.J.: Prentice Hall.

Bogdan, R. & Taylor, S. (1975). *Introduction to qualitative research methods.* New York: John Wiley & Sons, Inc.

Brim, O. (1969). Socialization through the life cycle. In O. Brim & S. Wheeler, (Eds.), *Socialization after childhood.* New York: John Wiley & Sons, Inc.

Bullough, R. V. (1989). *First year teacher: a case study.* New York: Teachers College Press.

Bullough, R. V. & Knowles, G. J. (1991). Teaching and nurturing: Changing conceptions of self as teacher in a case study of becoming a teacher. *International Journal of Qualitative Studies in Education* 4 (2): 121–140.

Carnegie Forum on Education and the Economy, Task Force on Teaching as a Profession (1986). *A nation prepared: Teachers for the 21st century.* New York: Author.

Carter, K. (1990). Teachers' knowledge and learning to teach. In W. R. Houston (Ed.), *Handbook of research on teacher education.* New York: Macmillan.

Central Council of Education (Japan) (1971). *Basic policies for comprehensive expansion and improvement of school education.* Tokyo: Ministry of Education.

Cooley, C. H. (1956). *Human nature and the social order.* Glencoe, Ill.: Free Press.

Crow, N. A. (1986). The role of teacher education in teacher socialization: A case study. Paper presented at the meeting of the American Educational Research Association, San Francisco.

————. (1987). Preservice teacher's biography: A case study. Paper presented at the American Educational Research Association, Washington, D.C.

Cuban, L. (1984). *How teachers taught.* New York: Longman.

Cummings, W. (1980). *Education and equality in Japan.* Princeton, N.J.: Princeton University Press.

Dahrendorf, R. (1978). *Life chances: Approaches to social and political theory.* Chicago: University of Chicago Press.

Darling-Hammond, L. & Berry, B. (1988). *The evolution of teacher policy.* New Brunswick, N.J.: Rand Corp.

Denscombe, M. (1982). The work context of teaching: An analytic framework for the study of teachers in classrooms. *British Journal of Sociology of Education* 1: 279–292.

Dewey, J. (1930). *Human nature and conduct.* New York: Modern Library.

Doyle, W. (1986). Classroom organization and management. In M. Wittrock (Ed.), *Handbook of research on teaching.* New York: Macmillan.

Duke, B. (1986). *The Japanese school: Lessons for industrial America.* New York: Praeger.

Edgar, D. & Warren, D. (1969). Power and autonomy in teacher socialization. *Sociology of Education* 42: 386–399.

Education Commission of the States, Task Force on Education for Economic Growth (1983). *Action for excellence: Comprehensive plan to improve our nation's schools.* Denver: Author.

Elbaz, F. (1983). *Teacher thinking: A study of practical knowledge.* New York: Nichols.

Erickson, F. (1986). Qualitative methods in research on teaching. In M. Wittrock (Ed.), *Handbook of research on teaching.* New York: Macmillan.

Etheridge, C. P. (1989). Acquiring the teaching culture: How beginners embrace practices different from university teaching. *International Journal of Qualitative Studies in Education* 2: 299–313.

Evertson, C. M. & Harris, A. H. (1990). *Classroom organization and management program: Workshop manual for elementary teachers.* Nashville, Tenn.: Vanderbilt University.

Feinman-Nemser, S. & Floden, R. E. (1986). The culture of teaching. In M. Wittrock (Ed.), *Handbook of research on teaching.* New York: Macmillan.

Fukutake Shoten Kyoiku Kenkyu-jo (1992). *Monograph on contemporary elementary school students [Monografu shogaku-sei now]* 14. Tokyo: Fukutake Shoten.

Fullan, M. G. & Stiegelbauer, S. (1991). *The new meaning of educational change.* New York: Teachers College Press.

Furhman, S., Clune, W. H. & Elmore, R. F. (1988). Research on education reform: Lessons on the implementation of policy. *Teachers College Record* 90 (2): 237–257.

Goffman, E. (1959). *The presentation of self in everyday life.* Garden City, N.Y.: Doubleday.

Goodlad, J. I. (1984). *A place called school: Prospects for the future.* New York: McGraw-Hill.

———. (1990). *Teachers for our nation's schools.* San Francisco: Jossey-Bass.

Green, M. (1973). *Teacher as a Stranger.* Belmond, Cal.: Wadsworth.

Hamaguchi, E. (1988). *Rediscovery of 'Japanese-ness' ['Nihon-rashisa' no sai-hakken].* Tokyo: Kodansha.

Hammersley, M. (1980). Classroom ethnography. *Educational Analysis* 2: 46–75.

Hargreaves, D. H. (1980). The occupational culture of teachers. In P. Woods, (Ed.), *Teacher strategies.* London: Croom Helm.

Haring, M. & Nelson, E. (1980). A five-year follow-up comparison of recent and experienced graduates from campus and field-based teacher education programs. Paper presented at the American Educational Research Association, Boston.

Haruta, M. (1983). *An introduction to the educational guidance [Seikatsu shido nyumon].* Tokyo: Meiji Tosho.

Hata, M. & NHK Kyoiku Project (1992). *What to do with public junior high schools? [Koritsu chugaku wa korede yoi-noka].* Tokyo: Nippon Hoso Shuppan Kyokai.

Hess, R. D. & Azuma, H. (1991). Cultural support for schooling: Contrasts between Japan and the United States. *Educational Researcher* 20 (9): 2–8.

Hida, D. (1989). The new entrance examination era for junior high schools [Chugaku juken: shin juken jidai no shin chugaku juken]. *Journal of Nanzan Junior College [Nanzan Tanki Daigaku Kiyo]* 17: 65–90.

Holmes Group (1986). *Tomorrow's teachers: A report of the Holmes Group.* East Lansing, Mich.: Author.

Holmes Group (1989). *Work in progress: The Holmes Group one year on.* East Lansing, Mich.: Author.

Hoy, W. (1968). Pupil control ideology and organizational socialization: A further examination of the influence of experience on the beginning teacher. *School Review* 77: 257–265.

Hsu, F. (1963). *Clan, caste & club.* New York: Van Nostrand.

———. (1975). *Iemoto: The heart of Japan.* Cambridge, Mass.: Schenkman.

Hurling-Austin, L. (1990). Teacher induction programs and internships. In W. R. Houston (Ed.), *Handbook of Research on Teacher Education.* New York: Macmillan.

Imazu, K. (1978). Internal career of student teachers [Gakusei no uchigawa kara mita kyoshi yosei katei]. *Bulletin of the Faculty of Education of Mie University (Educational Science) [Mie Daigaku Kyoiku Gakubu Kenkyu Kiyo],* 29 (4): 17–33.

———. (1979). Occupational socialization of teachers 1. [Kyoshi no shokugyo-teki shakaika 1]. *Bulletin of the Faculty of Education of Mie University (Educational Science) [Mie Daigaku Kyoiku Gakubu Kenkyu Kiyo]* 30 (4): 17–24.

Ishii, H. (1978). A history of school cleaning [Gakko soji no rekishi]. In Y. Okihara, (Ed.), *School cleaning: Its role in the formation of character [Gakko soji].* Tokyo: Gakuji-shuppan Co.

Ito, K. (1980). A consideration on professional socialization of students of the Faculty of Education [Kyoiku-gakubu gakusei no shokugyo-teki shakaika ni kansuru ichikosatsu]. *Bulletin of the Faculty of Education of Shizuoka University (Liberal Arts and Social Sciences) [Shizuoka Daigaku Kyoiku Gakubu Kenkyu Hokoku: Jinbun Shakai Kagaku Hen]* 30: 99–119.

———. (1981). Developmental process of professional orientation of students of the Faculty of Education [Kyoiku-gakubu gakusei no kyoshoku shiko-sei no tenkai katei].

Bulletin of the Faculty of Education of Shizuoka University (Liberal Arts and Social Sciences) [Shizuoka Daigaku Kyoiku Gakubu Kenkyu Hokoku: Jinbun Shakai Kagaku Hen] 31: 115–128.

Ito, K. & Yamazaki, J. (1986). Research on anticipatory socialization in the teaching profession 1 [Kyoshoku no yoki-teki shakaika ni kansuru chosa kenkyu 1]. *Bulletin of the Faculty of Education of Shizuoka University (Liberal Arts and Social Sciences) [Shizuoka Daigaku Kyoiku Gakubu Kenkyu Hokoku: Jinbun Shakai Kagaku Hen]* 37: 117–127.

Jackson, P. W. (1990). *Life in classrooms.* New York: Teachers College Press (originally published in 1968).

Janesick, V. (1978). *An ethnographic study of a teacher's classroom perspective.* East Lansing, Mich.: Institute for Research on Teaching, Research Series No. 33.

Japan Society of Educational Sociology (1986). *New dictionary of sociology of education [Shin kyoiku shakaigaku jiten].* Tokyo: Toyokan Publishing Co.

Jinnouchi, Y. (1987). Preservice and in-service teacher training in career development [Kyoshi 'career' no keisei ni okeru kyoin yosei to kyoin kenshu]. *Japanese Journal of Educational Research [Kyoiku Gaku Kenkyu],* 54 (3): 300–309.

Johnson, W. R. (1989). Teachers and teacher training in the twentieth century. In D. Warren (Ed.), *American teachers: Histories of a profession at work.* New York: Macmillan.

Kano, Y. (1984). A study on the development of teaching competence [Kyoshoku noryoku no keisei katei ni kansuru chosa kenkyu]. *Kagawa University Studies on Educational Practice [Kagawa Daigaku Kyoiku Jissen Kenkyu]* 2: 29–37.

Kataoka, T. (1992). Class management and student guidance in Japanese elementary and lower secondary schools. In R. Leestma and H. J. Walberg (Eds.), *Japanese educational productivity.* Ann Arbor, Mich.: University of Michigan Press.

Knowles, J. G. (1992). Models for understanding pre-service and beginning teachers' biographies. In I. Goodson (Ed.), *Studying teachers' lives.* New York: Teachers College Press.

Kojima, H. & Shinohara, S. (1985). A study of the development of career consciousness of college students: An analysis of career consciousness of the students at the Faculty of Education *[Daigakusei no shokugyo ishiki keisei katei no kenkyu]. Bulletin of the Faculty of Education of Ibaragi University (Educational Science). [Ibaraki Daigaku Kyoiku Gakubu Kiyo]* 34: 281–296.

Lacey, C. (1977). *The socialization of teachers.* London: Methuen.

Lambert, M. (1985). How do teachers manage to teach?: Perspectives on problems in practice. *Harvard Educational Review* 55: 178–184.

Lebra, Takie, S. (1976). *Japanese patterns of behavior.* Honolulu: University of Hawaii Press.

LeCompte, M. & Ginsburg, M. (1987). How students learn to become teachers: An exploration of alternative responses to a teacher training program. In G. W. Noblit & W. T. Pink (Eds.), *Schooling in social context: Qualitative studies.* Norwood, N.J.: Ablex Publishing Co.

Lessinger, L (1970). *Every kid a winner: Accountability in education.* New York: Simon & Schuster.

Levine, R. & White, M. (1986). *Human conditions: The cultural basis of educational development.* New York: Routledge.

Lewis, C. (1989). From indulgence to internalization: Social control in the early school years. *Journal of Japanese Studies* 15 (1): 139–157.

Liguana, J. (1970). *What happens to the attitudes of beginning teachers?.* Denville, Ill: Interstate Printers.

Lortie, D. C. (1975). *Schoolteacher: A sociological study.* Chicago: The University of Chicago Press.

Maki, M. (1988). Implementation of internship for beginning teachers. *Educational Law* 75: 17–29.

Mardle, G. & Walker, M. (1980). Strategies and structure: Critical notes on teacher socialization. In P. Woods (Ed.), *Teacher strategies.* London: Croom Helm.

Mead, G. H. (1934). *Mind, self, and society.* Chicago: University of Chicago Press.

Ministry of Education (Japan) (1989a). *Education in Japan.* Tokyo: Gyosei.

Ministry of Education (Japan) (1989b). *Outline of education in Japan.* Tokyo: UNESCO Asian Cultural Center.

Ministry of Education (Japan) (1992). *Basic survey report on schools [Gakko Kihon Chosa Hokokusho].* Tokyo: Mombusho.

Miwa, S. (1988). The problematic internship program [Gimon darake no shonin-sha kenshu]. *Educational Law [Kikan Kyoiku Ho],* 75: 11–16.

Miyasaka, T. (1959). *Educational guidance and moral education [Seikatsu shido to dotoku kyoiku].* Tokyo: Meiji Tosho.

Monbusho (1982). *Understanding and guiding children: a resource book for educational guidance at an elementary school 1 [Jido no rikai to shido].* Tokyo: Okurasho Insatsu-kyoku.

Munby, H. (1986). Metaphor in the thinking of teachers: An exploratory study. *Journal of Curriculum Studies* 18: 197–209.

————. (1989). Reflection in action and reflection on action. Paper presented at the meeting of the American Educational Research Association, San Francisco.

Naigai Kyoiku (Domestic and Foreign Education), Bi-weekly newspaper, December 12, 1989.

Nakane, Chie (1970). *Japanese society.* Berkeley: University of California Press.

Nakatome, T. (1988). How to develop the internship program for beginning teachers. *Educational Law* 75: 17–29.

National Center for Education Statistics (1993). *America's teachers: Profile of a profession.* Washington, D.C.: U.S. Government Printing Office.

National Commission on Excellence in Education (1983). *A nation at risk: The imperative for educational reform.* Washington, D.C.: U.S. Government Printing Office.

National Council on Educational Reform (Japan) [Rinji Kyoiku Shingikai] (1988). *Recommendations for education reform [Kyoiku kaikaku ni kansuru toshin].* Tokyo: Okurasho Insatsu-kyoku.

National Science Foundation (1983). *Educating Americans for the 21st century: A report to the American people and the National Science Board.* Washington, D.C.: Author.

Nippon Nyushi Center (1991). *The 1990–1991 university entrance examination research [90–91 daigaku nyushi data research].* Tokyo: Yoyogi Zeminaru.

Nishi, K. (1988). *A teacher who is able to see children: How to develop ability and sensitivity in understanding children [Kodomo ga mieru kyoshi].* Tokyo: Kyoiku Shuppan.

Nosow, S. (1975). Students' perceptions of field education. *Journal of College Student Personnel* 16 (6): 508–513.

Otsuki, T. (1982). *The history of the postwar voluntary education movement [Sengo minkan kyoiku undoshi].* Tokyo: Ayumisha.

Peak, L. (1991). *Learning to go to school in Japan.* Berkeley: University of California Press.

Petty, H. & Hogben, D. (1980). Explorations of semantic space with beginning teachers: A study of socialization into teaching. *British Journal of Teacher Education* 3: 19–37.

Pollard, A. (1982). A model of classroom coping strategies. *British Journal of Sociology of Education* 3 (1): 19–37.

Reid, I. (1986). *The sociology of school and education.* London: Fontana Press.

Rohlen, T. P. (1983). *Japan's high schools.* Berkeley: University of California Press.

———. (1989). Order in Japanese society: Attachment, authority, and routine. *Journal of Japanese Studies* 15 (1): 5–40.

Ross, E. W. (1987a). *Preservice teachers' responses to institutional constraints: The active role of the individual in teacher socialization.* Albany, N.Y.: The State University of New York at Albany, Department of Teacher Education.

———. (1987b). Teacher perspective development: A study of preservice social studies teachers. *Theory and Research in Social Education* 5 (4): 225–243.

Russell, T. (1989). The roles of research knowledge and knowing-in-action in teachers' development of professional knowledge. Paper presented at the meeting of the American Educational Research Association, San Francisco.

Ryan, K. (1986). *The induction of new teachers.* Bloomington, Ind.: Phi Delta Kappan Educational Foundation.

Sakai, A. & Shimahara, N. (1991). An inquiry into the process of learning teaching methods: Sociology of knowledge on teaching [Gakushu shido hoho no shutoku katei ni kansuru kenkyu]. *The Journal of Educational Sociology [Kyoiku Shakaigaku Kenkyu]* 49: 135–153.

Sato, N. & McLaughlin, M. (1992). Context matters: Teaching in Japan and in the United States. *Phi Delta Kappan* 73 (5): 359–366.

Schon, D. (1983). *The reflective practitioner: How professionals think in action.* New York: Basic Books.

Schoppa, L. J. (1991). *Education reform in Japan: A case of immobilist politics.* New York: Routledge.

Sharp, R. & Green, A. (1975). *Education and social control.* London: Routledge and Kegan Paul.

Shimahara, N. (1979). *Education and adaptation in Japan.* New York: Praeger.

———. (1986). Japanese education reforms in the 1980s. *Issues in Education* 4 (2): 85–100.

———. (1991). Teacher education in Japan. In E. Beauchamp (Ed.), *Windows on Japanese education.* New York: Greenwood Press.

———. (1993). Teacher education reforms: Salient issues in a sociopolitical context. Paper presented at the Rutgers Invitational Seminar on Education, Rutgers University, New Brunswick, N.J.

Shimahara, N. & Sakai, A. (1990). Teacher internship and educational reform in Japan [Nippon ni okeru kyoin kenshu to kyoiku kaikaku]. *Bulletin of the Faculty of Education of University of Tokyo [Tokyo Daigaku Kyoiku-gakubu Kiyo]* 30: 83–93.

————. (1992). Teacher internship and the culture of teaching in Japan. *British Journal of Sociology of Education* 13 (2): 147–162.

Shintani, T. (1983). Classroom and school management [Gakkyu Gakunen Keiei to Gakko Keiei]. In J. Nagaoka, (Ed.), *School management [Gakko keiei]*. Tokyo: Yushindo.

Sikula, J. (1990). National commission reports of the 1980s. In W. R. Houston (Ed.), *Handbook of research on teacher education*. New York: Macmillan.

Smyth, J. (1989). Developing and sustaining critical reflection in teacher education. *Journal of Teacher Education* 40: 2–9.

Spindler, G., Spindler, L., Trueba, H. & Williams, M. D. (1990). *The American cultural dialogue and its transmission*. London: The Falmer Press.

Spradley, J. P. (1980). *Participant observation*. New York: Holt.

Stevenson, H. W. & Stigner, J. W. (1992). *The learning gap: why our schools are failing and what we can learn from Japanese and Chinese education*. New York: Summit Books.

Tabachnick, B. R. & Zeichner, K. (1984). The impact of the student teaching experience on the development of teacher perspectives. *Journal of Teacher Education* 35: 28–36.

————. (1985). *The development of teacher perspectives: Final report*. Madison, Wisc.: University of Wisconsin Center for Education Research.

Tanaka, I. (1974). The process of occupational socialization of beginning teachers: a school organizational approach [Shinnin kyoin no shokugyo teki shakaika katei: Gakko soshiki ron teki kosatsu]. *Research Bulletin of the Faculty of Education of Kyushu University [Kyushu Daigaku Kyoiku Gakubu Kiyo]* 20: 137–152.

Tobin, J., Wu., D. Y. H. & Davidson, D. H. (1989). *Preschool in three cultures: Japan, China, and the United States*. New Haven: Yale University Press.

Tsuchiya, M. (1984). *Japanese teachers: Teacher education, certification, and in-service training*. Tokyo: Shin Nippon Shuppan.

Tsuneyoshi, R. (1992). *Personality formation—A Japan-U.S. comparison of the hidden curricula [Ningen-keisei no nichibei hikaku—Kakureta karikyuramu]*. Tokyo: Chuo Koron Sha.

Twentieth Century Fund Task Force on Federal Elementary and Secondary Education Policy (1983). *Making the grade*. New York: Author.

Tyler, W. (1988). *School organization: A sociological perspective*. London: Croom Helm.

U.S. Department of Education (1984). *The nation responds: Recent efforts to improve education*. Washington, D.C.: U.S. Government Printing Office.

U.S. Department of Education (1987). *Japanese education today*. Washington, D.C.: U.S. Government Printing Office.

U.S. Department of Education (1988). *Fifth annual wall chart of state education statistics*. Washington, D.C.: U.S. Government Printing Office.

U.S. Department of Education (1993). *America's teachers: Profile of a profession*. Washington, D.C.: U.S. Government Printing Office.

Veenman, S. (1984). Perceived problems of beginning teachers. *Review of Educational Research* 54 (2): 143–178.

Waller, W. (1967). *The sociology of teaching*. New York: John Wiley.

Weick, K. (1982). Administering education in loosely coupled schools. *Phi Delta Kappan* June 673–676.

Weinstein, C. (1991). The classroom as a social context for learning. *Annual Review of Psychology* 42: 493–525.

Wells, K. (1984). *Teacher socialization in the educational organization: A review of the literature*. Seattle: University of Washington.

White, J. J. (1989). Student teaching as a rite of passage. *Anthropology and Education Quarterly* 20 (3): 177–195.

White, M. (1987). *The Japanese educational challenge: A commitment to children*. New York: The Free Press.

Yokohama National University Institute for Modern Education [Ed.] (1983). *Central council of education and educational reforms*. Tokyo: Sanichi Shobo.

Yuki, M. (1992). Teacher behavior and intention in education for preschoolers [Shudan hoikuni okeru hoikusha no hoiku kodo to ito]. In T. Kuze & M. Nishito (Eds.), *Human Relations* [Ningenkankei] Tokyo: Fukumura Shuppan.

Zeichner, K. (1984). *Individual and institutional influences on the development of teacher perspectives.* Madison: Wisconsin Center for Education Research.

Zeichner, K. & Gore, J. M. (1990). Teacher socialization. In R. Houston (Ed.), *Handbook of research on teacher education.* New York: Macmillan.

Zeichner, K. & Tabachnick, B. R. (1981). Are the effects of university teacher education "washed out" by school experience? *Journal of Teacher Education* 32 (3): 7–11.

Index

About the Authors

Nobuo K. Shimahara is currently a professor of education at the Graduate School of Education and a member of the graduate faculty of the Anthropology Department at Rutgers University. He has also served as acting dean and associate dean at the GSE. He was a visiting professor at the University of Tokyo in 1989. His publications include six books and numerous monographs and articles, many of which focus on Japanese education. Since 1976 the author has done ethnographic research on various aspects of Japanese education, including university entrance examinations, minority education, adolescent socialization, teaching, and the socialization of beginning teachers. He is an editor of *Teacher Education in Industrialized Nations* (1994). He is now conducting research on the culture of teaching in a changing social context in Japan.

Akira Sakai is a lecturer on the sociology of education in the Faculty of Literature, Nanzan University, Nagoya, Japan. He completed the Ph.D. program in sociology of education at the University of Tokyo in 1991. He was a recipient of a fellowship from the Japan Society for the Promotion of Science. He has done research on the culture of teaching, teacher socialization, and student subculture and has published nearly 20 articles on these topics. He spent one year at Rutgers University in 1990–1991 and participated in a research project on teacher socialization directed by Nobuo K. Shimahara. The author is currently doing research on the culture of teaching in the Nagoya area, Japan.

REFERENCE BOOKS IN
INTERNATIONAL EDUCATION

EDWARD R. BEAUCHAMP
Series Editor